The Expressive Organization

Linking Identity, Reputation, and the Corporate Brand

edited by

MAJKEN SCHULTZ, MARY JO HATCH, AND
MOGENS HOLTEN LARSEN

OXFORD
UNIVERSITY PRESS

OXFORD

UNIVERSITY PRESS

Great Clarendon Street, Oxford OX2 6DP

Oxford University Press is a department of the University of Oxford.
It furthers the University's objective of excellence in research, scholarship,
and education by publishing worldwide in

Oxford New York

Auckland   Cape Town Dar es Salaam   Hong Kong   Karachi
Kuala Lumpur Madrid Melbourne Mexico City   Nairobi
New Delhi Shanghai Taipei Toronto
With offices in
Argentina Austria Brazil Chile Czech Republic France Greece
Guatemala Hungary Italy Japan South Korea Poland Portugal
Singapore Switzerland Thailand Turkey Ukraine Vietnam

Oxford is a registered trade mark of Oxford University Press
in the UK and in certain other countries

Published in the United States
by Oxford University Press Inc., New York

© The several contributors 2000

The moral rights of the author have been asserted

Database right Oxford University Press (maker)

Reprinted 2009

ISBN 978-0-19-829779-6

Printed in the United Kingdom by
Lightning Source UK Ltd., Milton Keynes

CONTENTS

LIST OF FIGURES

LIST OF TABLES

LIST OF BOXES

ABBREVIATIONS

CMD	Committee of Managing Directors
CPA	certified public accountant
CSP	common starting point
FTTD	fiber-to-the-desk
IP	Internet Protocol
IT	information technology
KI	Koch Industries
MBM	market-based management
ROIT	Rotterdam Organization Identification Test
OI	organizational identity
UAW	United Auto Workers
UOVP	unique organization value proposition
USP	unique selling proposition

NOTES ON THE CONTRIBUTORS

Paul A. Argenti has been Professor on the faculty at Dartmouth's Tuck School of Business for the last nineteen years. Prior to that he taught at Columbia and Harvard. His Communication Department has been named number one in the nation by *US News & World Report*. His research and extensive consulting practice are in the area of corporate communication. He has published several articles and books, including most recently a second edition of his *Corporate Communication* textbook (Irwin/McGraw-Hill, 1998). Argenti serves on the editorial board for *Management Communication Quarterly* and is Associate Editor for *Corporate Reputation Review*. Paul may be reached at: paul.a. argenti@dartmouth.edu.

Jay B. Barney is Professor of Management and holder of the Bank One Chair for Excellence in Corporate Strategy at the Max M. Fisher College of Business, Ohio State University. His research focuses on the relationship between firm skills and capabilities that are costly to copy, as well as sustained competitive advantage. He has published over forty articles in a variety of journals on management, strategy, and business. He has been Associate Editor at the *Journal of Management*, and Senior Editor at *Organization Science*. He has published three books: *Organizational Economics* (with William G. Ouchi), *Managing Organizations: Strategy, Structure and Behavior* (with Ricky Griffin), and *Gaining and Sustaining Competitive Advantage*. Jay Barney has consulted with a wide variety of public and private organizations, including Westinghouse Electric, the Masonite Corporation, McDonnell-Douglas, Wells Fargo Bank, Honeywell Information Systems, Mead, Hewlett-Packard, Texas Instruments, Tenneco, Arco, Koch Industries Inc., and others. Jay may be reached through: Hutton.2@osu.edu.

Suzanne M. Carter is Assistant Professor at the University of Notre Dame. She received her MBA and Ph. D. in Strategic Management from the University of Texas at Austin. Her research interests are primarily in the management of corporate reputation, with an emphasis on how organizational members communicate and respond to multiple stakeholders. She has published several articles on the subject of reputation management in *Corporate Reputation*

Review and in The Wiley Strategic Management Series. Suzanne may be reached at: Suzanne.M.Carter.34@nd.edu.

George Cheney is Professor in the Department of Communication Studies at the University of Montana-Missoula, USA, and Adjunct Professor in the Department of Management Communication in the Waikato Management School, Hamilton, NZ. He has published over fifty articles and chapters on such topics as organizational identification and commitment, power in organizations, public relations and marketing, workplace democracy, and business ethics. His latest book, *Values at Work* (Cornell, 1999), analyzes the 'marketization' of employee participation programs. He is past Chair of the Organizational Communication Division of the National Communication Association, and Co-Editor of the research annual *Organization ← → Communication: Emerging Perspectives* (Ablex/Elsevier). George may be reached at: Gcheney@selway.umt.edu.

Lars Thøger Christensen is Associate Professor and Chair of the Department of Marketing, University of Southern Denmark. He specializes in the study of corporate communications and has published articles and book chapters in the fields of advertising, semiotics, image/identity formation, managerial discourse, communication technology, public relations, and issue management. He is also the author of *Marketing Communication as a Way of Organizing: A Cultural Theoretical Analysis* (in Danish) (Akademisk Forlag, 1994), a book that discusses the discourse of marketing and its implications for contemporary management and communication practices. Lars may be reached at: ltc@sam.sdu.dk.

Barbara Czarniawska holds the Skandia Chair in Management at Gothenburg Research Institute, School of Economics and Commercial Law, Göteborg University, Sweden. Her research focuses on control processes in complex organizations, most recently in the field of big city management. In terms of methodological approach, she combines institutional theory with the narrative approach. She has published in the area of business and public administration in Polish, her native language, as well as in Swedish, Italian, and English. Her most recent positions are stated in *Narrating the Organization: Dramas of Institutional Identity* (University of Chicago Press, 1997), *A Narrative Approach to Organization Studies* (Sage, 1998) and *Writing Management* (Oxford University Press, 1999). Barbara may be reached at: barbara.czarniawska@gri.gu.se.

Paul du Gay is Senior Lecturer, Faculty of Social Sciences, Open University (UK). His background is within the discipline of sociology, and his research areas are the sociology of economic and organizational life, and cultural studies. He has published a number of articles and several books, including *Consumption and Identity at Work* (Sage, 1996) and *Production of Culture/*

Cultures of Production (Sage, 1997). His latest book *In Praise of Bureaucracy: Weber/Organization/Ethics* is scheduled to be published by Sage in 2000. Paul may be reached at: p.l.j.Dugay@open.ac.uk.

Janet M. Dukerich is Associate Professor in the Management Department at the University of Texas. She received her Ph. D. in Organizational Behavior from the University of Minnesota. Her current research interests focus on the images that individuals develop of their work organization and how these images affect the degree to which these individuals identify with their organization. She has published a number of papers in journals within organization studies, business ethics, psychology, and organizational behavior, including a study of identity–image adaptation in the New York–New Jersey Port Authority (with Jane Dutton). Janet may be reached at: janet.dukerich@mail.utexas.edu.

Charles I. Fombrun is Professor of Management and Director, Stern Management Consulting Program, New York University, Stern School of Business. He is also Executive Director of the Reputation Institute, a research organization devoted to the study and analysis of corporate reputations. His research interests include organization theory and strategy, specializing in the study of corporate reputations and change management. He is the author of three books, most recently *Reputation: Realizing Value from the Corporate Image* (Harvard Business School Press, 1996), and over fifty articles. Charles may be reached at: cfombrun@stern.nyu.edu.

Janis Forman is Professor at, established, and now directs the Management Communication Program for the Anderson School of Management at UCLA. In 1995 she was named outstanding researcher by the International Association for Business Communication, based on her entire publication record. She has published several books, including *The Random House Guide to Business Writing and New Visions of Collaborative Writing*, as well as numerous articles on management communication. Her current research focuses on the role of communication in the implementation of organizational strategy, as well as the uses of storytelling for producing effective strategic communications. Janis may be reached at: janis.forman@anderson.ucla.edu.

Mary Jo Hatch is a Professor for the McIntire School of Commerce at the University of Virginia and Visiting Professor of Organization Theory at Cranfield School of Management (UK). She is also a Director of the Reputation Institute. She specializes in the application of culture-based organization theory to the study of leadership and change management as well as to the areas of organizational identity and corporate branding. She has published numerous articles in academic journals and a textbook, *Organization Theory: Modern, Symbolic and Postmodern Perspectives* (Oxford University Press, 1997). She is also European Editor of the *Journal of*

Management Inquiry. Mary Jo may be reached at: m.j.hatch@cranfield. ac.uk.

Mogens Holten Larsen is Managing Director and owner of Bergsøe 4 A/S, a leading Danish communication consultancy specializing in corporate branding and reputation management. For the last twenty years he has worked with companies such as AstraZeneca, Renault, Unibank, Statoil, and Maersk. He is the author of *The Red Thread* (1993, in Danish), *The Value of a Mission Statement* (1996), and, together with Majken Schultz, 'The Expressive Company' (1998, in Danish), all www.bergsoe4.dk. Mogens may be reached at: ml@bergsoe4.dk.

Kevin Lane Keller is the E. B. Osborn Professor of Marketing at the Amos Tuck School of Business at Dartmouth College. An academic pioneer in the study of integrated marketing communications and brand equity, Keller has served as brand confidant to marketers for some of the world's most successful brands, including Disney, Ford, Intel, Levi Strauss, Nike, and Starbucks. His *Strategic Brand Management: Building, Measuring, and Managing Brand Equity* (Prentice Hall, 1998) has been heralded as 'a rare success at combining practical advice and real substance'. Keller's academic résumé includes award-winning research and an eight-year stint on the faculty of the Stanford Business School, where he served as the head of the marketing group. Kevin may be reached at: kevin.l.keller@dartmouth.edu.

Simon Knox is Professor of Brand Marketing at the Cranfield School of Management, and consultant to a number of multinational companies, including McDonald's, Levi Strauss, DiverseyLever, and the Ocean Group. Prior to joining Cranfield, Simon worked for Unilever in a number of senior marketing roles in both detergents and foods. He publishes extensively on brand equity issues and customer purchasing styles, and is co-author of *Competing on Value*, published by Financial Times Pitman Publishing (http://www.competingonvalue. com). Simon may be reached at: s.knox@cranfield.ac.uk.

Stan Maklan holds a B. Sc. and an MBA. He is a managing consultant with the European Customer Relationship Management Practice at CSC Computer Sciences, one of the world's largest IT and Management Consulting firms, and is a regular contributor to international conferences and seminars. He has been a director at operating companies for Unilever and Burson-Marsteller, as well as a marketing manager for Cable & Wireless (telecommunications). Stan ran his own consultancy, specializing in business-to-business marketing, before joining CSC. He was awarded honors for academic excellence when he obtained a Masters of Business Administration from the University of Western Ontario (Canada). He is co-author of *Competing on Value*, published by Financial Times Pitman Publishing (http://www.competingonvalue.com). Stan may be reached at: smaklan@csc.com.

Jan Mouritsen is Professor in the Department of Operations Management at the Copenhagen Business School. His research interests include management control and accounting, technology management, performance management, manufacturing strategy, and immaterial assets and intellectual capital. He is in charge of a large longitudinal research project on intellectual capital, involving a selection of distinguished Scandinavian companies. He has published a number of journal articles within the areas of accounting, management, and management control. His most recent book in English is *Accountability: Power, Ethos and Technologies of Managing* (edited with R. Munro) (Thomson Publishers, 1996). Jan may be reached at: jm.om@cbs.dk.

Wally Olins is co-founder of Wolff Olins, the branding and identity consultancy based in the UK. He was educated at Oxford University. He has advised many of the world's leading organizations both in the public and private sectors on identity, branding, communication, and related issues. Among others, he has worked with BT, Repsol (Spain), Renault, and Volkswagen. He has written several books on these subjects, including *Corporate Identity*, which have been translated into many languages, including Chinese. He is a visiting professor at three universities: the Copenhagen Business School, Denmark, Lancaster University, UK, and Duxx, Mexico. He lectures and holds seminars on branding issues around the world, and was awarded a CBE in 1999. Wally may be reached at: w.olins@wolff-olins.com.

Violina. P. Rindova is Assistant Professor in Entrepreneurship and Strategy at the School of Business, University of Washington. Her work focuses on the socio-cognitive dynamics of competition and market creation. In particular, she studies how processes of communication between firms and constituents affect competitive positions in various markets. She has published several book chapters, as well as articles in scholarly journals, such as *Corporate Reputation Review, Journal of Management Inquiry, Journal of Management Studies*, and *Strategic Management Journal*. Violina may be reached at: vrindova@u.washington.edu.

Majken Schultz is Professor in the Department of Intercultural Communication and Management at the Copenhagen Business School. She is also a Director of the Reputation Institute. Her research interests are located at the interface between organization theory, strategy, and communication studies, and include the interplay between organizational culture, identity and image, corporate branding, and reputation management. She has published numerous articles in international journals within management, organization studies, marketing, and reputation. She is the author and editor of several books, one of which has been published in English: *On Studying Organizational Cultures: Diagnosis and Understanding* (Walter de Gruyter, Berlin, 1995). Majken has worked with a number of leading Danish companies, including

Bang & Olufsen, Danfoss, and Unibank. Majken may be reached at: ms.ikl@cbs.dk.

Gordon Glen Shaw was formerly Executive Director of Planning and International within the 3M company, USA. He is now retired, but has recently published an article in *Harvard Business Review* (May–June 1998). His areas of professional and managerial interest include management, strategic planning, and marketing. He holds an MBA from the University of Michigan. Gordon may be reached at: CandGinAZ@aol.com.

Alice C. Stewart is Assistant Professor of Management in the Fisher College of Business and Director of the Office of Strategic Analysis and Planning for Ohio State University. She received her degree from the University of North Carolina, and was a faculty member at the University of Pittsburgh prior to joining Ohio State University in 1995. Alice's research interests include organizational learning processes and the creation and usage of knowledge for organizational competitive advantage. She is currently advising Ohio State University on its strategic positioning as a twenty-first-century university. Thus, strategic management in higher education has become one application of her more theoretical work on organizational learning and strategy. Alice may be reached at: Stewart@cob.ohio-state.edu.

Keith E. Thompson is Senior Lecturer in Management and Marketing at Cranfield University. He teaches buyer behavior and international marketing, following several years in marketing management, notably with Spillers and IBM. Since joining Cranfield, Keith has published thirty papers on buyer behavior and marketing strategy, and has undertaken academic and consulting work in Eastern Europe and North America. His current field of research encompasses the roles of attitudes, values, risk, and trust in buyer behavior. Keith may be reached at: k.e.thompson@cranfield.ac.uk.

Cees B. M. van Riel is Professor of Corporate Communication and Director of the Corporate Communication Center in the Graduate Business School at Erasmus University, Rotterdam, the Netherlands. He is also a Director of the Reputation Institute. He obtained his Ph. D. from Erasmus University in 1986. Cees has published several books and articles about the interaction between corporate strategy and reputation management. Together with Charles Fombrun, he launched the academic journal *Corporate Reputation Review*. His book *Principles of Corporate Communication* has been translated into Dutch, Spanish, and Bahassa. He has published numerous articles in journals on communication, marketing, branding, and public relations. Cees may be reached at: criel@fac.fbk.eur.nl.

1

Introduction: Why the Expressive Organization?

Majken Schultz, Mary Jo Hatch, and Mogens Holten Larsen

INTRODUCTION

Ideas such as organizational identity, reputation, and corporate branding have been around for a long time. But never before have the interests that promote these ideas within business—the functions of HRM, communication, marketing, strategy, and accounting—been in greater need of one another's support. For example, if corporate identity is to attract top-level employees to the firm, then potential employees must hear good things about the company from trusted sources. Recruiting brochures are no longer sufficient. Web sites and corporate advertising are equally important, leaving HRM departments increasingly dependent on marketing for their recruiting success. Good corporate advertising does not hurt motivation once employees are inside the firm either.

This is not a one-way street, however. For a corporate brand to be more than an empty promise to customers, employees have to follow through on the images marketers put forth. If the corporate brand rests on images of superior technical performance of products, then employees have to deliver that superior technical performance. If the image rests on friendly and efficient customer service, then employees had better be friendly and efficient.

But it is not enough to insist on employee behavior that fits whatever management deems a desirable image. Setting up systems to control behavior with rewards simply gets businesses superficial compliance. The behavior that supports a corporate reputation or brand needs to be more deeply rooted, it needs to rest in the organization's identity. Employees must feel the message they are sending with their behavior, not just go through the motions. Thus, increasingly organizations compete based on their ability to express who they are and what they stand for. Emotional and symbolic expressiveness is becoming part of the experience of doing business, which is why we chose the title of our book: *The Expressive Organization*.

This concern for expressiveness is the reason why we chose a painting by David Hockney for the cover of our book. The most obvious reason for the choice of *A Walk around the Hotel Courtyard, Acatlan* (1985) is the expressiveness of the primary colors of red, yellow, and blue that predominate in this painting; primary colors bring out the strongest emotions. But beyond color, there are many layers to our interpretation of the painting, just as we hope you will find many layers to interpret in our book. For us, the imagery of the painting suggests many associations to the work we are presenting. For example, the columns around the courtyard represent different concepts, different disciplines, and multiple perspectives. All of these are part of what the contributing authors bring to the book. Furthermore, depending on your location in the courtyard, the arch in the middle might be regarded as identity, reputation, or the corporate brand. The connections between identity, reputation, and the corporate brand are symbolized when you take a walk in the hotel courtyard.

One implication of the new emphasis on expressiveness is that strategy must serve all stakeholders and that means employees as well as customers, shareholders, creditors, suppliers, local communities, and the media. If the corporate reputation is to be maintained, all these relationships have to be nurtured and sustained over the long run. The whole company has to work together for effective performance to be achieved. This has been said before, of course. But what is different this time is that the coming-together of stakeholder interests has an expressive (symbolic and communicative) dimension that has not been emphasized in the past. What for the moment seems to be pushing us towards a renewed concern for integration is captured in the convergence of the issues of identity, reputation, and the corporate brand. These are matters of meaning as much as or more than they are technical concerns, and this is changing everything.

Let's back up a moment. Pressures to pull together stakeholder interests in organizations have produced at least two decades of insistence by managers on greater teamwork across functions. Functional specialists have had to learn the skills of collaboration or have been pushed aside as organizations have responded to increased competitive pressures. This has produced cross-functional thinking not only in businesses, but in business schools. Not surprisingly, the first areas tackled were technical. Just-in-time management, business process re-engineering, and value-chain management have each helped organizations to integrate across their technical functions. But the human and relational aspects of these changes have not yet come together in a similar fashion, and this is hampering not only technical integration, but strategic effectiveness as well. We believe the growing concern that strategic planning does not work anymore is a symptom of this deeper problem.

The authors of this book have come together to face the crisis in strategy by creating integration at the strategic level of thinking about organizations. By pooling our knowledge and experience about identity, reputation, and the corporate brand we hope to offer fresh insight and new direction to theory, research, and practice. We believe that this insight will help to integrate technical and expressive interests.

The authors of this book come from most of the disciplines of business studies—organization studies, communication, marketing, strategy, and accounting—and we have each done extensive research on at least one of the key ideas mentioned in the subtitle of the book, and/or have been involved in the application of these ideas in various companies. In discussions about our research at several conferences (most notably the annual Corporate Reputation, Identity, and Competitiveness conferences) we have discovered how similar our approaches to organizational strategy are. But we have also discovered differences in our interests, differences imposed on us by our various disciplines and functions. Thus, the task of integrating our knowledge is going to be strenuous. We agreed to write this book together as a means of collecting in one place the relevant ideas, knowledge, and experience each of us brings. The contours of the new perspective we hope to produce together are outlined in Fig. 1.1.

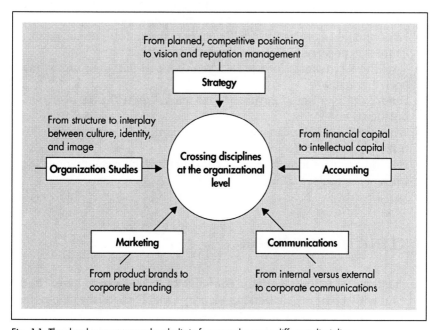

Fig. 1.1. The development towards a holistic framework across different disciplines

In addition to presenting the latest thinking from our disciplines and business fields, we have each been engaged in our own interdisciplinary activities. We share a belief in the necessity of collaboration across disciplinary and functional borders and we hope you will also find in the pages of this book traces of these struggles and ideas for confronting your own. For instance, we have had to confront some long-standing dilemmas such as those between the hard and soft sides of management, controlling and communicative functions, and rational and symbolic approaches. As you can easily see in this list of dilemmas and in Fig. 1.1, we do not pretend the sort of integration we are after will be easy, either for academics or for practitioners, but we do claim that progress has been made and you will see it in the pages of this book.

This book is just such an effort at interdisciplinary, cross-functional understanding. But it is more. We have, through the influence of close collaboration with practitioners, some of whom you will meet in the pages of this book, tried to carry the effort as far as possible in the direction of practical application. So, not only will you find integrative ideas in this book; you should also find ideas that can be implemented. Some of the questions you will find addressed include:

- How do organizations discover their identities?
- How do you broaden a growing organization's identity so that it embraces its expanding variety of businesses?
- What are the processes by which an organization changes its identity?
- How does an organization create a strong reputation?
- What should organizations deliberately communicate about themselves in order to positively influence their reputation?
- How should organizations react when they feel that their reputation has been threatened?
- Does corporate branding imply that marketing will take over business organizations?
- What are the implications of corporate branding for organizational structures and processes?
- How do organizations determine the difference between credible expressions of themselves and self-seduction?

OUTLINE OF THE BOOK

The chapters that follow fill out the contours we have sketched here. The book starts out with a part on 'Rethinking Identity', which establishes the notion of identity at the organizational level. The section offers a rethinking of identity from two different points of view, one based in cross-disciplinary theory building, the other arguing the strategic role for identity. The chapter by Mary Jo Hatch and Majken Schultz introduces the reader to the various conceptualizations of corporate and organizational identity found within the multiple disciplines addressed in this book. They combine these insights into a conceptual framework of identity and define a set of differences for mapping identity against culture and image. Jay B. Barney and Alice C. Stewart focus on the value-based foundations of identity. They show how identity operates as a source of competitive advantage and claim that the complexity of highly diversified firms pushes identity in the direction of moral philosophy. They argue that only abstract moral imperatives are able to unite a variety of business areas and serve as a shared platform for strategic decision-making.

Part Two, on 'The Symbolic Marketplace', introduces the symbolic dimensions of the new marketplace and offers a reconceptualization of the relations between market and organization. This marketplace is loaded with meanings, emotions, and symbols and it is here that organizations learn to express themselves. Wally Olins presents a historical perspective, showing how the roles of brands and branding processes changed completely in the last quarter of the twentieth century. Once dominant only in the minds of consumers, brands are increasingly taking over the minds of all stakeholders. As this change occurs, brands are becoming the company's most critical source of distinctiveness and value creation. Paul du Gay argues that the boundaries between consumers and organizational members are becoming blurred, as perceptions of organizing and work are re-imagined in terms of consumption. Du Gay points to the multidisciplinary theme of the book by showing how the symbolic expertise from marketing, communication, and design has extended market rationality and 'enterprising manners' to organizational life in general.

One of the most crucial accomplishments of organizations in the transparent marketplace is establishing reputation. Recently the definition of reputation has changed from an output measure of organizational performance to a strategic construct, which includes deliberate attempts to manage and monitor relations between organizations and their multiple stakeholders. Part Three, entitled 'Reputation as Strategy', includes two views of reputation, each analyzing the implications of considering reputation to be a corporate strategy. Reputation as strategy means that concern for corporate reputation drives organizational and managerial processes both within corporations and between corporations and their stakeholders. Charles J. Fombrun and Violina P. Rindova offer an extensive empirical analysis of the transformation of Royal Dutch Shell into a more transparent and expressive organization by the use of a comprehensive reputation management process. They introduce a learning model for reputation management and describe the managerial and organizational processes needed to support reputation as strategy. Dukerich and Carter focus on what they label reputation repair strategies—that is, organizational actions designed to repair damaged corporate reputations. They argue that organizational identity and image frame situations involving a damaged reputation and discuss the kinds of resources organizations allocate to reputation repair activities.

As branding travels from products and services to the corporation, the ways in which we discuss brand building and brand equity change. In 'Organizations as Brands' the authors invite the reader to explore the implications of branding organizations, each adding a different perspective to the argument. The chapter by Kevin Lane Keller uses the brand hierarchy to position the corporate brand and shows how different kinds of images can be associated with corporate brands. He offers a framework for designing a branding strategy illustrating the variety of ways in which corporate brands can be expressed. Simon Knox, Stan Maklan, and Keith E. Thompson argue that many brand tools are dated as they cease to create value for the customer across the organization. They offer an integrative framework as well as a methodology for organizational brand building based on what they label the Unique Organizational Value Proposition®, thereby expanding the marketing mix to include reputation as a core element.

In their search for efficient modes of expressing themselves, organizations have become more evocative in applying ideas, concepts, and tools not usually associated with business behavior, generating an increasing level of creativity and playfulness. Part Five, entitled 'The Value of Storytelling', exposes the reader to one of the most recent forms of expression. This part not only demonstrates that storytelling is an imaginative and creative source of organizational expression; it also argues why storytelling has relevance to business. The chapters by Cees B. M. van Riel, Gordon G. Shaw, and Mogens Holten Larsen all focus on narrative forms of expression by showing how corporate stories can stimulate organizational vision, challenge strategic position, and enhance cross-functional organizational processes. Van Riel offers an analytical framework for formulating and applying a sustainable corporate story, mapping the stages of storytelling as an organizational process. His chapter includes a rich empirical illustration of each stage. Shaw's chapter is based on his managerial experiences from 3M. He argues that strategic storytelling is fundamentally different from strategic planning, and challenges the myth that stories are inappropriate for business. He argues that many areas within large corporations will benefit from storytelling and gives examples from his own rich experience to bolster his point. Mogens Holten Larsen addresses the managerial implications of storytelling, and describes how to reconceptualize core organizational and communicative processes in order to express the corporate story. Finally, the chapter by Jan Mouritsen expands our understanding of the ways in which organizations tell their story by using visual expressions, such as models, sketches, and drawings, along with digits. He discusses how value is being created within organizations by introducing the concepts of intellectual capital and proposes the use of intellectual capital statements. This value-creating process is illustrated in a number of companies by tracing the interplay between the various kinds of expression and their related organizational processes.

The last part, 'Communicating Organizations', has a deliberate focus on the communicative processes of the expressive organization. It challenges our understanding of how organizations communicate about themselves. All three chapters in this part restate the foundations for communication in terms of the transparency of post-industrial organizations and offer provocative reflections on the meaning and expression of identity in the post-industrial era. Paul A. Argenti and Janis Forman claim that the role of communication is often overlooked in the formulation and implementation of strategy. Based on

Aristotle's insights about rhetoric, their argument suggests a constituency-based approach to communication that bridges the gap between communication and strategy. Lars Thøger Christensen and George Cheney challenge the role of constituents in communicating identities. They argue that the articulation and expression of identity more often reflect the needs and feelings of organizational members than those of their external constituents. They demonstrate a set of communication strategies that companies apply in order to seduce themselves into believing that what they want to say matters in a cluttered marketplace. The last chapter by Barbara Czarniawska brings the reflection on narrating identity into the sphere of cyberspace. She argues that the postmodern era calls for restating the issues of identity and claims that, rather than being concerned with authenticity and fragmentation, expressive organizations concern themselves with new virtual constructions of identity. By the use of examples from science-fiction novels, she shows how these virtual identities challenge the perception of identity itself.

As you can see, the book offers a palette of the most recent thinking and ideas that challenge a number of well-established theories and concepts within a variety of disciplines and business fields. Thus, we have intended *The Expressive Organization* to be a reader with cross-disciplinary application to organization studies, strategy, accounting, marketing, and communication studies. Although the majority of our authors are based in academia, they all have rich practical experience and are thus able to bring life into the conceptual arguments. By the same token, the authors coming out of business demonstrate their ability to make more general conceptualizations based on their insights and experiences. The authors have taken great care to produce personal statements, and we, the editors, have taken care to preserve their voices. Even so, we hope you will see how together these chapters weave a holistic understanding to support the emerging expressive organization.

I

RETHINKING IDENTITY

2

Scaling the Tower of Babel: Relational Differences between Identity, Image, and Culture in Organizations

Mary Jo Hatch and Majken Schultz

Corporate and organizational identity have attracted considerable attention from both academics and practitioners whose efforts to explain, control, and/or exploit them offer us a multiplicity of issues, concepts, and theoretical perspectives. This multiplicity is broadly based, because of the multidisciplinary appeal of the identity concept as it applies to organizations. In this chapter we examine different approaches to the study of the identity of organizations within the fields of marketing, organization studies, organizational communication, and strategy. On the one hand, the multidisciplinarity of these approaches creates considerable conceptual confusion, leading to what we describe as the Tower of Babel in identity research. On the other hand, the variety and richness that come from such diversity provide valuable input to our theorizing.

Our use of the Babel image is meant to acknowledge the frustration we and other identity researchers feel whenever the problem of defining our terms is confronted. There seem to be too many interests all trying to define a single set of concepts in their own preferred language. The cry for simplification by these same identity researchers indicates belief in a lost (or not yet found) common language, hence the invocation of the Babel myth. However, the problem with simplification is that it throws information richness away. We believe the reason no common language has yet been accepted is that the identity concept is informed by this richness. Although we feel that simplification is too high a price to pay, we persevere in our pursuit of an alternative. The solution we pursue in this chapter is to try to work through the theoretical complexity of the identity concept to see if it is possible to gain clarity in the face of this confusion.

In pursuit of our ambition to articulate the theoretical domain of identity without sacrificing multidisciplinary richness, we introduce the method of relational differences. This method is based on Saussure's (1966) observation that words are defined by their relationships to other words. In the context of this chapter the method involves comparing and contrasting identity with organizational image and culture—two concepts with which identity holds much in common. The method allows us to treat identity as a reference point within this rich multidisciplinary theoretical domain rather than as a concept standing in isolation. In our view, the understanding afforded by conceptualizing identity through relational differences offers a way out of what we feel is an unnecessary trade-off between simplification and overwhelming complexity.

In the first section of the chapter we will define corporate and organizational identity in the terms provided by their respective disciplinary origins and point out the divergence as well as the growing convergence in the ongoing development of their meanings. From a perspective of combined corporate and organizational identity, we will next explore the relationships identity shares with image and culture. Using our method of relational differences, we will map and analyze the multidisciplinary theoretical domain of identity, image, and culture, revealing six comparison/contrasts. Three of these define image in relation to identity (external/internal perspective, other/self, and multiplicity/singularity) and three define identity in relation to culture (textual/contextual, explicit/tacit, and instrumental/emergent). We conclude the chapter by deriving a relational definition of identity and by suggesting how the method of relational differences might help to develop empirical measures.

IDENTITY: CORPORATE AND ORGANIZATIONAL

As it relates to organizations, the concept of identity emerged simultaneously along two relatively distinct paths, one known as corporate identity and the other as organizational identity. The roots of corporate identity are primarily found in consultancy practice and the field of marketing, whereas organizational identity traces its heritage within the field of organization studies. The fields of strategy and communication have contributed to both the corporate and organizational identity literatures. So far only a few authors have addressed both concepts (Balmer 1995; Hatch and Schultz 1997; van Riel and Balmer 1997; Rindova and Schultz 1998) and we will draw heavily on their research below. We believe it is important to pursue insights from both the corporate and organizational identity literatures, since we believe they are addressing the same phenomenon, even though they do so from different perspectives.

Corporate Identity

In general, the field of corporate identity has been concerned with the notion of the central or distinctive idea of the organization and how this idea is represented and communicated to a variety of audiences (Margulies 1977; Olins 1989, 1995; Fombrun 1996). Thus the concept of corporate identity refers to how an organization expresses and differentiates itself in relation to its stakeholders (Alvesson 1990; Olins 1995; van Riel and Balmer 1997). For example, Olins (1995: 3) wrote that corporate identity 'can project four things: Who you are, what you do, how you do it and where you want to go'. Originally, corporate identity programs were targeted to external stakeholders or audiences (e.g. customers, investors, the public), but recently the target has been expanded to include employees (i.e. internal stakeholders).

Nearly all writing on corporate identity is focused on its business relevance, which is argued in several ways. The most widely used economic argument is that a distinctive and recognized corporate identity offers added value that attaches not only to the share price of a publicly traded firm but also to a firm's products in the form of premium prices and enhanced sales volumes (Greyser 1996).[1] What is more, marketers and strategists argue that, as products and services become increasingly indistinguishable, corporate identity carries a bigger share of the responsibility for sustaining margins.

According to this view, the economic value of a firm dealing in commoditized products or services is based on generating strong corporate images or corporate brands. Although marketers are often most concerned with projecting corporate distinctiveness to the marketplace by means of communication and impression management, some recognize that identity is the foundation of this distinctiveness (Abratt 1989; Olins 1989; Barich and Kotler 1991; Upshaw 1995; Aaker 1996; Fombrun 1996; Baker and Balmer 1997; van Riel and Balmer 1997).

Several authors point to the difference between what Balmer (1995) labeled the visual and the strategic schools of corporate identity. The visual school focuses on visible and tangible manifestations of what the company is and on the implications of these manifestations for leadership behavior and company structure. Balmer traced the roots of the 'visual school' to the graphic design community, which traditionally concerned itself with the creation of a company name, logo, color, house style, trademarks, and other elements of the visual identity program (e.g. Mollerup 1997). The tangible aspects of corporate identity also include buildings, corporate architecture, design, and decor of retail outlets, and aspects of products and services such as product design, packaging, and ritualized behavior (Olins 1995; Argenti 1998). Recently, sound, touch, and smell have been added to the corporate identity mix. For example, Schmitt and Simonson (1997) noted that the characteristic scents of a Body Shop retail outlet are an intrinsic part of the identity of the Body Shop. Thus, these authors replaced the term 'visual identity' with the 'look and feel' of the organization.

The 'strategic school' focuses on the central idea of the organization, which includes the vision, mission, and philosophy of the company (Olins 1989, 1995; van Riel 1995). In this school, corporate identity is conceptualized as part of the strategic process linking corporate strategy to company image and reputation (van Riel 1995; Fombrun 1996). In communication studies the strategic role of corporate identity is defined in terms of integrated communication, issue management, and public relations activities (e.g. Argenti 1998; Cheney and Christensen, forthcoming). We argue that the strategic school is shifting the intention of corporate identity programs from helping organizations to define 'who they are' to helping them project a vision of 'what they will become' (Collins and Porras 1994). It is this shift that introduces companies to ideas about the internal marketing of corporate vision such as with corporate stories, or scenario exercises. The strategic use of corporate identity can be seen in recent mergers where the companies involved have exercised great care in explaining the merger in terms of the company's new identity—for example, Daimler-Chrysler, PriceWaterhouseCoopers, and Diagio.

Another framing of the corporate identity literature focuses on identity structure and the ways in which corporate identity influences how companies communicate about themselves. In offering this framework, van Riel and Balmer (1997) distinguished between graphic design and integrated communication. The graphic design approach, which is similar to the visual school described above, focuses on identity structures. The concept of identity structure articulates the ways in which some companies present subsets of their identity as different product or business lines. For instance, Olins (1989; 1995: 20–4; van Riel 1995; see also Aaker 1996; Mollerup 1997) distinguished between three types of identity structure: (1) monolithic identity, where companies use one name and a consistent visual identity to 'promote a special idea about themselves' (e.g. Virgin, Shell); (2) endorsed identity, defined as a multi-business identity, where companies use a combination of an overall company identity (e.g. Nestlé) and a series of business line names (e.g. KitKat, Lyons Maid); and (3) branded identity, where companies manifest their identity only at the product brand level, making it less than obvious that all the different brands are related to the same organization (e.g. Procter & Gamble, Unilever, Diageo).

The integrated communication approach builds on a monolithic identity structure. Because of the explosion in messages, communication channels, and media awareness, proponents of integrated communication have argued the need to create consistency between visual and marketing communication, public relations, and corporate advertising. They claim that consistency creates a reliable, recognizable, and distinctive portrait of the organization across its communication channels and messages (van Riel and Balmer 1997). This approach focuses attention on the problem of aligning all the elements of the 'corporate identity mix' propounded by the graphic design or visual school.

Organizational Identity

In general, the concept of organizational identity refers to how organizational members perceive and understand 'who we are' and/or 'what we stand for' as an organization. Most views of organizational identity are built upon a version of social identity theory (Albert and Whetten 1985). Social identity theory emphasizes social interaction as the site of individual identity formation processes (e.g. Cooley 1902; James 1890/1918; Goffman 1959; Erickson 1964). By comparison with individual identity theories (see Gergen 1991 or du Gay 1996 for recent reviews), organizational identity is a young field, tracing its roots only as far back as Albert and Whetten (1985: 292), who defined organizational identity as the organization's 'central, distinctive and enduring aspects'. This definition has been reiterated throughout much of the organizational identity literature (e.g. Dutton and Dukerich 1991; Fiol and Huff 1992; Dutton *et al.* 1994; Reger *et al.* 1994; Ashforth and Mael 1996; Gioia *et al.* 1998).

Albert and Whetten (1985: 292) defined organizational identity as: 'A particular kind of question. The question, "What kind of organization is this?" refers to features that are arguably core, distinctive, and enduring and reveal the identity of the organization.' They went on to tackle the difficult issue of multiple identities that arises from the observation that 'organizations are capable of supplying multiple answers for multiple purposes'. In relation to multiple identities, they developed a model of the dual identity organization (e.g. universities, cooperatives). The dual identity organization is both normative (centered on cultural, educational, and expressive functions) and utilitarian (oriented towards economic production). Recently, Whetten and his co-authors (Whetten *et al.* 1992; Whetten 1997; Whetten and Godfrey 1998) framed one of the differences in approaches to organizational identity by distinguishing between researchers interested in 'identity of' and those concerned with 'identification with' the organization.

For those interested in 'identification with' the organization, a key issue is the interrelationship between personal and social aspects of identity construction (e.g., Ashforth and Mael 1989, 1996; Mael and Ashforth 1992; Brewer and Gardner 1996). For example, Dutton, Dukerich, and Harquail (1994: 239) defined organizational identification as 'the degree to which a member defines him- or herself by the same attributes that he or she believes define the organization'. Building on Mael and Ashforth (1992), van Riel (1995) operationalized the organizational identification concept with the Rotterdam Organizational Identification Test (ROIT). The ROIT measures the affinity of individuals with their organization along nine dimensions: perception of belonging, congruence between goals and values, positive evaluation of membership, need for affiliation, perceived benefits of membership, and perceived support, acknowledgment, acceptance, and security. In later work, three factors have emerged from their measures of these dimensions: pride and involvement; acknowledgment and perceived opportunities; and likemindedness/congruence (Smidts *et al.* 1998).

Concern with the 'identity of' the organization is not unrelated to that of identification, for the identity of the organization is believed to create a basis for member identification with the organization. That is, as the object of belonging and commitment, organizational identity provides a cognitive and emotional foundation on which organizational members build attachments and with which they create meaningful relationships with their organization. Evidence of this relationship between identity and identification is often found in large, visible, and highly articulate companies such as Shell and Virgin, but may also be significant in start-up companies—for example, within the IT industry. In general, however, 'identity-of' research is organizationally focused, while 'identification-with' research focuses on the relationship between the individual and the group or organization. Thus organizational identity in the 'identity-of' literature tends to concern itself with definitions of how organizational members see themselves as an organization (that is, its perspective lies internal to the organization and is rooted in organizational members' perceptions and understandings).

There appears to be increasing contention over Albert and Whetten's somewhat static notion of identity as that which is central, distinctive, and enduring about an organization. For instance, Gioia and Thomas (1996) have raised the question of how enduring identity really is, and Gioia, Schultz, and Corley (2000) present the concept of adaptive instability to address the same concern. Critiquing another aspect of the definition, Sevon (1996) questions whether identity is distinctive or whether organizational identities are institutionally determined via imitation processes.

Other dynamic views of identity take a narrative or storytelling approach. Czarniawska (1997; see also Czarniawska-Joerges 1994) has been a particularly forceful proponent of this approach, asserting that organizational identity, like individual identity, has a 'narrative character' that 'persists through an ability to narrate one's life, formulate it into a narrative composed of terms that will be accepted by the relevant audience' (Czarniawska-Joerges 1994: 196). In the narrative approach, different aspects of identity are highlighted at different moments depending upon who is speaking and who is listening, what speakers and listeners communicate in their exchanges, and how they react to and thus further influence the tale as it is told.

More radical dynamic views portray the essence, coherence, and continuity of identity as illusions created and maintained by processes of social construction. In denying that identity has an essence, they align with postmodernist views. Postmodern views of the self define identity as the product of cultural and social contexts and of the language that grants the subject position (for example, 'I' or 'we') around which notions of identity can be formed (e.g. Gergen 1991; Bauman 1992; Hall 1996). Bauman (1996: 18) explained the postmodern view this way: 'If the *modern* "problem of identity" was how to construct an identity and keep it solid and stable, the *postmodern* "problem of identity" is primarily how to avoid fixation and keep the options open.' In this view, identity is a mask that can be changed according to context or whim.

Contrasting Corporate and Organizational Identity

As can be seen from the discussion above, the difficulty with integrating corporate and organizational identity is that their proponents come from different disciplinary discourses so that, although there is considerable overlap in their efforts to theorize identity, there are also significant differences. The primary differences we find between corporate and organizational identity are summarized in Box 2.1. Below we describe these contrasts and deconstruct them in order to indicate why we believe identity is both corporate and organizational.

Box 2.1. Contrasts between corporate and organizational identity that need to be deconstructed

Dimensions of identity	Corporate identity	Organizational identity
Perspective	Managerial: top managers and their advisers	Organizational: all members of the organization
Recipients	External stakeholders or audiences	Organization members or internal stakeholders
Communication channels	Mediated	Interpersonal

Perspective

One difference lies in the perspective from which identity is defined. Corporate identity involves choosing symbols to represent the organization (for example, logo, name, slogan, livery). These choices are most often made by top management and their advisers, although these decision-makers increasingly take the perceptions and reactions of organizational members into consideration in their formulation of corporate identity (for example, via surveys or data collected through interactive media). Organizational identity, on the other hand, consists of the myriad ways that organizational members throughout the organization perceive, feel, and think of themselves as an organization. Organizational identity is most often projected in statements about 'who we are' or in stories that reveal the organization. These expressions are informal rather than planned or deliberate and thus agreement among organizational members is not an issue except insofar as researchers, managers, or consultants attempt to describe or articulate what 'the identity' of the organization 'is'. To fully appreciate corporate identity requires taking a managerial perspective, while appreciation of organizational identity requires an organizational perspective.

It should be recognized, however, that managerial and organizational perspectives on identity are not independent of one another. Top management's contributions to identity, such as via corporate identity programs, become part of organizational identity when members of the organization use these proffered corporate symbols in their everyday organizational lives. What is more, the symbols of identity and narratives about themselves that organizational members produce can be, and in some cases are, resources top managers use when they develop corporate identity statements, symbols, and/or programs.

Recipients

Corporate and organizational identities also differ in relation to how the recipients of identity messages are conceptualized. Originally, research on corporate identity was focused on enhancing the visibility and attractiveness of the organization and its products and services. Corporate identity researchers saw the recipients of identity messages as audiences to be persuaded (or seduced) or as stakeholders whose interests needed to be addressed. In contrast, organizational identity researchers concerned themselves with how organizational members perceived themselves as an organization and how those perceptions influenced their identification with the organization. Thus, as opposed to the concern with audiences or external stakeholders found in corporate identity research, organizational identity researchers conceptualized the recipients of identity messages as organizational members or internal stakeholders. As some researchers have pointed out, this characteristic of organizational identity research renders organizational identity a reflexive concept that sees recipients of identity messages as the same people who send them (this is the concept of auto-communication proposed by Broms and Gahmberg 1983 and Christensen 1994).

Increasingly the distinction between recipients of identity messages as external and internal stakeholders is being muddied by the amount of overlap between these groups. The overlap can be illustrated by the way in which relationship marketing repositions customers as organizational members or the way in which advertisers are increasingly treating employees as prime audiences for advertising messages. Another illustration is found in the taking-up of multiple roles by some individuals who are simultaneously employees, customers, investors, and members of the public. This muddying of categories and interests creates ambiguity about where the organizational boundary lies and who has responsibility for monitoring and managing these different groups and their perceptions of the organization.

Communication Channels

A final difference between corporate and organizational identity is that corporate identity expressions are frequently mediated whereas expressions of organizational identity are unmediated or direct.[2] In other words, external stakeholders receive official corporate identity expressions via communication channels that are mediated by television, newspapers, magazines, video, and the Internet. Organizational identity, on the other hand, tends to be directly experienced through everyday behavior and language. Communication of organizational identity to external stakeholders therefore requires opportunities for interpersonal interaction with them.

Acknowledging that organizational members may also belong to various external stakeholder groups (for example, customers, investors, the public) means that organizational members receive mediated communications of corporate identity just as other external stakeholders do. Their joint status as internal and external stakeholders may even make them more attentive to these mediated messages than other stakeholders are. This means they are likely to carry their impressions of corporate identity into their organizational lives and compare them to their understanding of organizational identity as it derives from their direct experience. They may even share these comparisons with other organizational members or stakeholders. Similarly, any interaction between internal and external stakeholders (e.g. customer service, information exchange) brings external stakeholders into direct contact with the organizational identity that organizational members carry and express. Like employees who are also customers, investors, or members of special interest groups, these external stakeholders will make comparisons between corporate and organizational identity as a natural consequence of these interactions. Thus it is not possible to maintain a clean distinction between mediated and direct communication.

Identity is both Corporate and Organizational

We conclude on the basis of our analysis above that the concepts of corporate and organizational identity, though representing different perspectives, targeting different recipients, and making use of different communication channels, do not represent different phenomena. Instead of choosing between corporate or organizational identity, we advocate combining the understandings offered by all the contributing disciplines into a single concept of identity defined at the organizational level of analysis. Doing this, of course, demands combining perspectives and practices originating in marketing, strategy, communication, and organization studies.

In this regard we propose taking a view of identity that encompasses the interests of all stakeholders including managers (strategy), customers (marketing), organization members (organization studies), and all other stakeholder groups (communication). To articulate this expanded concept of identity requires some effort at redescription. To achieve this we turn to the two other concepts to which identity has most often been related in both the theory and practice of organizing: the concept of image, which addresses the impressions and perceptions of the organization formed and held by external stakeholders; and the concept of culture, which refers to everyday organizational life as it is experienced by organizational members.

RELATING IDENTITY TO IMAGE AND CULTURE

Almost all corporate and organizational identity researchers link identity to image and always have. Similarly, culture has appeared regularly in discussions of corporate identity (e.g. Abratt 1989; Desphande and Webster 1989; Dowling 1993), although it has only recently been made an explicit part of theorizing about organizational identity (e.g., Hatch and Schultz 1997; Fiol *et al.* 1998; Rindova and Schultz 1998; van Rekom, n.d.). In this section of the chapter we will turn to identity's associations with image and culture in order to expand our search for the best terms in which to define identity at the organizational level of analysis.

Saussure (1966) observed that words are defined, not in relation to what they are believed to represent in the world, but how they affect each other in use. We apply this aspect of Saussurian logic as a method of theoretical development, in that we discriminate the key concepts of identity, image, and culture by focusing on their theoretical interdependence, or what we call their relational differences. Because the key concepts of identity, image, and culture help to define one another, we use the term 'relational differences' to emphasize that the discriminations we make are relative rather than absolute. Below we present six relational differences that have helped us to clarify the concept of identity in relation to image and culture by articulating how their meanings color one another (see Fig. 2.1).

For example, the meaning of identity seems to change depending on which position in Fig. 2.1 you assume. One way to imagine this is to use a spatial metaphor. Imagine that the theoretical domain of identity defined at the organizational level of analysis is a geographical territory. Using the spatial metaphor, you can then see Fig. 2.1 as a map of the theoretical domain, which facilitates imagining a variety of 'moves' between perspectives, each of which influences the meaning of identity. For instance, from the 'image' side, identity and culture seem almost equivalent, as both appear to be relatively tacit and internally focused. Similarly, from the 'culture' side of the 'map', identity and image are difficult to distinguish, as both seem to lie beyond the cultural core and to be relatively more superficial in the sense of being more concerned with appearances. However, when one takes the 'middle view' from the identity position, identity is simultaneously distinguishable from both

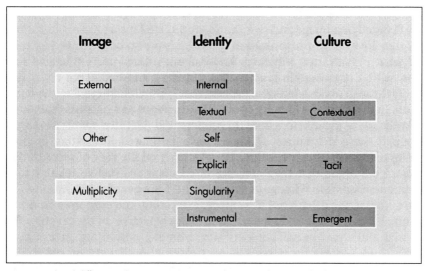

Fig. 2.1. Related differences between organizational image, identity, and culture

image and culture; hence the premise of our defining identity in relation to these two concepts and our use of the method of defining relational differences.

Linking Organizational Image to Identity

We will first restrict our 'movements' to the left side of Fig. 2.1. In this section we define identity as it compares and contrasts with image and find that the relational differences between image and identity include: external/internal perspective, other/self, and multiplicity/singularity.

External/Internal Perspective

Perhaps the most difficult distinction we can make between image and identity involves the perspective within which conceptualizations of these phenomena are formed. Organization studies researchers have contributed a notion of identity that rests on an internal perspective—that is, the perspective of organizational members or insiders (as is seen in their emphasis on the word 'we'). These researchers typically extend or project this internal perspective to image. For example, within organization studies, Dutton and Dukerich (1991) claimed that organizational image is what organizational members think that external constituencies think of them. Also, when Gioia and Thomas (1996) defined image in relation to identity change, they argued that the future image of the university they studied was constructed by top management as a driver for changing present identity. Whetten (1997) similarly claimed that image and reputation are situated inside the organization in that they involve how organization members want to be perceived by others and what organization members know about others' perceptions of them. Thus, within organization studies, both identity and image are constructed largely through a self-referential process that is situated internal to the organization. In this field, the identity concept is privileged and image is defined secondarily as a means to come to understand identity more thoroughly. Although these definitions of image have facilitated interesting empirical studies of identity–image relations based strictly on the view of organizational insiders, we argue that they are very often counter-intuitive relative to the common-sense view of image as externally held images of organizations.

In contrast, the disciplines of strategy, marketing, and corporate communication all locate image and reputation in the perspectives of the organization's external audiences or stakeholders (for example, customers, investors, the media) and address the ways different external audiences or stakeholders interpret and perceive the organization. For example, Barich and Kotler (1991) define image in relation to customers' levels of awareness and attraction to the organization (see also Aaker 1996; van Riel and Balmer 1997). Proponents of these disciplines then define identity as a foundation for images in the sense that identity influences both what is being projected to different external stakeholders, and how the organization is being interpreted and perceived by those stakeholders. In what nearly seems the antithesis of developments in organization studies, these researchers assume identity as a necessary antecedent of the observable phenomenon of image: stakeholders must have an image of something and they assume that something is identity. For them, image is privileged and identity is of secondary importance. This privileging has a tendency to make identity a black box.

A major challenge in defining identity across disciplinary borders thus involves grappling with the relationship between internal and external perspectives. As Jenkins (1994: 199) put it: 'It is in the meeting of internal and external definitions of an organizational self that identity, whether social or personal, is created.' In other words, the processes of identity construction and formulation blend both internal and external perspectives, just as do the processes of image creation. However, we argue that the meaning of the identity concept is associated with internal perspectives in a way that image is not. Those situated on the inside have a privileged claim on their own identity, and this claim is the organizational foundation for identity.

Similarly, the strong association of image with the perspectives of those external to the organization affects the meaning of the image concept. Thus, we accept the distinction between identity and image suggested by marketing and communication studies, while we argue the need to further open the black box of identity processes and acknowledge that it is a complex phenomenon that is influenced by the interaction of both internally and externally informed views (Hatch and Schultz 1999).

Other/Self

The starting points for identity and image studies differ. Organizational identity researchers are typically concerned with how organizational members develop, express, and project their organizational sense of self. Organizational image researchers, on the other hand, ask how organizational self-expressions and identity projections (e.g. corporate identity campaigns) are interpreted and perceived by others (van Riel 1995; Argenti 1998). Scholars within marketing and communication claim that organizational members often compare themselves to other organizations in order to grasp the uniqueness and distinctiveness of their own identity (e.g. Aaker 1996; Argenti 1998). Identity fundamentally addresses 'who we are', whereas image is concerned with either 'how we perceive others' or 'how we are perceived by others'.

As argued above, who we are cannot be separated from the perceptions others have of us, just as our perceptions of others are influenced by who we are. For example, Dutton and Dukerich (1991) found that mirrored (negative) images of perceived external prestige challenged the New York/New Jersey Port Authority's sense of itself as effective and hurt its organizational pride. This caused organizational members to act to change their organization's image. By the same token, deliberate reflection on the differences between self and other helps an organization define itself. For instance, Gioia and Thomas (1996) found that administrators in a US university made deliberate comparisons of their university with the images of its competitors within the 'Top Ten'. These comparisons generated reflection on their own university's non-Top Ten status, prompting the administration to initiate change.

In defining identity it is important to construct or confront a notion of self as that to which one's own identity refers. However, this self can be considered from both the position of the self and the position of the other. According to the definitions we are giving these terms, images are formed when a self is considered from the position of the other. That is, 'the other' is a position different from the self from which an image of the self (again different from the self and its identity) can be formed. Although it is possible for a single individual to take both the positions of self and of other (a detached position from which the self is viewed as if it were another), this does not negate the importance of recognizing the difference between the two positions.

Multiplicity/Singularity

In general, image analysis focuses on the multiplicity of audiences likely to form images of the organization and be affected by them and/or affect the organization with their subsequent reactions or actions. Image analysts generally offer conceptual frameworks highlighting the differences between these audiences. For example, in corporate communication studies, audience analysis involves segmenting different audiences (e.g. customer, community, investor, media, employee, or partner) and analyzing how each perceives and judges an organization (van Riel 1995; Fombrun 1996). Similarly, in marketing studies segmentation of customers is typically carried out on the basis of differences in attitudes, lifestyles, and consumer behavior.

In contrast to image, there is a singularity attributed to organizational identity that is not expected from organizational images. That is not to say that identity cannot be multiple, fragmented, and even contradictory, but even so the concept of identity refers to a focal (or single) organization, albeit one possibly having multiple identities (e.g. Albert and Whetten 1985; Markus and Wurf 1987; Cheney 1991; Gergen 1991). Postmodernists have taken the most extreme position so far on this point, arguing that, since what is claimed as identity changes with circumstances, a single self cannot be postulated (e.g. Markus and Wurf 1987; Gergen 1991). That is, the varied roles of an individual or organization give rise to many identities readily available to interested parties for their myriad constructions of the individual or organizational self. However, we feel it is important also to observe that the multiple identities of an individual or organization are rarely mistaken for different individuals or organizations; instead they are described as multiple identities or images *of the same* individual or organization. Thus, the very notion of multiple identities points, in Derridian fashion, to an underlying (though possibly absent) singularity.

Virgin offers an example. Virgin's self-projected image of being 'on your side against the fat cats' turns out to be interpreted by its multiple stakeholders as anything from a playful and hip anti-authoritarian statement to a vulgar example of overextended (British) youth culture. Furthermore, within the organization, interpretations of Virgin may differ significantly by business area. People working in Mega-Stores, in the Virgin Direct insurance company, and the Virgin Atlantic and Virgin Express airlines operate in different business contexts that require different competencies and affiliations, which means they will interpret Virgin's identity in different ways. Yet, in spite of the variety of these interpretations, they all point to Virgin as their single source and target.

Linking Organizational Identity to Culture

We now turn to the right side of Fig. 2.1 in order to define identity in relation to culture. In this section of the chapter we find three more relational differences: textual/contextual, explicit/tacit, and instrumental/emergent.

Textual/Contextual

Several researchers have argued that organizational culture provides local context for addressing the central question of organizational identity (who are we?) and contributes a great deal of symbolic material to its construction (Fiol and Huff 1992; Hatch 1993; Hatch and Schultz 1997; Fiol *et al.* 1998). As Hatch (1993) explained, identity involves how we define and experience ourselves and this is at least partly influenced by our activities and beliefs, which are grounded in and interpreted using cultural assumptions and values. What we care about and do defines us to ourselves and thereby, to some extent, forges our identity in relation to our culture. Along similar lines, Fiol, Hatch, and Golden-Biddle (1998: 56) proposed that: 'An organization's identity is the aspect of culturally embedded sense-making that is self-focused. It defines who we are in relation to the larger social system to which we belong.'

As opposed to organizational identity, the concept of organizational culture broadly concerns all aspects of everyday organizational life, in which meaning, values, and assumptions are expressed and communicated via the behavior and interpretations of organizational members and their artifacts and symbols (Geertz 1973; Schein 1992). Organizational culture is situated in patterns of taken-for-granted assumptions (Schein 1981, 1992; Schultz 1994), world views (Weber 1968/1978; Geertz 1973), and tacit mental frameworks (Hofstede 1980; Sackmann 1997) that are more or less shared among organizational members. Insofar as cultural assumptions, meanings, world views, and tacit knowledge shape answers to 'who are we?', culture contextualizes identity (or is one context for it). Of course, less consistency or more complexity may occur where there are multiple subcultures or fragmented cultures (e.g. Gregory 1983; Young 1989; Martin 1992; Martin and Frost 1997).

The idea that organizational identity is constituted within cultural contexts by organizational members' reflections on 'who we are' opens the way to a narrative view. In this view, identity is formed by a text or story about 'who we are' that is articulated in relation to cultural context (e.g. Czarniawska-Joerges 1994; Czarniawska 1997); however, the focus of identity texts can shift within contexts.[3] To give just one example, Virgin's anti-authoritarian style acts as a context for different stories about itself as an airline, a cola-maker, an insurer, and a train company.

Explicit/Tacit

Reflections on the organization's identity are assumed to take place at a more conscious level than that at which cultural knowledge resides, because they involve organizational members being explicit about the existence of an organization and/or what it means to them to form a relationship with that organization. In contrast to organizational identity, organizational culture neither demands nor necessarily provokes such reflexivity. In organizational culture studies, organizational reflexivity (or explication in this case) has typically been observed in the construction and development of corporate value statements (that is, corporate identity) rather than in the expression of deeper patterns of assumption and meaning presumed to constitute the cultural paradigm or core (e.g. Schein 1985, 1992; Hatch 1993; Martin and Frost 1997).

The relative explicitness of identity can be seen in terms provided by Schein's three-level model of culture. As Rindova and Schultz (1998) argued, the concept of organizational identity belongs at the more consciously accessible and explicable value level as opposed to the tacit level of taken-for-granted cultural assumptions. Even though organizational identity has also been associated with the unconscious and with psychodynamic processes of defensive behavior (e.g. Argyris 1990), the relative accessibility to consciousness enjoyed by identity (psychodynamic processes can be exposed and altered), in our view, renders identity the more explicit of the two phenomena, and culture the more tacit. However, it should be acknowledged that there may be aspects of identity that run as deep or deeper than the tacit levels of culture (e.g. soul), just as some aspects of culture may be made explicit (e.g. artifacts, value statements).

Instrumental/Emergent

In relation to identity, symbols are often used instrumentally to raise consciousness of a preferred or desired organizational self or to express that self to others. This is most significant in corporate identity programs, which include the deliberate creation of a mix of different artifacts like name, slogan, graphics, house style, and dress code, which are then used to communicate the organization's identity (for example, Virgin's red logo; IBM's blue suits and white shirts). By contrast, artifacts are symbolic materials used for sense-making purposes within organizations. The everyday life of the organizational culture emerges from these sense-making activities (for example, Virgin's aggressive yet playful attitude towards doing business and Branson's woolly jumpers). A focus on culture emphasizes how organizational members accomplish the emergent, local constructions of symbols from artifacts and meanings, whereas a focus on identity emphasizes the use of these same artifacts and symbols to express and/or communicate answers to the question 'who are we?'.

In their expressions of 'who we are' organizational members use various artifacts and symbols produced within the organizational culture but are also influenced by the ways in which others view the organization and interpret its symbols and values. Thus cultural analysis focuses on how organizations maintain their interpretive systems as a context for organizational sense-making activities, while identity analysis focuses on how the symbols and values of the organization, in combination with external influences, are used as resources for constructing organizational identity and projecting it to others.

HOW RELATIONAL DIFFERENCES CONTRIBUTE TO UNDERSTANDING IDENTITY: NEW THEORETICAL AND METHODOLOGICAL POSSIBILITIES

Box 2.2 shows aspects of image or culture (column 1) and identity (column 2) that refer specifically to the six dimensions of relational difference our analysis of the identity literature revealed (listed in the stub). The first three rows of column 1 taken together can be read as a definition of image and the last three as a definition of culture. Column 2 describes the identity concept as it has previously been explained by organizational researchers, while column 3 redescribes identity using the relational differences approach.

In column 2, identity is opposed either to image or to culture, whereas in column 3 parts of what we mean by image or culture elaborate the identity concept. In other words, in column 3 we employed both/and rather than the either/or thinking of column 2. This does not mean that we abandon the concepts of image and culture, but rather that we recognize and theorize the points of articulation between these three concepts in order to advance

Box 2.2. How relational differences contribute to understanding identity

Dimension	Image/culture	Identity as previously understood	Identity using the method of relational differences
External/internal	Images are formed from the positions of external stakeholders	Identity is a privileged claim of organizational members	Identity is formed from both internal and external positions
Other/self	Images are perceptions and interpretations made by others	Identity is a projection of an organizational self	Who we are cannot be completely separated from the perceptions others have of us and that we have of others
Multiplicity/singularity	Images are multiple when audiences are diverse	Identity refers to a single organization	Multiple images of identity refer to the same organization
Contextual/textual	Culture provides the symbolic backdrop against which meaning-making occurs	Identity is a story about who we are as an organization	Identity is a text that is read in relation to cultural context
Tacit/explicit	Culture is patterns of taken-for-granted beliefs and assumptions more or less shared among members	Identity is symbolized by artifacts such as logo, name, slogan, house style	Tacit understandings sit alongside overt expressions of identity (e.g. artifacts)
Emergent/instrumental	Culture is the product of sense-making activities in everyday life	Questioning identity invites comparisons with the desired self	Identity involves the instrumental use of emergent cultural symbols

theory. It is in this sense that we claim to have applied Saussure's (1966) idea that words (or concepts) are defined in relation to how they affect each other. By this logic, the method of relational differences could just as well be used to advance theorizing about image (for example, in relation to identity and reputation) or culture (for example, in relation to organizational identity and structure).

Comparison of columns 2 and 3 reveals what our relational differences contribute to understanding identity. In all cells of column 2, identity is depicted as organizationally self-focused, whereas identity defined through the relational differences shown in column 3 expands the focus on identity to include all stakeholders. Perhaps it goes without saying that column 3 also represents a relational stand on identity. Given its genesis in relational differences, this should come as no surprise; however, the cells in column 3 do give us some sense of the specific relationships to focus upon when striving to understand identity relationally. Relationships with and between stakeholders and their organizational symbols appear to be the primary concerns revealed by our analysis.

We believe the broader, more relational focus of identity, as depicted in column 3, is due to the influence of allowing all the fields of marketing, strategy, organization studies, and communication to play a role in defining identity. Thus we believe that, if all the items in column 3 were taken into account, we would have a truly multidisciplinary theory of identity at the organizational level of analysis. Although it is beyond the scope and intention of this chapter to present such a theory, we believe that clarifying the identity concept through the method of relational differences is a step in this direction (see also Hatch and Schultz 1999 for our first attempt at building this sort of theory).

Our articulation of the theoretical domain of identity (summarized in Box 2.2) not only provides a common theoretical map of the territory identity covers; it also suggests ways in which it might be useful to refocus measurement efforts. So far, the empirical measurement of identity has received less attention than its conceptual underpinnings. The most extensive efforts have been made by Ashforth and Mael (1996) and van Riel and his colleague (1995, 1997), who have developed survey techniques to measure the degree of identification of individuals with the company in question. Most recently, van Rekom (n.d.) has developed a laddering technique that elicits the actions, goals, and values that he claims provide the foundation for corporate identity. Organizational self-diagnostic tools have also been offered, such as Bernstein's (1984) cobweb method for eliciting descriptions of a company's identity along eight predefined dimensions: integrity, quality, imagination, reliability, service, social responsibility, technical innovation, and value for money.

In contrast to these existing approaches to measuring identity, an approach suggested by the relational difference of external/internal would be to ask organizational stakeholders to finish the following sentences: 'I feel like an insider in this organization when . . .' and 'I feel like an outsider to this organization when . . .'. The same questions could be asked of members of all key stakeholder groups such as managers, employees, customers, investors, suppliers, and the public. This approach overcomes the limitations of predefining internal and external stakeholder groups by allowing individuals to self-define their categories. What is more, the technique reveals situational information about when insider and outsider self-definitions are likely to be adopted. This approach could reveal differences in degree of belongingness that might then be correlated, for instance, with propensities to act (e.g. buy products, invest in stocks, seek employment, support initiatives).

The relational difference of other/self suggests asking multiple stakeholders of the focal organization to define the organization's identity in relation to that of others. This is a well-known technique used in strategy research to define the competitors of a firm and their relative strengths and weaknesses. However, we advocate adapting the method to articulate the identity of the organization. For example, first one would ask, 'When you think about this organization (e.g. Virgin), what other organizations come to mind (e.g. British Airways)?'.

We do not expect all stakeholders to define the organization in relation to its competitors; they may use other comparative foundations such as admired firms or firms they have worked for. This information in itself could be analyzed to reveal information about how identity is formed by different stakeholder groups. For example, in the case of Virgin some stakeholders may associate Virgin with other companies having casual and charismatic leaders (e.g. Steve Jobs at Apple Computer), while others may associate it with other challenger brands (e.g. Amazon).

Another elicitation technique would be to use metaphor (for example, which animal, automobile, or plant best describes this organization?). Using metaphor introduces an element of playfulness into the exercise and taps into a different sort of associative imagery than does elicitation of comparison companies. Either or both elicitation techniques could be used (company and/or metaphoric comparisons), but in all cases next you would query the respondent, using one elicited 'other' at a time: 'Compared to (e.g. British Airways/Coke/spider/Volkswagen camper/jade plant) Virgin is similar in the following ways (ask respondent to list comparisons), and different in the following ways (respondent to list contrasts).' You should bear in mind that these elicitation techniques will not give a reliable answer to the identity of the organization in question (the descriptive terms will no doubt shift over time and with the participants in the exercise). However, the point is not to label identity with accuracy, but to tap the rich imagery by which the identity of the organization is constructed in the imaginations of its stakeholders. Reviewing a tabulated list of the terms elicited from stakeholders should reveal thought-provoking images of identity reflected in the words offered.

To take the analysis further, a comprehensive list of comparisons and contrasts could be formed from the responses of a representative sample of stakeholders to elicitation exercises like those described above. Such a list could be presented in a survey instrument that asks stakeholders to assess the extent to which each term describes the focal organization (including spaces for 'other' in which the respondent can specify additional terms). With a broad enough sample and used over time, this technique might expose differences in the perceptions of different groups of stakeholders and shifts in their perceptions over time.[4] If so, changes could be keyed to events such as competitor moves, corporate advertising, organizational change initiatives, and the like to see if these events influence those aspects of identity that can be reached by tapping stakeholder images.

Finally, the relational difference of multiplicity/singularity suggests asking respondents to take all the descriptive terms they identified as relevant to the organization in the survey mentioned above and suggest anything that ties the terms (or subsets of them) together in their mind. The widely used card-sorting technique (one descriptive term pre-written on each card with the respondent's own suggested terms written on additional cards) might prompt respondents to form subsets of descriptors that cohere in their mind. Analysis of the data generated by this or a similar sorting method should reveal the extent to which identity is seen to be multiplicitous and/or highlight gaps (inconsistencies) between different aspects of identity. Researchers could then probe the respondents to find either an underlying singularity or evidence of multiple identities.

Cultures are less amenable to direct questioning than are images, so different techniques of measuring identity are suggested by the relational differences between identity and culture. We suggest that a combination of ethnographic and text-based methods may be best suited to addressing the right half of the domain of identity shown in Fig. 2.1. Here, the focus would be primarily on internal stakeholders, but some of the methods apply equally to external stakeholders, particularly when they are interacting with members of the organization. For example, using participant observation, one could collect narratives of organizational identity on occasions when stories about the organization are normally told, such as at organizational celebrations, anniversaries, during internal training programs or meetings, or at sales presentations or press conferences. Statements of identity could also be drawn from secondary sources such as minutes of meetings, employee newsletters, summaries of strategy formulation sessions, public relations bulletins, sales reports, and the like.

Meanwhile ethnography would offer the researcher an understanding of the cultural context of these expressions based on collection and description of artifacts and symbols of identity in use. For example, the people of Virgin may have created a rich collection of artifacts describing the history of their company that to them are profound symbols of what Virgin is (e.g. the first cut of Tubular Bells by Mike Oldfield, documents of the legal fight with British Airways, or an invitation to the grand opening of the first Virgin Records Mega-Store in London). By the same token, one could discover whether different stakeholder groups also become engaged by Virgin artifacts to support their feeling of belonging to the organization. For example, do music-lovers, train passengers, or airline travelers collect Virgin memorabilia? Asking stakeholders for their interpretations of collected identity symbols could reveal much about what identity in organizations consists of and how it is formed and maintained (or changed). Although cultures are obviously much more difficult to measure than are images, we find that the richness of well-established cultural methods of study could be used to inform identity research by providing a systematic approach to studying how stakeholders construct identity from cultural/symbolic material and what they use identity symbols for.

Finally, the data from all of these different techniques and methods could be brought to bear on discovering what the identity of the organization is and how it is being influenced by interpretive and associative processes linked to the concepts of culture and image. These are only preliminary suggestions for refocusing and integrating methods already used in strategy, communication, marketing research, and organizational culture studies, but the adaptations we suggest above illustrate the methodological possibilities of the relational differences approach when applied to the empirical study of identity.

CONCLUSION

The 'map' presented in Fig. 2.1 and the relational differences summarized in Box 2.2 present the theoretical contribution of this chapter towards articulating the identity concept at the organizational level of analysis. We feel that the map and the relational differences are important, since the increasing complexity of multidisciplinary theorizing about organizational life may sometimes seem like an endless parade through the Tower of Babel. We believe that our method of crossing different disciplines by defining relational differences can make a contribution toward scaling the Babel Tower of uni-disciplinary theorizing and towards promoting more cross-disciplinary empirical research. Ideas to inspire the development of identity measures based on the relational differences presented in the chapter were offered in order to encourage cross-disciplinary study. Not only will development of such measures encourage empirical research; they should also make it possible to test the theory we hope will evolve from the work we have started here.

NOTES

1 In the field of branding this added value is known as brand equity, the foundation of which is claimed to be brand identity. Brand identity, like corporate identity, is built upon the distinctiveness and reliability of core values, though in the case of brand identity these values are presumed to be expressed by the brand (Aaker 1996; Keller 1998), whereas in corporate identity they are communicated by name, logo, livery,

architecture, advertising, and other public statements made by the company about itself.

2 We are indebted to Craig Carroll for pointing out this distinction.

3 We believe that differing cultural contexts are what give rise to the perception of multiple identities discussed earlier under the heading of multiplicity/singularity.

4 If combined with the external/internal technique offered earlier, respondents' self-defined categories could be used as a basis of the groups to see if these groups have more coherent perceptions than do those constructed demographically.

REFERENCES

Aaker, D. (1996), *Building strong brands* (New York: Free Press).

Abratt, R. (1989), 'A New Approach to the Corporate Image Management Process', *Journal of Marketing Management*, 5: 63–76.

Albert, S., and Whetten, D. A. (1985), 'Organizational Identity', in L. L. Cummings and M. M. Staw (eds.), *Research in Organizational Behavior, Volume 7* (Greenwich, Conn.: JAI Press), 263–95.

Alvesson, M. (1990), 'Organization from Substance to Image?', *Organization Studies*, 11/3: 373–94.

Argenti, P. (1998), *Corporate Communication*, 2nd edn. (Boston: Irwin/McGraw-Hill).

Argyris, C. (1990), *Overcoming Organizational Defenses* (Boston: Allyn & Bacon).

Ashforth, B. E., and Mael, F. (1989), 'Social Identity Theory and the Organization', *Academy of Management Review*, 14/1: 20–39.

———— (1996), 'Organizational Identity and Strategy as a Context for the Individual', in J. A. C. Baur and J. E. Dutton (eds.), *Advances in Strategic Management, Volume 13* (Greenwich, Conn.), 19–64.

Baker, M., and Balmer, J. (1997), 'Visual Identity: Trappings or Substance', *European Journal of Marketing*, 31/5–6: 366–83.

Balmer, J. (1995), 'Corporate Branding and Connoisseurship', *Journal of General Management*, 21/1: 22–46.

Barich, H., and Kotler, P. (1991), 'A Framework for Marketing Image Management', *Sloan Management Review*, Winter: 94–104.

Bauman, Z. (1992), *Intimations of Postmodernity* (London: Routledge).

—— (1996), 'From Pilgrim to Tourist—or a Short History of Identity', in S. Hall and P. du Gay (eds.), *Questions of Cultural Identity* (London: Sage), 18–36.

Bernstein, D. (1984), *Company Image and Reality: A Critique of Corporate Communications* (Eastbourne: Holt, Rinehart & Winston).

Brewer, M., and Gardner, W. (1996), 'What is this "We"? Levels of Collective Identity and Self-Representations', *Journal of Personality and Social Psychology*, 71/1: 83–93.

Broms, H., and Gahmberg, H. (1983), 'Communication to Self in Organizations and Cultures', *Administrative Science Quarterly*, 28: 482–95.

Cheney, G. (1991), *Rhetoric in an Organizational Society: Managing Multiple Identities* (Columbia, SC: University of South Carolina Press).

—— and Christensen, L. T. (forthcoming), 'Identity at Issue: Linkages between "Internal" and "External" Organizational Communication', in F. M. Jablin and L. L. Putnam (eds.), *New Handbook of Organizational Communication* (Thousand Oaks, Calif.: Sage).

Christensen, L. T. (1994), *Markedskommunikation som Ørganiseningsmåde: En Kultur-teoretisk analyse* (Copenhagen: Akademisk Forlag).

Collins, J. C., and Porras, J. I. (1994), *Built to Last: Successful Habits of Visionary Companies* (New York: Harper Business).

Cooley, C. H. (1902), *Human Nature and the Social Order* (New York: Scribner).

Czarniawska, B. (1997), *Narrating the Organization: Dramas of Institutional Identity* (Chicago: University of Chicago Press).

Czarniawska-Joerges, B. (1994), 'Narratives of Individual and Organizational Identities', in S. A. Deetz (ed.), *Communication Yearbook 17* (Thousand Oaks, Calif.: Sage), 193–221.

Desphande, R., and Webster, F. (1989), 'Organizational Culture and Marketing: Defining the Research Agenda', *Journal of Marketing*, 53: 3–15.

Dowling, G. R. (1993), 'Developing your Company Image into a Corporate Asset'. *Long Range Planning*, 26/2: 101–9.

du Gay, P. (1996), *Consumption and Identity at Work* (London: Sage).

Dutton, J. E., and Dukerich, J. M. (1991), 'Keeping an Eye on the Mirror: Image and Identity in Organizational Adaptation', *Academy of Management Journal*, 34/3: 517–54.

—— —— and Harquail, C. V. (1994), 'Organizational Images and Member Identification', *Administrative Science Quarterly*, 39: 239–63.

Erickson, E. (1964), *Identity and the Life Cycle* (New York: Norton).

Fiol, C., and Huff, A. (1992), 'Maps for Managers: Where Are We? Where do We Go from Here?', *Journal of Management Studies*, 29: 267–85.

—— Hatch, M. J., and Golden-Biddle, K. (1998), 'Organizational Culture and Identity: What's the Difference Anyway?', in D. A. Whetten and P. Godfrey (eds.), *Identity in Organizations: Developing Theory through Conversations* (Thousand Oaks, Calif.: Sage), 56–9.

Fombrun, C. J. (1996), *Reputation: Realizing Value from the Corporate Image* (Boston: Harvard Business School Press).

Geertz, C. (1973), *The Interpretation of Cultures* (New York: Basic Books).

Gergen, K. J. (1991), *The Saturated Self: Dilemmas of Identity in Contemporary Life* (New York: Basic Books).

Gioia, D., and Thomas, J. B. (1996), 'Image, Identity and Issue Interpretation: Sensemaking during Strategic Change in Academia', *Administrative Science Quarterly*, 41: 370–403.

—— Bouchikhi, H., Fiol, M., Golden-Biddle, K., Hatch, M. J., Rao, H., Rindova, V., and Schultz, M., with Fombrun, C., Kimberly, J., and Thomas, J. (1998), 'The Identity of Organizations', in D. A. Whetten, and P. Godfrey (eds.), *Identity in Organizations: Developing Theory through Conversations* (Thousand Oaks, Calif.: Sage), 33–80.

—— Schultz, M., and Corley, K. (2000), 'Organizational Identity, Image and Adaptive Instability', *Academy of Management Review: Special Topic Forum on Identity and Identification*, 25/1: 63-81.

Goffman, E. (1959), *The Presentation of Self in Everyday Life* (New York: Doubleday).

Gregory, K. L. (1983), 'Native-View Paradigms: Multiple Cultures and Culture Conflicts in Organizations', *Administrative Science Quarterly*, 28: 359–76.

Greyser, S. A. (1996), 'Reputation: Aid to Growth and Shield', *Reputation Management*, 1/1: 73–4.

Hall, S. (1996), 'Introduction: Who Needs Identity?', in S. Hall and P. du Gay (eds.), *Questions of Cultural Identity* (London: Sage), 1–17.

Hatch, M. J. (1993), 'The Dynamics of Organizational Culture', *Academy of Management Review*, 18: 657–93.

Hatch, M. J. and Schultz, M. (1997), 'Relations between Organizational Culture, Identity and Image', *European Journal of Marketing*, 31/5–6: 356–65.

—— —— (1999), 'A Process Model of Organizational Identity', paper presented to the Academy of Management, OMT Division, Chicago.

Hofstede, G. (1980), *Culture's Consequences* (Beverly Hills, Calif.: Sage).

James, W. (1890/1918), *The Principles of Psychology*, i (New York: Holt).

Jenkins, R. (1994), 'Rethinking Ethnicity: Identity, Categorization and Power', *Ethnic and Racial Studies*, 17: 197–223.

Keller, K. L. (1998), *Strategic Brand Management: Building, Measuring and Managing Brand Equity* (Upper Saddle River, NJ: Prentice Hall).

Mael, F., and Ashforth, B. E. (1992), 'Alumni and their Alma Mater: A Partial Test of the Reformulated Model of Organizational Identification', *Journal of Organizational Behavior*, 13: 103–23.

Margulies, W. (1977), 'Make the Most of Your Corporate Identity', *Harvard Business Review*, July–Aug.: 66–72.

Markus, H., and Wurf, E. (1987), 'The Dynamic Self-Concept: A Social Psychological Perspective', *Annual Review of Psychology*, 38: 299–337.

Martin, J. (1992), *Cultures in Organizations* (Oxford: Oxford University Press).

—— and Frost, P. (1997), 'The Organizational Culture War Games: A Struggle for Intellectual Dominance', in S. R. Clegg, C. Hardy, and W. Nord (eds.), *Handbook of Organization Studies* (Thousand Oaks, Calif.: Sage Publications), 599–621.

Mollerup, P. (1997), *Marks of Excellence: The History and Taxonomy of Trademarks* (London: Phaidon).

Olins, W. (1989), *Corporate Identity: Making Busines Strategy Visible through Design* (Boston: Harvard Business School Press).

—— (1995), *The New Guide to Identity* (London: Gower).

Reger, R. K., Gustafson, L. T., DeMarie, S. M., and Mullane, J. V. (1994), 'Reframing the Organization: Why Implementing Total Quality is Easier Said than Done', *Academy of Management Review*, 19/3: 565–84.

Rindova, V., and Schultz, M. (1998), 'Identity within and Identity without: Lessons from Corporate and Organizational Identity', in D. A. Whetten, and P. Godfrey (eds.), *Identity in Organizations: Developing Theory through Conversations* (Thousand Oaks, Calif.: Sage), 46–51.

Sackmann, S. (1997) (ed.), *Cultural Complexity in Organizations* (London: Sage).

Saussure, F. (1966), *Course in General Linguistics* (New York: McGraw Hill).

Schein, E. H. (1981), 'Does Japanese Management Style have a Message for American Managers?', *Sloan Management Review*, 23: 55–68.

—— (1985), *Organizational Culture and Leadership* (San Francisco: Jossey-Bass).

—— (1992), *Organizational Culture and Leadership*, 2nd edn. (San Francisco: Jossey-Bass).

Schmitt, B., and Simonson, A. (1997), *Marketing Aesthetics: The Strategic Management of Brands, Identity, and Image* (New York: Free Press).

Schultz, M. (1994), *On Studying Organizational Cultures: Diagnosis and Understanding* (Berlin: Walter de Gruyter).

Sevon, G. (1996), 'Organizational Imitation in Identity Transformation', in B. Czarniawska and G. Sevon (eds.), *Translating Organizational Charge* (Berlin: Walter de Gruyter).

Smidts, A., van Riel, C. B. H., and Pruyn, H. (1998), 'The Impact of Employee Communication and External Prestige on Organizational Identification', working paper, Erasmus University, Rotterdam, the Netherlands.

Upshaw, L. (1995), *Building Brand Identity* (New York: John Wiley & Sons).

van Rekom, J. (n.d.), 'Corporate Identity: Development of the Concept and a Measurement Instrument', Ph.D. dissertation (Erasmus University, Rotterdam, the Netherlands).

van Riel, C. B. M. (1995), *Principles of Corporate Communication* (London: Prentice Hall).

—— and Balmer, J. M. T. (1997), 'Corporate Identity: The Concept, Its Measurement and Management', *European Journal of Marketing*, 31/5–6: 340–56.

Weber, M. (1968/1978), *Economy and Society*, ed. G. Roth and C. Wittich (Berkeley and Los Angeles: University of California Press).

Whetten, D. A. (1997), 'Theory Development and the Study of Corporate Reputation', *Corporate Reputation Review*, 1/1: 26–34.

—— and Godfrey, P. C. (eds.) (1998), *Identity in Organizations: Building Theory through Conversations* (Thousand Oaks, Calif.: Sage).

—— Lewis, D., and Mischel, L. J. (1992), 'Towards an Integrated Model of Organizational Identity and Member Commitment', paper presented to the Academy of Management annual meeting, Las Vegas.

Young, E. (1989), 'On the Naming of the Rose: Interests and Multiple Meanings as Elements of Organizational Culture', *Organization Studies*, 10: 187–206.

3

Organizational Identity as Moral Philosophy: Competitive Implications for Diversified Corporations

Jay B. Barney and Alice C. Stewart

This chapter argues that organizational identity (OI) can, in some circumstances, be a source of competitive advantage for firms. This chapter also argues that, as the level of diversification in a corporation increases, OI must be defined in increasingly abstract terms. One way firms can define an abstract identity is as moral philosophy—statements of right and wrong around which employees can rally and which can influence a broad range of business decisions. In this sense, OI as moral philosophy can become a source of sustained competitive advantage for firms.

ORGANIZATIONAL IDENTITY AS DECISION FRAME

In their definition of OI, Albert and Whetten (1985) emphasize three important defining attributes: claimed central character, claimed distinctiveness, and claimed temporal continuity. By claimed central character, Albert and Whetten (1985) mean that an organization's identity must focus on an attribute or attributes of a firm that are, in some sense, fundamental in understanding why a firm exists, its purpose or its mission. Ashforth and Mael (1996) refer to central character as an internally consistent system of beliefs, values, and norms that inform sense-making and action of organizational members.

By claimed distinctiveness, Albert and Whetten (1985) argue that, whatever these fundamental attributes are, they must be perceived as unique by those who espouse an OI. This perception of distinctiveness suggests that organizations actively seek to distinguish themselves from other comparable organizations (Messick and Mackie 1989). By identifying 'who they are' the organization is also determining 'who they are not'. These distinctions allow organizations to demarcate and sustain the boundaries of the organization (Ashforth and Mael 1996), clearly identifying which members stand within firm boundaries and which do not.

By claimed temporal continuity, Albert and Whetten (1985) emphasize the longevity of OI—that an organization's identity will remain unchanged over time, regardless of objective changes in the environments within which a firm operates and regardless, even, of the businesses within which a firm is operating. Though facets of the OI may evolve, the more clearly articulated and consensual the OI, the more likely that changes in OI will be path dependent. Present identity will not be inconsistent with past identity; rather the past may be reinterpreted in the light of the present.

The three characteristics described above suggest that the nature of OI has a strong cognitive component (Reger *et al.* 1994). In some ways, OI operates as a shared organizational schema that guides decision-making within organizations (Dutton and Dukerich 1991; Fiol and Huff 1992). A schema is a stored framework or body of knowledge (Ashcraft 1993) that consists of a set of concepts, relationships among the concepts, and information embedded in them (Medin 1989; Leahey and Harris 1993). Empirical research (e.g. Barr *et al.* 1992; Calori *et al.* 1994) has established connections between the shared or collective schemas of an organization and strategies adopted by the organization. The power of a collective schema is also demonstrated by Hall (1984), who documented how strongly an organization's strategy is influenced by a dominant schema or mental model.

If OI is the central, distinctive, and continuous core of a shared organizational schema, it can act as a framing mechanism for organizational decision-making. Consistency of organizational action resulting from this dominant mental model may be reflected in the core competencies that emerge within organizations.

ORGANIZATIONAL IDENTITY AND CORE COMPETENCE

Prahalad and Hamel (1990) define a firm's core competence as 'the collective learning in the organization, especially concerning how to coordinate diverse production skills and integrate multiple streams of technologies'. For Prahalad and Hamel, core competencies are, in an important sense, shared belief systems that specify *how* a firm will compete in its markets. Similar to OI, the definition of core competence implies a consistent application of an implicit organizational schema. Thus, one conclusion is that OI and core competence are both organizationally shared schemas that act to influence strategic decisions within a firm. Indeed, Sarason (1995) found that, when asked what was 'central, distinctive, and enduring' in their organizations, most managers responded by citing some firm attribute consistent with firm strategy or core competence. Similarly, Ashforth and Mael (1996) suggest that strategy and OI often become more tightly coupled over time. Though OI and core competence are related, what is unclear are the circumstances under which these two organizational schemas work together to reinforce consistent strategic action.

OI, as an organizational schema, is values based (Ashforth and Mael 1996). It reflects what is central, distinctive, and enduring about the organization (Ashforth and Mael 1989). For organizational members who adopt this schema (e.g. become strongly identified with the organization), OI provides direction about *what* events in the competitive or operating environment 'must be attended to'. OI suggests what is appropriate, legitimate, and feasible (Elsbach and Kramer 1996). Conversely, OI also determines what is inappropriate, illegitimate, and infeasible. The impact of OI, then, is that of ultimately aligning members' goals with the goals of the organization (Cheney 1983).

Core competencies are knowledge-based organizational schema that may be most effective when aligned consistently with the overarching OI. Core competencies are schemas and belief systems about *how* to 'attend to' certain events. For example, an organizational identity as a low-cost manufacturer will elicit knowledge-based competencies associated with maximized efficiency in firm processes. Efficiency-effectiveness decisions will tend to favor those activities that lower costs relative to the value created. Thus, while OI aligns member goals, core competencies align member behaviors, such as the means to achieve the goals. The tighter the coupling between OI and core competence, the greater the consistency among the strategic actions undertaken by a firm. Success of these strategic actions will tend to reinforce both the OI schema as well as the core competency schema.

THE ECONOMIC VALUE OF ORGANIZATIONAL IDENTITY

Though tight coupling between OI and core competence schemas may create consistent strategic action within a firm, this alone is not a sufficient condition to create economic value within a firm. For OI to add economic value to a firm, the identity must have *specific* implications for operational and strategic decisions. Indeed, if an organizational identity does not have such implications then it is either probably not widely shared among a firm's employees or it is irrelevant to business decisions made in a firm. In either case, organizational identity will not have a positive impact on the economic value of a firm. Indeed, efforts to leverage weak or inappropriate organizational identities will probably reduce economic value.

To add economic value, not only must an organizational identity affect decisions; it must affect those decisions in a way that enhances the ability of a firm both to conceive of and implement strategies that exploit environmental opportunities and/or neutralize environmental threats. In this sense, an organization's identity can help managers in a firm see opportunities for growth and profitability that they would not otherwise have seen or see potential threats that they would not have seen without this identity.

As a device to facilitate the conception and implementation of strategic action, OI can have a profound influence on a firm. However, an OI not only helps managers see some opportunities and threats, but it simultaneously makes it more difficult for these managers to see other opportunities and threats (Gioia and Thomas 1996). Indeed, it may well be the case that OI helps managers focus on certain opportunities and threats by eliminating from consideration other types of opportunities and threats. The value of focus is that it helps managers see options they would not otherwise see. However, focus means that managers will not be able to see options that fall *outside* the range defined by the organizational identity (Reger *et al.* 1994).

Put differently, there are significant opportunity costs associated with organizational identity. These opportunity costs are equal to the value of the opportunities forgone because they are outside the range of focus framed by a particular OI. To add economic value, not only must an organization's identity enable it to see and exploit/neutralize opportunities and threats, but, because of this focus, the value of the opportunities forgone must be less than the value of the opportunities exploited.

For these reasons, it is not possible to make general statements like: firms with a clear organizational identity will outperform firms without a clear organizational identity. The impact of an OI on the economic value of the firm will be a function of (1) the strength of the organizational identity, (2) the content of organizational identity as translated through core competencies into strategic actions, and (3) the value of the opportunities forgone by applying existing OI schema to the evaluation of environmental opportunities and threats.

ORGANIZATION IDENTITY AND SUSTAINED COMPETITIVE ADVANTAGE

To extend this discussion, assume that a particular OI is economically valuable, in that the value of opportunities created by this identity is greater than the value of the opportunities forgone because of this identity. To be a source of sustainable competitive advantage, not only must an organization's identity be valuable, but it must also be rare and costly to imitate (Barney 1991).

The condition of rareness is closely associated with Albert and Whetten's (1985) notion of claimed distinctiveness. To generate competitive advantages, however, OI must move beyond 'claimed' distinctiveness to actual distinctiveness. This is problematic, since many firms may think they possess a distinctive identity when, in fact, they do not (Reger *et al.* 1994). Indeed, research in cognitive psychology (Kahneman *et al.* 1982) suggests that all individuals tend to think they are more distinctive than they actually are. Just because employees in a firm think they are distinctive does not mean that they are actually distinctive. Organizational identities can fail to be distinctive in at least two ways.

First, it may be the case that competing firms possess similar OIs. This could happen for several reasons. For example, if many firms in an industry were founded at roughly the same time and in a similar geographic location, these firms could possibly generate very similar OIs. Moreover, if these firms draw employees from a common labor pool, OIs can become homogeneous. If large numbers of employees obtain personal identity from a common professional base (that is, computer software developers, CPAs, engineers), that professional identity may have a homogenizing effect on many competing organizations. Indeed, much of the new institutional school in organizational theory is based on the observation that important components of the organizational identities of competing firms will tend to converge over time as firms seek to attain organizational legitimacy (DiMaggio and Powell 1983). Thus, the extent to which a firm has the opportunity to create 'distinctiveness' may be increasingly limited as competitive terms are more clearly defined and resources and processes used by firms converge towards similarity.

Second, while it may be the case that a particular organizational identity appears to be distinctive, strategically equivalent substitutes for this identity may exist in other organizations. For example, a component of one firm's identity might be: 'We will not pollute because it is morally wrong.' Other competing firms may have, as part of their identities: 'We will make decisions that maximize the present value of our firm.' In a setting where polluting firms are subject to significant fines and adverse publicity, these two types of identity will often lead to the same competitive behaviors, although the motivations behind these behaviors may be very different. In a competitive context, however, what matters most is *what* a firm does, not *why* it does what it does. If two very different organizational identities end up motivating similar sets of behaviors, with perhaps similar core competencies, then those identities are strategic substitutes and cannot be a source of competitive advantage.

If, however, an OI is both valuable and rare, then it seems likely that it will also be costly to imitate. An organization's identity is likely to reflect its unique history—the unique people, personalities, and technologies that have existed in a firm over time. In this sense, OI is also likely to be path dependent (Arthur 1989). Path dependence is one reason a firm resource or capability may be costly to imitate (Barney 1991). Moreover, once established, organizational identity is also likely to be a socially complex phenomenon, involving numerous tacit agreements and understandings. Social complexity is another resource attribute that often increases the cost of imitation (Barney 1991).

That OI may be costly to imitate has both positive and negative implications for firms. On the positive side, if a firm's identity is valuable, rare, and costly to imitate, it can be a source of sustained competitive advantage. However, should a firm's competitive environment change dramatically, and should the value of a firm's identity disappear, costly imitation will often imply that it will be difficult for a firm to change. It is, perhaps, ironic that the very attributes that make it possible for OI to be a source of sustained competitive advantage can also make OI a source of sustained competitive *dis*advantage should it become less valuable.

ORGANIZATIONAL IDENTITY IN A DIVERSIFIED ORGANIZATION

In many ways it is easy to show a relationship between the concepts of OI and economic value. It is also easy to show that OI can be a source of sustained competitive advantage in some circumstances. This can be done by applying the criteria developed in the resource-based view of the firm to the concept of OI. While it cannot be argued that OI will always be a source of sustained competitive advantage, it is clear that in some circumstances (i.e. when it is valuable, rare, and costly to imitate) it will be.

As traditionally discussed, both OI and core competence apply very well to the single business firm as well as for firms pursuing strategically related businesses. For single business firms, identity and core competencies are often tightly coupled (Ashforth and Mael 1996). OI is a powerful organizational schema that defines *what* 'must be attended to' in the environment. Core competencies are knowledge-based schemas that influence *how* organizations react to the environment. Often, these two schemas are articulated in the context of the product market of the firm. For example, Nucor Steel defines its identity in terms of the steel product market as: 'We build plants economically and run them efficiently' (Ghemawat and Stander 1992). WalMart, another single business firm, defines its identity in terms of the discount retail market as 'low prices everyday' and generates organizational competencies in all components of its business to be consistent with this identity (Ghemawat 1986).

Since firms pursuing *related* diversification strategies often operate in multiple product markets, it is usually difficult for these firms to define their identities and core competencies in terms of a single product market. The nature of the environment is more diverse, suggesting that 'what must be attended to', as a practical matter, must be more general—not specifically determined by the competitive characteristics of a particular product market. In this case, the relatedness of the markets may allow emergence of identities associated with particular organizational characteristics. For example, Cooper Industries define their identity as a company that acquires underperforming firms with well-known name brands and creates value through applying their core competencies in state-of-the-art manufacturing and other management processes to these firms. Managers at Cooper call this the 'Cooperization Process'. 'Cooperization' is a complex set of organizational routines used by Cooper

Industries to integrate firms into the Cooper family of business units. Once 'Cooperized', a firm comes to understand what it means to become part of this corporation, meaning it comes to understand and share Cooper's OI (Collis 1991).

As a firm becomes progressively more diversified, however, defining a firm's identity in terms of either product markets or common organizational processes becomes more difficult. By definition, highly diversified firms operate in multiple product markets. The diversity of markets makes it virtually impossible to apply the same organizational processes or core competencies across all operations. A market-based OI that may be valuable in one industry could be meaningless or even detrimental in a second industry, and yet one firm may own businesses operating in both. These complexities can be multiplied many times as firms become diversified and operate in multiple businesses around the world.

The characteristics of diversified firms suggest that the tightly coupled schematic linkage between OI and core competence that forms the basis for strategic action in single industry firms does not apply in highly diversified firms. The linkage for diversified firms will be, at best, loosely coupled. The values-based schema of OI must be broad; it must encompass a wide variety of contexts. The common denominator must be large. The definition of what 'must be attended to' should provide an umbrella schema broad enough to process information about a multitude of operating environments. In addition, the knowledge-based schemas upon which core competencies are based may not be the same in all subsidiaries of a highly diversified firm. Thus the cognitive linkages that reiterate the OI as part of core competencies are less likely to be present in a highly diversified firm. The problem within diversified firms is that the values-based OI must be broad enough to signal convergent goals while clear enough to support a wide variety of knowledge-based means (i.e. core competencies) to achieve those goals.

THE NEED FOR ORGANIZATIONAL IDENTITY IN THE HIGHLY DIVERSIFIED FIRM

One response to this situation is simply to argue that highly diversified firms do not need a single identity or core competence that cuts across all the businesses they own. This assertion, though, is inconsistent with how capital markets operate throughout the world. Essentially, managers of firms should engage in diversification strategies only when those strategies (1) exploit real economies of scope that (2) cannot be exploited by outside investors on their own at low cost. Real economies of scope exist when the combined value of the businesses pursued by a firm is greater than the value of each of these businesses separately. However, if outside investors can obtain these economies on their own (through, for example, holding a diversified portfolio of stocks), they have no need to hire managers to gain these economies for them. This implies that diversified firms that fail to exploit the economies of scope that cannot be duplicated by outside investors will be under enormous pressure either to discover some real economies or to split the corporation into separate businesses (Barney 1996).

There are numerous potential economies of scope for firms pursuing multiple businesses in closely related product markets. As diversification increases, however, many of these economies can no longer be realized. When this occurs, firms must seek economies of scope that exploit more intangible aspects of the organization. The more highly diversified a firm is, though, the more abstract these economies of scope must be—while still adding real value to the organization.

In the extreme, highly diversified firms may create economies of scope from defining a common OI. Such OI, however, cannot be constructed from values based on the attributes of a particular product market. Thus the approach utilized by Nucor Steel and WalMart to define their respective identities cannot apply in the highly diversified case. Nor can OI focus on values defined by specific operating resources and capabilities common across all firm businesses—since there are no such common frames of reference. Thus Cooper Industries' approach to defining their identity cannot apply in the highly diversified firm. In the extreme, to generate the necessary breadth, highly diversified firms may have to create an OI that is defined in terms of moral philosophy—a statement about the right and wrong ways to behave in society and in a company. Managers can then take these moral imperatives and apply them in managing their particular subsidiary business.

EXAMPLES OF ORGANIZATIONAL IDENTITY AS MORAL PHILOSOPHY

While the idea of a moral philosophy may be highly abstract, it is none the less real. An example of a firm that is highly diversified and uses a particular moral philosophy to define its organizational identity is Koch Industries (KI). KI is a highly diversified firm headquartered in Wichita, Kansas. The firm operates in the oil, gas, oil and gas derivatives, and agricultural products industries. KI is the second largest privately held company in the USA. Eighty-five percent of KI stock is owned by Charles Koch, who is currently the CEO and Chairman of the Board. Since inheriting the company at the time of his father's death in 1967, Charles Koch has presided over a one-hundred-fold increase in sales at KI. In 1966, KI had $177 million in sales; in 1998, it had over $37 billion in sales. In 1967, KI employed 650 people; by the mid-1990s KI employed over 13,000.

Charles Koch attributes much of the success at KI to a management style he calls 'market-based management'. Market-based management (MBM), in turn, is Charles Koch's solution to a fundamental conundrum. On one hand, the virtues of market capitalism—as an engine of progress, as a way to allocate scarce resources, and as a way to promote individual freedom—are impossible to deny. On the other hand, even casual observation suggests that the simple market capitalism described by Adam Smith—with small shopkeepers and manufacturers responding to the 'invisible hand' of supply and demand—does not exist. Instead, huge multinational corporations, some with sales in excess of the gross national products of many medium-sized countries, compete in global markets. The sheer size of these corporations suggests that much value creation in the modern economy occurs within managerial hierarchies and not across markets. Many of these managerial hierarchies are characterized by highly centralized decision-making, a change-resistant bureaucracy, and uninformed and under-appreciated workers. Is it really possible to have market capitalism when markets are populated with inefficient and bureaucratic, centrally planned corporations?

MBM is Charles Koch's answer to this question. MBM does not seek to recreate market exchanges within organizations. After all, as Williamson (1975) has shown, if it were possible to create perfect market exchanges within a corporation, then these exchanges should not occur within the corporation, but should occur across a market. Rather MBM seeks to derive principles from the analysis of market efficiency and to adapt those principles in the context of an organization. Some of the key tenets of MBM, derived from an analysis of market efficiency, include:

1. all decisions made in an organization should focus on maximizing the net present value of the firm,
2. decisions should be made by those people in an organization who have the local knowledge necessary to make present value maximizing decisions, regardless of their rank or status,
3. compensation should be tied directly to the ability of individuals in a firm to maximize the net present value of the firm,
4. management control mechanisms should focus on measuring those aspects of behavior that are most directly linked to maximizing present value (i.e. focus on economic value added, not accounting measures of performance),
5. present value maximizing decisions need to be consistent with rules of just conduct to ensure that fair and appropriate decisions are made, and
6. success is possible only if employees are intellectually honest and humble and respect the contributions made by unique individuals throughout the firm.

These principles lead to what many firms might conclude are unusual management practices at KI. For example, KI invests heavily in training its employees. Much of this training focuses on microeconomic theory and net present value analysis—training provided to employees at all levels—from managers to secretaries and janitors. KI's objective is that employees see their job in terms of how it affects the present value of the firm, no matter what that job is.

One recently hired manager at KI was about to make some copies when his secretary stopped him and observed, 'The opportunity cost for me making these copies is $50; the opportunity cost for you making these copies is $175. I will make the copies. In the mean time, you need to discover ways you can add at least $175 in value to the firm.'

KI has no budgets or budget systems. Senior management at KI decided to abandon budgets for several reasons. First, they concluded that budgeting, *per se*, makes no money for KI. Second, they observed that budgets assume that all the critical information needed to make a decision is available at the time a budget is set in stone. That assumption is simply not true in most of KI's markets. Rather than engaging in the fiction adopted by most firms—where budgets are set and then adjusted when new information becomes available—KI simply does not have budgets. Finally, budgeting is, according to KI management, inconsistent with delegating decision-making authority to those people with the local knowledge needed to make a decision. Rather than constraining those individuals to budget targets, KI expects its employees to constantly make decisions that maximize the present value of the firm. Indeed, the only way to ensure long-term employment at KI is to demonstrate the ability to add economic value to the firm over the long run.

Despite being highly diversified, KI has not adopted a multi-divisional organizational structure. Rather it has adopted a functional organizational structure that requires employees at KI to coordinate with numerous other employees in numerous different functions in order to accomplish anything. This helps ensure the free flow of ideas that is necessary if KI is to take full advantage of its economic opportunities and the skills and knowledge of its employees.

In the end, MBM is more than just a management system derived from the study of market economies. As Charles Koch says, MBM is a 'framework, a philosophy, a methodology'. It is an organizational identity that employees can accept and believe in, something greater than their narrow self-interests, something that connects employees to each other and to Charles Koch. It is a statement of values and beliefs and helps define a code of 'moral' behavior within the firm. MBM goes beyond describing an economically efficient way to manage a diversified corporation—it helps define the 'right and wrong' of working in this modern corporation. The power of this philosophy is perhaps best revealed in a common answer to a simple question often addressed to Koch employees: 'Why do you work so hard?' The answer is, more often than not: 'I just can't imagine letting Charles Koch down.'

MBM is just one example of organizational identity raised to the level of moral philosophy. There are other examples of identities that are broad enough to shape the schema of widely diversified firms. Johnson & Johnson is a diversified firm in the health-care and pharmaceutical industries. Several decades ago, Johnson & Johnson senior management developed something called 'the Credo'. The Credo is a statement of values and beliefs around which Johnson & Johnson tries to operate. Every few years, senior managers at

Johnson & Johnson go through a process of evaluating the Credo, assuring that managers throughout the company understand its intent and purpose. There are times when specific business decisions may violate one or another tenet of the Credo. When this happens, managers throughout the organization are empowered to declare a decision a 'Credo issue', at which time the discussion shifts from the short-term economics of a decision to a discussion of its broader moral implications (Aguilar and Bhambri 1983).

CONCLUSION

The common theme in these two examples is that the values-based foundation of OI must have a moral tone in highly diversified firms. In single businesses the values-based foundation may often be defined in terms of competitive position or strength. The tight coupling between OI and core competence frames strategic action. In highly diversified firms, the values associated with a particular product market may not be easily translated across subsidiaries. Thus managers must seek a broader schematic framework in which to couch the organizational identity. A moral philosophy, with its emphasis on right and wrong, can be just such an umbrella theme to unite a variety of business operations. A morality-based organizational identity identifies more subtle issues that 'must be attended to' within the environment. This attention may provide unique economies of scope for diversified firms.

REFERENCES

Albert, S., and Whetten, D. A. (1985), 'Organization Identity', in L. L. Cummings and M. M. Staw (eds.), *Research in Organizational Behavior, Volume 7* (Greenwich, Conn.: JAI Press), 7: 263–95.

Arguilar, F. J., and Bhambri, A. (1983), 'Johnson & Johnson (A)', Harvard Business School Case, no. 9–384–053.

Arthur, W. (1989), 'Competing Technologies, Increasing Returns, and Lock-In by Historical Context', *Economic Journal*, 99/394: 116–31.

Ashcraft, M. A. (1993), *Human Memory and Cognition* (New York: Harper Collins).

Ashforth, B. E., and Mael, F. (1989), 'Social Identity Theory and the Organization', *Academy of Management Review*, 14/1: 20–39.

—— —— (1996), 'Organizational Identity and Strategy as a Context for the Individual', in J. A. C. Baur, and J. E. Dutton (eds.), *Advances in Strategic Management, Volume 13* (Greenwich, Conn.: JAI Press), 19–64.

Barney, J. (1991), 'Firm Resources and Sustained Competitive Advantage', *Journal of Management*, 17: 99–120.

—— (1996), *Gaining and Sustaining Competitive Advantage* (New York: Addison Wesley).

Barr, P., Stimpert, J., and Huff, A. (1992), 'Cognitive Change, Strategic Action, and Organizational Renewal', *Strategic Management Journal*, 13: 15–36.

Calori, R., Johnson, G., and Sarnin, P. (1994), 'CEO's Cognitive Maps and the Scope of the Organization', *Strategic Management Journal*, 15: 437–58.

Cheney, G. (1983), 'On the Various and Changing Meanings of Organizational Membership: A Field Study of Organizational Identification', *Communication Monographs*, 50: 342–62.

Collis, D. (1991), 'Cooper Industries' Corporate Strategy', Harvard Business School Teaching Note, no. 5–391–281.

DiMaggio, P., and Powell, W. (1983), 'The Iron Cage Revisited: Institutional Isomorphism and Collective Rationality in Organizational Fields', *American Sociological Review*, 48: 147–60.

Dutton, J. E., and Dukerich, J. M. (1991), 'Keeping an Eye on the Mirror: Image and Identity in Organizational Adaptation', *Academy of Management Journal*, 34/3: 517–54.

Elsbach, K., and Kramer, R. (1996), 'Members' Responses to Organizational Identity Threats: Encountering and Countering the Business Week Rankings', *Administrative Science Quarterly*, 41/3: 442–76.

Fiol, C., and Huff, A. (1992), 'Maps for Managers: Where are We? Where do we Go from Here?', *Journal of Management Studies*, 29: 267–85.

Ghemawat, P. (1986). 'Sustainable Advantage', *Harvard Business Review*, 64: 5.

—— and Stander III, H. J. (1992), 'Nucor at a Crossroads', Harvard Business School Case, no. 9–793–039.

Gioia, D., and Thomas, J. B. (1996), 'Identity, Image, and Issue Interpretation: Sensemaking during Strategic Change in Academia', *Administrative Science Quarterly*, 41/3: 370–403.

Hall, R. I. (1984), 'The Natural Logic of Management Policy Making: Its Implications for the Survival of an Organization', *Management Science*, 30: 905–27.

Kahneman, D., Slovic, P., and Tversky, A. (1982), *Judgement under Uncertainty: Heuristics and Biases* (Cambridge: Cambridge University Press).

Leahey, T. H., and Harris, R. J. (1993), *Learning and Cognition* (Englewood Cliffs, NJ: Prentice Hall).

Medin, D. L. (1989), 'Concepts and Conceptual Structure', *American Psychologist*, 44: 1469–81.

Messick, D., and Mackie, D. (1989), 'Intergroup Relations', in M. R. Rosenzwieg, and L. W. Porter (eds.), *Annual Review of Psychology* (Palo Alto, Calif.: Annual Reviews), 40: 45–81.

Prahalad, C. K., and Hamel, G. (1990), 'The Core Competence of the Corporation', *Harvard Business Review*, 68/3: 79–91.

Reger, R. K., Gustafson, L. T., DeMarie, S. M., and Mullane, J. V. (1994), 'Reframing the Organization: Why Implementing Total Quality is Easier Said than Done', *Academy of Management Review*, 19/3: 565–84.

Sarason, Y. (1995), 'Operationalizing Organizational Identity: The Case of the Baby Bells', paper presented at the Organizational Identity Conference, Deer Valley, Utah.

Williamson, O. (1975), *Markets and Hierarchies: Analysis and Antitrust Implications* (New York: Free Press).

II

THE SYMBOLIC MARKETPLACE

4

How Brands are Taking over the Corporation

Wally Olins

In the *Financial Times*, 4 August 1999, a headline proclaimed: 'Ford to outsource important parts of car assembly.' This apparently modest announcement concealed extraordinary news. According to one executive quoted in the article, 'The manufacture of cars will be a declining part of Ford's business. They will concentrate in the future on design, branding, marketing, sales and service operations.'

Even allowing for some hyperbole, this is an apocalyptic observation. Ford's business was created and sustained above all around its unassailable manufacturing superiority. In its early days nobody built cars faster, better, or more economically than Ford. It was historically the most admired manufacturing company in the world. Now it seems Ford is shifting its center of gravity so far that in the long term it may do everything with its products except manufacture them. Ford will not make but it will brand. This shows how far branding has come in a very few years—and it also shows how the world is going.

The first, industrial, revolution was based around product innovation and manufacturing expertise. If someone invented a machine or a system that could do things better, faster, and cheaper, an advantage was gained until someone else improved on it. In today's knowledge revolution, innovation remains very important, but since everyone knows everyone else's secrets almost as soon as they appear, organizations keep looking for ideas that give them an advantage that they do not have to share. They look for intangible factors that are unique. The only intangible factors that no company needs to share are its brands. And that in essence is why branding is becoming such an important issue for the corporation.

In the 1970s when I first started putting down my thoughts on branding it never occurred to anyone, and certainly not to me, that the brand would become so important that it would challenge the identity of the corporation itself. 'Theoretically,' I said in *The Corporate Personality* (published by the

Design Council in 1978), 'the dividing line between a brand identity and company or corporate identity is very clear: a brand is a wholly concocted creation that is devised solely to help sell and it has no life of its own.' In those days, in theory at any rate, the brand identity was aimed only at the consumer, while the corporate identity was aimed at many audiences, including its own staff, shareholders, suppliers, governments, opinion-formers, and others.

Of course in reality things were never that simple. Some corporations, like Ford, used their names on products so that they were brand names too. Some brands, like Johnnie Walker whisky, at that time part of Distillers, had their own factories, workforces, and internal focus and therefore still had a real existence. But in the main the situation that I described in the 1970s was one in which the corporation wholly or largely controlled the brand's identity.

In the last quarter of the twentieth century the position of brands and branding changed completely. Brands became dominant in the minds of the consumer and increasingly in the minds of all the other audiences of the corporation, including shareholders and employees. Financial audiences now know that brands are an intangible asset that raises share price. People like to work for companies whose brands are well known and respected. Above all consumers have fallen in love with brands. By the turn of the century, brands had been established as the greatest gift that commerce had brought to popular culture. In the twenty-first century, brands have acquired a place in the world unimaginable in any previous period of history.

Many factors conspired to bring about this dramatic change. My intention in this chapter is to trace them. I start with consumer brands, because that is where branding began. I then move on to retail brands, because there is a kind of symbiosis in the relationship between consumer and retail brands. After that I look at manufacturers' product brands. This is a sector in which branding, in its more sophisticated form, arrived relatively recently. Its impact still varies greatly between countries and areas of activity. Then, to conclude the brief historical survey, I look at corporate branding. The issue here is whether corporate branding is just another more fashionable name for corporate identity, or whether the brand has truly subsumed the identity of the corporation. This is a new and in my judgment significant and immediate topic. Next, under the heading 'Brands in the Public Mind', I examine aspects of the relationship between brands and the consumer. Finally, in the section 'What is a Brand Worth', I look at the impact of all this on the stock market value of the company.

CONSUMER BRANDS

Brands in a modern sense emerged to serve a literate industrial proletariat in the late nineteenth century. Using revolutionary techniques like advertising and distribution on a vast scale, huge companies grew up, initially in the USA, that created a new world for the housewife. Uncontaminated factory-fresh products of consistent quality were made available at the nearest shop, heavily and clearly branded and backed up by powerful and imaginative advertising. The brand was the major engine of their success.

Although a few of the great companies that created the consumer goods business used their own names on their products, like Heinz, most of them—Procter & Gamble, Lever Brothers, and the others—created brands with unsubtle but powerful associations such as Lifebuoy and Sunlight, designed to drive home the virtues and strengths of their simple domestic products to a credulous but literate audience.

The brands these companies created were mostly mundane everyday items: soap, jam, toothpaste, washing powder, breakfast cereals—packaged goods aimed at the housewife. For about the first 100 years of their existence brands and perishable household commodities were largely synonymous—and the formula used to market them was both rigid and vigorously applied. Although there were, and for that matter still are, genuine differences in performance between brands, these were often difficult for the customer to discern. So, working with advertising agencies, the consumer goods companies developed a particular look, style, and tone for their brands, which emerged largely through advertising and packaging.

For about 100 years until the early 1970s, there was only one significant audience for the consumer brand—the housewife—and there was only one medium thought to be worth using—advertising, which was initially more or less neatly divided into press and posters, but later in that period also included radio and TV. Consumer goods manufacturers and their advertising agencies defined the branding idea. Although price and consistent high quality were an important part of the branding equation, emotional factors almost always came first. Advertising agencies developed a formula for promoting brands to housewives:

1. This product is better because it contains X (secret, magic, new, miracle) ingredient that will make it work more effectively.
2. If you use it, it will mean that your home will look more beautiful, or your food will taste much better, or you yourself will be even more glamorous than ever before.
3. This will leave you more time to remain even more desirable and attractive for your lovely husband and family.

This judiciously mixed formula, which eventually came to be known as a Unique Selling Proposition (USP), had a major impact on branding. In the 1920s Persil was advertised, for example, as 'an amazing Oxygen wash—Discovered by Scientific Experts'. Palmolive told housewives that 'The After-Sting of Harsh Soap is the sign of bad complexion to come'. Ovaltine was 'The Home Beverage for Health'. And so it went on.

Although in retrospect much advertising for consumer brands from say the 1920s to 1970s looks to our more sophisticated eyes like grotesque self-caricature, it worked. Advertising linked to overwhelmingly powerful distribution was the recipe for branded goods success. The retailer stocked and sold the brands created, manufactured, and promoted by fast moving consumer goods manufacturers.

Within this constricted, rigidly formalized battlefield the competition between manufacturers was murderous. In an attempt to dominate shelf space, they proliferated new products, and kept improving existing products. Watching their brand's positioning and personality closely, they extended the brand into related areas and spent increasing sums on advertising and promotion. The more successful brands you had, the more shelf space you took up. Easy, at least in retrospect. At the time it seemed very tough—product innovation, from both new and traditional competitors, together with tumultuous price competition kept the pace very lively. There seemed to be no end to this extraordinary business. And then it all began to change.

Starting in the 1970s and 1980s, a complex mix of interrelated, mutually reinforcing factors emerged that undermined the confined advertising-dominated world of household products branding, so that things could never be quite the same again. At the root of the changes and linked with each of them was the information technology (IT) revolution. IT overturned the traditional world of advertising and communication and is already making significant changes in distribution.

Towards the end of the twentieth century conventional paid advertising, the bedrock upon which traditional brand promotion was based, fragmented into shards. As we move into the twenty-first century, it is clear in an increasing number of countries that the old order has disappeared completely. There are hundreds of TV networks, some specializing in the most arcane topics. Satellite and cable TV have supplemented or replaced the three or four main TV channels. There are innumerable radio stations in every major marketplace. Newspapers still exist and are very powerful in some countries, so are magazines. Even here though there is much fragmentation, with an immense proliferation of specialist magazines. In addition, many publications and TV stations are attempting to cross national frontiers. Direct mail of various kinds and in various forms is becoming more significant. Events, sponsored and sometimes even controlled by corporations and brands, are attracting huge budgets. Promotion spend is moving increasingly below-the-line.

All this means that there are so many channels of communication, some so broad and others so specialized that consumer brand advertising using blanket coverage of all media has become both extremely expensive and in practical terms difficult to attain. The idea that consumer brands through advertising can reach into every potential customer's home simply does not work anymore.

What's more, there are all the new media. The ramifications of the IT jungle, the Internet, direct response, multimedia, and all the rest of it, are only just beginning to be grasped. The new media are fundamentally different from traditional media in one highly significant respect: they address individuals and not groups. Conventional advertising is for the most part, with the exception of a bit of coupon clipping here and there, passive; the new media are, for the most part anyway, interactive. It is the feelings and emotions of individuals as opposed to groups that are targeted. And that seems to have coincided with a significant change in the popular mood. Individuality, self-fulfillment, and self-expression seem to be emerging as significant phenomena for our epoch.

The new technologies, led by e-commerce, have made massive inroads into conventional retailing, and are busy creating new ways of managing relationships with customers. E-commerce can only be effective if it is heavily branded. Some activities, like buying books and holidays, are already affected, in a relatively minor way so far, but others, especially financial services, are changing radically. Retail banks, for over 100 years almost totally dependent on their high-street networks, are, with the emergence of a cashless society, lumbered with hundreds of branches they do not know what to do with, while the Internet has enabled new, nimble, heavily branded competitors to emerge.

So financial service businesses are now massive brand-builders. Solo in Finland, and First Direct in Britain, are major brands with advertising budgets comparable with traditional consumer brands. Entirely new service sectors like mobile phones directly derived from the link between deregulation and technology are also heavily and in many cases very innovatively branded. Orange in Britain and many other countries and Ono in Spain are just two of at least twenty new high-profile mobile phone brands aimed directly at the consumer. These brands are mutating into Internet channels that are, of course, also heavily branded because their need for differentiation is becoming increasingly acute.

Even fixed link telephones, dominated by monopolistic, introverted utilities until the 1980s, have now entered the branding war. Finish Telecom has become Sonera, with operations in Turkey and former Soviet Central Asia as well as in Finland; branding is becoming one of its major weapons. Since the 1980s BT has been one of the biggest spenders on advertising in the UK. Because it is very difficult for ordinary consumers to tell the difference between competitors, branding is a vital tool. On top of all this, makers of soft drinks, sporting gear, clothes, and other so-called lifestyle products have introduced a new dimension into branding. They have taken the brand out of the kitchen and the bathroom and made it a cult object. The brand as defined by Nike and others transmutes products into affiliations.

What all this means is that:

1. Consumer brands are no longer primarily associated with products. Consumer brands are services too. In fact, service brands are more innovative and becoming more dominant.
2. Brands are now promoted in a much more varied, various, and complex fashion than ever before. Conventional advertising using paid media remains significant, but multimedia promotion involving e-commerce is becoming very important too—in some situations it will no doubt become the lead medium;

3. Globalization is leading to the growth of major worldwide brands, an overall decline in the number of brands, and a growing flexibility and sophistication in the use of brands.

So the idea that a brand is simply a product that you buy in a shop is disappearing fast. And that in turn means that the traditional fast moving consumer goods companies like Procter & Gamble and Unilever, which once shaped the idea of branding, are losing the initiative they once had, which is passing to newer, faster, more innovative players with rapidly expanding brands. Nowadays innovation is much more likely to come from service brands aimed at the consumer than from traditional consumer products.

RETAIL BRANDS

And how are the retailers affected by all this change? Well, it is a very odd state of affairs; while some traditional retailers like banks are a bit lost and think they have to retreat from the retail world because e-commerce is taking over, other organizations not traditionally associated with retailing, such as Disney, Nike, and even VW with its Autostadt, are moving into it with what are increasingly being described as 'brand experiences' that vary in size from theme parks to quite small stores. Bluewater, in Kent, southern England, which when it opened in 1999 was the largest shopping complex in Europe, was intended to be just as much theme park and brand experience as shopping center.

Long-established retailers in the meantime are just beginning to realize that they have the potential to become major players in the world of branding too. Branded products were always sold through retailers. For the most part retailers, whether they positioned themselves as cheap or as classy, were primarily conduits through which manufacturers distributed their products. They felt inferior in both size and influence to fast moving consumer goods companies.

Although there have always been a few retailers who sold their own brands, such as Marks & Spencer or C & A Brenninkmeyer, these tended to be exceptions. It is only gradually, as the bigger retailers have gained more power, pushed the smaller shops to one side, and developed a massive physical and emotional relationship with customers, that they have come to realize that they can successfully sell high-quality products with their own name on them, because customers like and trust them. During the 1980s and 1990s many retailers (especially perhaps the major supermarket chains) began to appreciate the power and influence they have over their customers.

At first tentatively, almost apologetically, as a cheaper and by implication inferior substitute for manufacturers' products, and then with increasing confidence, retailers, particularly European supermarkets, have challenged the manufacturers who supply them. As their success and self-confidence have grown, they have moved from conventional household products like biscuits and detergents into fields that are traditionally quite distant from them, such as petrol and financial services. To do this successfully, retailers have also come to realize that they need to create a consistent, clear idea of who they are, and how they do things. Retailers have begun to understand the need to create brands. If the brand is strong enough, retailers are beginning to believe they can sell anything.

Retailers are in a position to create more powerful brands than manufacturers. They are physically and emotionally closer to the customer. The customer literally walks through the retailer's environment and deals with the retailer's staff. But to take advantage of this huge potential strength, the retailer has to think and act in an entirely new way. He or she has to make the store, products, and staff into one single, seamless, agreeable, even at times entertaining experience. As newcomers move into retailing and retail concepts like Niketown are launched, retailers are beginning to watch and learn.

Traditionally retailers are geared to selling on price and convenience. Fun has never entered into it. And not many are at all sure where to start now. So far, very few retailers have understood how to coordinate design of packaging, signing, and environments with training of staff or with consistent communication to suppliers and customers. Historically, different elements of the brand have been treated as separate, unrelated activities, which have been given varied measures of support and enthusiasm. Gap is a very interesting, unusual, and highly successful exception. Equally unusual, Gap is one of a very few retail brands that appears to be gaining global acceptance. Sales staff in Gap, young, attractive, and knowledgeable, ask customers whether anyone helped them get what they wanted, and seem really pleased when the answer is 'yes'.

Like so many organizations faced with the implications of branding, many retailers are bewildered and overwhelmed by what is going on around them. But there are some interesting signs of change. Sainsbury, Aldi, and Casino are still a long way from seeing Gap let alone Disney as a role model, but there is not much doubt that the direction has been set and that over the next few years there will be a massive change in retail branding. Price will remain an important factor, but entertainment will emerge alongside it.

PRODUCT BRANDS

Manufacturing companies have always expressed themselves primarily through their products. The product was the center of their life. From Mercedes to Apple it is the product, with its performance, appearance, price, and durability, that has been the vector through which the organization was largely perceived. That is why, in its heyday, Mercedes stood for the highest quality of automotive engineering, and Apple for innovative, easy-to-use, and good-to-work-with design.

Some of the world's greatest companies have been built around an absolutely unswerving dedication to the quality of the product. Siemens and Mercedes Benz in Germany, Hitachi and Kawasaki in Japan, SKF in Sweden, Pratt & Whitney and Otis (both now part of United Technologies) in the USA have all based their entire business philosophy around this straightforward idea. There is no doubt that for a very long time—the whole of the nineteenth century and most of the twentieth century—this system worked. The entire post-war German *wirtschaftswunder*, the remarkable recovery of German industry from zero to one of the world's top three economies, was based around this belief system. German companies tried to build the best products; German products were associated with the best quality; German products sold well, because, although prices were high, customers believed in German quality.

Gradually, though, all this began to change. In the 1970s, there began a major shift whose impact is still rumbling on. The key to this change, as in consumer brands, has been technological development. Every company has access to IT. If all companies have access to the same knowledge at the same pace, it is likely that, in the medium term, one product at a given price or quality is going to be pretty similar to another. Take a look at any product category—say, cameras. For $200 all cameras have similar features. What distinguishes one from another is what they look like, how they work ergonomically, and what they are called—in other words, the brand and the emotional qualities we associate with it.

Outsourcing accelerates this commoditization process. In the old days respectable manufacturers tried to be vertically integrated. Henry Ford was probably the greatest vertical integrator of them all. Iron ore went in at one end of his factories and completed cars came out at the other. Today, though, companies outsource more and more—that is, they buy components and even major systems from outside specialists, who will seek to manufacture in the country with the lowest cost base. We should not be surprised at the Ford move to outsource its manufacturing activity. It is the logical result of a development that has been going on for years. But inevitably the more you outsource the more likely your product is to behave and perform like those of your competitors. So, the more you have to design in difference to give your brand credibility and individuality.

In the automotive industry the current trick is to design in difference in order to make as many variations around as few basic elements as possible. That is what Ford is attempting to do with its various brands. The Jaguar S series, for example, shares a platform with Lincoln, another Ford brand. These two brands have completely different traditions of performance, appearance, and style. They appeal to quite different customers. It is important that they should continue to seem quite different from each other, even though they are very similar beneath the skin. So the Jaguar and Lincoln range of cars look different, feel different, and perform differently from each other, but this is because differences have been carefully created.

In former times products were genuinely different and the differences came from the inside and emerged outward. Today differentiation has to be deliber-ately introduced. When this does not happen, you can simply get identical products bearing different names. The Ford Maverick and the Nissan Terrano are exactly the same, assembled in the same factory, on the same production line in Portugal. The only difference between them is the trim and detail finish.

Another example of differentiation through branding is Rover. Rover in its glory days was a traditional British car, designed by Birmingham engineers for people with the same tastes, hobbies, and interests as themselves. That is why the Rover was all wood, leather, and eloquent understatement. Rover's man-agement in the 1930s, 1940s, and 1950s did not think that through; they simply created a product that they liked and they assumed that their neighbors, British bank managers, and doctors would like it too. Today in a more com-plex, knowing, self-aware age, BMW consciously tried to recreate that intuitive idea in its Rover brand. The Rover 75 in every detail of its appearance and per-formance had Englishness designed into it. It was not intuitive; it was con-trived to express a brand idea—an emotional idea of Englishness. Interestingly, it appears that what Ford made to work successfully with Jaguar, BMW failed to do with Rover. BMW's Rover 75 didn't sell well in its domestic UK market because although the product was fine, its image was poor. And that, in the end, despite all the excuses, is the real Rover failure. BMW, despite its brilliant record of making and sustaining an image with its own brand, couldn't make the magic work with Rover.

Brand building, which was traditionally so much taken for granted that most manufacturers were not even conscious of it, has become high on the corporate agenda of manufacturing companies. It is becoming the only way that they can demonstrate differentiation. And as the Jaguar and Rover stories show, branding makes the difference between success and failure.

This is not only true of products for consumers; it is equally true for makers of products for industry. Siemens, like many other major German companies, relied for over a century wholly on technical superiority for its success. Since the 1990s, it has been challenged by companies all over the world whose prod-ucts are just as good, whose prices are lower, and whose service is in many cases better. Initially Siemens found it almost impossible to believe that its technical superiority was no longer unassailable. Since the late 1990s, when it began to appreciate the critical nature of its difficulties, it has consciously begun brand building. It pays more attention to the shapes and ergonomics of its products. It designs Siemensness into dials, switches, and casings. Its liter-ature and other promotional materials emphasize the Siemens heritage. It has a good, informative website. It is even taking service seriously. It underlines Siemens brand characteristics as clearly as it can.

It is no exaggeration to say that, when companies whose belief system is built around design and manufacturing superiority discover that it has disap-peared, it creates a moral vacuum. At first they cannot and will not accept it. Management goes through a phase of denial. It sometimes takes years for top management to accept that product superiority has gone forever, and that a new corporate belief system has to be constructed, built around products that look and feel different from the competition, levels of service designed to support it, and environments and communication that are carefully crafted to sustain the brand idea.

Gradually though, and usually painfully, as management begins to understand the reality, great manufacturing enterprises take practical and active steps to look after their brand, to nurture it, to institutionalize and codify its characteristics, and therefore to professionalize its management.

Decisions about brands and branding begin to move up the corporate hierarchy. Branding and marketing are increasingly seen by CEOs as matters fit for their personal attention, because they realize that getting branding right is increasingly the difference between corporate life and death. A company's reputation is seen to depend on the values of its brand. This means that CEOs are increasingly drawn into concerns that only a few years before they would have regarded as peripheral, or even entirely irrelevant to their interests. And that is how words like vision, values, personality, marketing, product design, image, identity, and, above all, brand and brand values have entered the corporate bloodstream. Ford's move into branding and closer long-term customer relationships exemplifies this clearly. Not all manufacturing companies realize this yet. Not all CEOs are convinced, but those that are not are learning the hard way.

CORPORATE BRANDS

The brand, traditionally aimed only or largely at the customer, is increasingly taking over the corporation itself. Corporations have always dealt with a multiplicity of audiences: employees, shareholders and the financial community, suppliers and collaborators, and government and other regulatory bodies. Each of these was traditionally treated more or less separately. Differing messages, or messages with a quite separate emphasis, were sent to each.

Today this is no longer possible. Each of those audiences overlaps. Suppliers can also be partners or customers or shareholders. Employees can be shareholders too. In a world in which the media takes a lively interest in the corporation, in which environmentalists are alert for corporate misbehavior, and in which knowledge workers in particular are highly mobile and are quite ready to move on if they do not like their employers, there is an urgent requirement for some kind of coherence in projecting the identity of the corporation. When the corporation is in the public eye, it has to coordinate all aspects of its communication and behavior.

But there are other factors at work too. As the brand becomes more important in the marketplace and the cost of promotion drives organizations into brand extension, there is a huge temptation to use the corporate name to weld the brand portfolio together. The corporation, increasingly sensitive to the fact that its reputation has a direct impact on its share price, goes to extraordinary lengths to underline its position as a significant contributor to the welfare of its host community. Even Shell, not hitherto known for its sensitivity to environmental or human rights issues, is paying attention to this matter. In 1998 it issued its *Profits and Principles—Does there Have to be a Choice* publication. Subsequently, it launched a major advertising campaign emphasizing its concern with environmental issues.

Above all perhaps, as the Ford example so dramatically illustrates, the ground on which the corporation traditionally stood is shifting from making and selling to being—to representing a set of values. Virgin is perhaps the most high-profile early twenty-first-century example of this. It is not what Virgin does that defines it, it is how it does it. Virgin is hardly a corporation at all. It is really a brand that holds together a series of more or less otherwise completely unrelated products and services. Whenever any of them takes a dive or performs badly, which happens much more often than Virgin likes, all of them take a beating.

What this means is that corporations, as my former colleague Hans Arnold puts it, have 'to represent a compelling purpose that is widely understood'. In other words, the corporation increasingly has to manage itself, for all of its audiences, as a brand.

BRANDS IN THE PUBLIC MIND

Brands are much more important than they have ever been before. Their impact is overwhelming. What is it about brands that so intrigues us? Why are we so captivated by them? Why do more people in the USA drink Coca-Cola than water? There are I believe three complex interrelated reasons why brands have become so important, and why their influence will continue to grow.

First, in an extremely complex, noisy, almost insanely competitive world when there is much that is so similar to choose from, where choice based solely on rational factors is now almost impossible in most fields, brands make choice easier. Brands are the device we use to differentiate between otherwise almost indistinguishable competitors. Without clear branding, in some fields we literally could not tell one product or service from another.

Second, brands offer consistency. They give us the reassurance that what we have today is the same as we had yesterday and the same as we will have tomorrow. But consistency can also embrace variety even diversity. Disney is probably the most effective brand factory of its kind in the world. Every year Disney produces at least one major new brand linked to a supporting cast of minor brands; for example, Aladdin, Lion King, Beauty and the Beast (two brands here). Disney also assiduously recycles its older brands: Snow White plus all seven Dwarfs, Pinocchio and so on. Disney brands appear in every conceivable format. They are distributed through a mass of different channels:

films, ice shows, books, toys, theme parks, shops, and so on. Disney does not let us escape from its overpoweringly cuddly embrace. There is diversity and consistency both in the product and in distribution

Woody Allen's movies are just as consistently branded as Disney's, although there is no overt branding mechanism at work. Brand management in a conventional sense would no doubt be anathema to Woody Allen. Nevertheless, the music, the lighting, the plots, the jokes, the camera angles, and above all the characters all cohere. Although every film is different, we know what to expect and we get it. With Woody Allen as with Disney, it is the overall emotional and functional consistency, together with the minor but compelling variations, that cohere to make the brand so powerful.

The third and probably the most significant factor that makes brands so powerful is empathy. We enjoy their company and depend on their relationship because they help us to define who we are. We also shape brands into what we want them to be so that they can help us to tell the world about ourselves. A brand may reassure us and tell the world that we are fashionable (Max Mara) or sporty (Umbro) or preppy (Brooks Bros).

Branding enables us to define ourselves in terms of recognized standards and symbols. Lexus, Tommy Hilfiger, and Glenfiddich make precise and easily recognized statements about who they are and by inference about us, the people who buy them. Burberry, Dunhill, Daks, and Johnnie Walker are primarily about being British, male, middle aged, and well off. They trade in a kind of implicit fantastical British never-never land of Bertie Wooster, Sherlock Holmes, and Agatha Christie. Their strength lies in their ability to capture and make available something of this fantasy world at a high but not impossible price to a small, but large enough global market. Nobody claims that a Burberry raincoat keeps out rain better than its competitors, although no doubt Burberry uses high-quality fabrics. But a Burberry costs more not because of its fabric, but because of its style and the social and cultural implications that lie behind the style. And that is why Japanese executives like them. Rich people in East Africa who drive Mercedes cars are called WaBenzi—member of the Mercedes Benz tribe. You could not get a more powerful social comment than that. It is this third factor, the contribution that the brand makes to our ability to express who we are, to complement and reinforce our individuality, that makes branding such a potent and extraordinary force.

Brands are becoming increasingly divorced from the product/services with which they were originally associated. Caterpillar makes construction equipment, but by association the Cat brand turns up on boots and tough fashionable clothing. The rugged, outdoor, cigarette-puffing Marlboro man now appears on rugged outdoor Marlboro clothing. Some brands even stand for the nation from which they derive. Mercedes Benz and Germany are interchangeable, so are Sony and Japan. More people know about Daewoo than about South Korea, where the brand comes from. If there is nothing particular or special to say about the product's intrinsic qualities, clever brands develop an attitude. Benetton has used conventional advertising media to send strange and often disturbing messages about life, death, and the universality of suffering. Whatever else they are, those advertisements are not about selling clothes. They have social content.

The best and most successful brands can compress and express simple, complex, and subtle emotions. They can make those emotions immediately accessible, in many cases overriding mountainous barriers such as ethnicity, religion, and language. They have an immense emotional content and inspire loyalty beyond reason. Such brands can sweep across the world; their physical and emotional presence is ubiquitous; and they seem omnipresent, almost omnipotent. Disney, Coca-Cola, McDonalds, and Nike are such inclusive brands. They try to embrace as many people as possible, everywhere. A young athlete in the USA wears Nike shoes, both because he or she thinks they will help him or her perform better and because they are fashionable. They are both symbolic and functional. A young cleaner at Banjul airport in the Gambia scrapes and saves to buy the same shoes as a signal to him or herself and others that he or she is able to share some at least of the rich world's glamour. For the cleaner the shoes themselves are much more symbolic than functional. The brand idea has made them iconic.

Nike and brands like it appear to have this kind of spiritual power. They seem, in an individualistic, materialistic, acquisitive, egocentric era to have become some kind of replacement for or supplement to religious belief. Why else, one has to ask, are individuals prepared to demonstrate their allegiances to brands of soft drinks, cigarettes, and training shoes, by draping the insignia of these products all over their person? What satisfaction do they derive from it? This bizarre but entirely familiar pattern cuts across all ages, socio-economic groups, and cultures. It is not simply mass-market brands like Marlboro, Coca-Cola, and Nike that people bond with and display; flashy Moschino flaunts itself and by extension the people who buy the Moschino brand by scrawling its name in the largest possible size all over much of its clothing and accessories. Gucci, Prada, and others do the same thing a shade more discreetly.

People who buy these astonishingly self-promoting brands are not simply demonstrating that they can afford them. That may be significant, but it is not the only factor. Displaying the brand you have just paid money for, the brand that turns you into a perambulating advertisement, a sort of human poster site, is surely, above all, an attempt at self-definition. And that in turn relates to membership of a niche group, a club with a wide variety of nuances related to social, cultural, and economic status. Brands help us consumers, the people who buy them and use them, to express ourselves and cut through the clutter and noise that surrounds us. Brands represent a kind of shorthand, increasingly a global shorthand. No wonder that so many brands are outgrowing the products and services of which they originally consisted and no wonder that so many companies in manufacturing and service are so impressed and so bewildered by this new immense source of power and profit that they have created.

WHAT IS A BRAND WORTH?

If the brand is so important in the minds of consumers and increasingly of other audience groups too, it follows that some brands are worth a lot of money—much more than the physical assets with which they have traditionally been associated. Brands are becoming a significant contributor to the capital value of a company. Coca-Cola's value is many times greater than the total value of its tangible assets.

This is largely because, although it costs a great deal of money to sustain a brand, most brands can be marketed at a significant premium. One infallible guide to the power of a brand is to look at how much people are prepared to pay for it. A shirt with a little green embroidered crocodile costs three or four times as much as virtually the same article unadorned. Timberland deck shoes perform no better than, and look very little different from, similar products that cost a third as much. Watches are an even more instructive example. The Swiss company SMH owns a variety of watch brands including Omega, Longines, Tissot, and Swatch. All of the watches they make tell the time accurately. None of them breaks down. No doubt they have similar mechanisms inside. But these brands vary greatly in appearance—and of course in price. Some watches sell for up to a hundred times as much as others. Elaborate and expensive metals in complex and beautiful casings account for some of the differential; social and cultural implications for the remainder.

So, although, as customers, almost all of us want a bargain, we also evidently relish the vast price differentials that branding brings. I have never heard of a brand being driven out of business because it was too expensive. And this is a factor that has not escaped the notice of the people who market brands. No wonder that branding is becoming a major preoccupation of chief executives, who are increasingly concerned with putting a value on these immensely valuable, intangible brand assets, which they attempt to control.

How much is a brand worth? Accountants and others concerned with the financial evaluation of business have always been skeptical about intangible assets like brands. Traditionally, accountants gave short shrift to companies who wanted to put a value on 'goodwill' or 'reputation'. Since the mid-1990s though, things have been changing. It is becoming evident that intangible assets have real financial value. Just compare the net asset value of virtually any Fortune 500 company with its market capitalization. The gap between the two is presumably the value of its intangible assets. What else can it be? In almost every case, intangible assets greatly outweigh tangibles. In the view of the market, then, companies' intangible assets—that is, largely but not exclusively brands—have real value. The question is how much?

A brand, it appears, is worth as much as anybody is prepared to pay for it. Philip Morris paid more than four times book value for Kraft in 1988; Nestlé paid more than five times book value for Rowntree in the same year, and promptly replaced the Rowntree name with Nestle as a brand endorsement. At the time of these acquisitions, eyebrows were raised. But Nestlé took Kit-Kat, at one time a modest Rowntree brand, and turned it into a major global performer.

In 1987, when Jaguar made 49,000 cars, Ford paid $2.5 billion for the company. Jaguar was making losses, had a factory from hell, built a deeply unreliable product, and was saddled with a mediocre distribution system. The company predicts a rise to over 200,000 cars annually by 2002. Although under their skin, as I have indicated earlier, new Jaguars will be based on platforms shared with other Ford brands, Jaguars will continue to look very Jaguarish. Ford is turning the Jaguar brand into a huge success. And, of course, brand extension is also well under way. According to *Sovereign*, the glossy magazine of Jaguar Cars, 'A range of designer accessories from the Jaguar Collection is to be sold by retail giant Sogo from their prestigious store on Piccadilly Circus in London's West End. The range will sell alongside fragrances, luggage, jewelry and other products from the Jaguar Collection.' So what did Ford buy for its $2.5 billion: a clapped-out old car company, or a luxury brand with huge potential in cars, clothes, fragrances, shoes, pens, and other airport fodder?

As intangible values become increasingly significant in relation to tangible values, financial formulas will emerge to take this into account. A good solid financial formula, full of multiples, the discounting of key potential future cash flows to their present net value, and similar stuff all regularly under discussion by financial people in different countries will somehow give the illusion that the intangible is being made tangible. The fact of the matter, though, is that brands are increasingly emerging as the only way one company can distinguish itself from another. Brands are becoming fundamental to the way a company operates. They have influence over all audiences: customers, partners, staff, and shareholders.

Increasingly, brands are emerging as the company's unique asset. And the reason for that is that we, consumers from all over the world, have fallen in love with the idea of brands and branding. The affiliation that the individual makes with the brand is a unique and amazing characteristic of our time—a cultural and sociological phenomenon. And that is why, like them or loathe them, brands are unstoppable.

5

Markets and Meanings: Re-Imagining Organizational Life

Paul du Gay

According to the French philosopher and cultural theorist Gilles Deleuze (1992: 6), 'marketing has become the soul of the corporation'.[1] A provocative statement certainly, but one that, at first sight, appears to founder upon the rock of empirical verification. In the UK, for example, marketing, along with other disciplines of symbolic expertise such as design and communication, still seems to suffer a subordinate professional and organizational status in comparison to that enjoyed by the expertise of finance, production, and accounting (Armstrong 1989). However, to dismiss Deleuze on these grounds alone could be a mistake, for might there not be developments afoot that, amongst many other things, are in the process of problematizing traditional hierarchies of organizational expertise? Certainly, many contemporary programmes of organizational reform contain an explicit critique of finance and accounting, for example. What has been represented, and accepted in many countries, for many years as the strengths of finance and accounting—namely, their ability to manage by numbers alone—is now turning out increasingly to be viewed as their major weakness (Miller and O'Leary 1993). In other words, as maps of the organizational world have been redrawn around the figure of the 'sovereign consumer', those disciplines able to indicate 'knowledge' of, and the potential to exercise power in relation to the needs, desires, and aspirations this creature have begun to achieve increased visibility (du Gay 1996; Nixon 1997a).[2] While the installation of a new norm of organizational governance—what I have termed elsewhere 'the cult[ure] of the customer'—may not effect an immediate translation of comparative professional advantage from finance and accountancy to other forms of expertise, it nonetheless remains as something in terms of which individuals and groups are judged and judge themselves and to which appeals can be made (du Gay and Salaman 1992).

This suggests that, rather than viewing Deleuze's statement as a theoretical flight of fancy devoid of empirical substance, it might be more productive to examine the conditions of possibility of the statement itself. In what sense might it be possible to say that forms of 'symbolic expertise' such as marketing have become the ' "soul" of the corporation'? What might this tell us about the conduct of organizational life in the present? Indeed, what might it say to us about ourselves as persons and the sorts of social formation we inhabit in the present?

RE-IMAGINING ORGANIZATIONAL LIFE

Throughout the twentieth century a range of discourses has emerged, each of which has offered a certain way of drawing the map of the organizational world. By 'discourse', I do not simply mean 'speech and writing'. Rather, I refer to 'discourse' in a rather more specialized sense. A discourse, I suggest, is a group of statements that provide a way of talking about and acting upon a particular object. When statements about an object or topic are made from within a certain discourse, that discourse makes it possible to construct that object in a particular way. It also limits the other ways in which that object can be thought about and acted upon. Thus managerial discourses such as 'scientific management', 'human relations', and 'quality of working life', to name but a few, have all offered novel ways of imagining 'organization' and have played an active role in constructing new ways for people to conduct themselves at work. In other words, by elaborating particular ways of conceptualizing, documenting, and acting upon organizations, these discourses have served to transform the meaning and reality of organizational life.

During the 1980s and 1990s, the character of organizational life has once again undergone considerable reinterpretation. The dominant discourses of organizational reform throughout this period—'excellence', 'business process re-engineering', 'value chain management' to name some of the most obvious—have all placed considerable emphasis upon the development of more 'organic', 'flexible' organizational forms, structures, and processes that would overcome the perceived stasis, rigidity, and inefficiency of existing organizational arrangements.

These new discourses of organizational reform are related to a number of developments often gathered together under the heading of 'globalization'. While proponents of these discourses use this term to highlight differing combinations of phenomena—such as those associated with a rapid deployment of new information and communication technologies; or those associated with competitive pressures resulting from global systems of trade, finance, and production—they all agree that an intensification of patterns of global interconnectedness has serious repercussions for the conduct of organizational life—in both the private and public sectors (Kanter 1989; Osborne and Gaebler 1992).

If 'globalization' constitutes the key predicament, then the figure of the 'customer' is often positioned as a crucial organizational mechanism for the successful management of its effects. Globalization, it is argued, creates an environment of massive uncertainty. In such an environment, only those organizations that can 'stay close to the customer'—reflexively reconstituting their conduct to become evermore enterprising and innovative—will survive and prosper. In other words, the successful management of globalization and its effects requires constant 'creativity' and the continuous construction and reconstruction of organizational forms that rest less and less upon 'mechanistic', bureaucratic practices and increasingly upon the development of more flexible, reflexive, and hence 'entrepreneurial' organizational forms and modes of conduct.

If the winners and losers in this new global economy are to be determined largely, if not exclusively, by their competitiveness, then it comes as no surprise to learn that 'enterprise' is regarded as a quality that no player in the global market game can afford to be without, whether nation, firm, or individual. In contemporary discourses of organizational change, 'enterprise' occupies an absolutely crucial position, providing both a critique of contemporary organizational practices and offering itself as a solution to the problems posed by globalization through delineating the essential principles of a new art of governing organizational conduct. As Colin Gordon (1991) has suggested, 'enterprise' refers to a subtle suffusion of 'economic rationality' and cultural meaning to produce a novel method for programming the totality of governmental action.[3] No longer simply implying the creation of an independent business venture, 'enterprise' now refers to the progressive enlargement of market mechanisms by a series of redefinitions of their object.[4]

So what are the essential principles of 'enterprise' and in what ways do these redefine the conduct of organizational life? Quite obviously, one crucial feature of enterprise as a principle of organizational governance is the role it accords to the 'commercial enterprise' as the preferred model for any form of institutional organization and provision of goods and services (Keat 1990). However, of equal importance is the way in which the term also refers to the 'kind of action' or project that displays 'enterprising' qualities or characteristics on the part of those concerned, whether they be individuals, groups, or organizations. Here, enterprise refers to a plethora of characteristics such as initiative, self-reliance, and the ability to accept responsibility for oneself and one's actions.

As Colin Gordon (1991) has also suggested, in this latter manifestation, 'enterprise' as a principle of governance is intimately bound up with 'ethics'. By 'ethics', Gordon is referring to the means by which individuals come to understand and act upon themselves in relation to the true and the false, the permitted and the forbidden, the desirable and the undesirable.[5] Thus, 'enterprise' as an art of governing organizational and personal conduct promotes a conception of the individual as an 'entrepreneur of the self' (Gordon 1987).

This idea of an individual human life as an 'enterprise of the self' suggests that there is a sense in which, no matter what hand circumstance may have dealt a person, he or she remains always continuously engaged (even if technically unemployed) in that one enterprise, and that it is 'part of the continuous business of living to make adequate provision for the preservation, reproduction and reconstruction of one's own human capital' (Gordon 1991: 44). As I have argued elsewhere, an 'enterprising self' is a calculating self—a self that calculates about itself and works upon itself in order to better itself (du Gay 1996; see also Rose 1990).

Governing organizational life in an 'enterprising' manner therefore involves the reconstruction of a wide range of institutions and activities along the lines of the commercial firm, with attention focused, in particular, on its orientation towards the 'sovereign consumer'. In other words, the market system with its emphasis upon consumer sovereignty provides the model through which all forms of organizational relation should be structured. At the same time, however, guaranteeing that the optimum benefits accrue from the restructuring of organizational life according to the logics of market rationality necessitates the production of certain forms of conduct by all members of an organization. Reconstructing organizational life in this sense involves 'making up' new ways for people to be; it refers to the importance of individuals acquiring and exhibiting particular 'enterprising' capacities and dispositions.

THE CULT(URE) OF THE CUSTOMER

As I indicated above, governing organizational life in an enterprising manner is intimately bound up with a pronounced blurring between 'production' and 'consumption' and between the 'corporate' and 'culture'. As the language of the market becomes an increasingly important, if not dominant, vocabulary of moral and social calculation, the 'privilege of the producer' is superseded by the 'culture of the customer', with citizens reconceptualized as 'enterprising consumers' (Keat 1990; du Gay and Salaman 1992).

As Nikolas Rose (1990) has indicated, the primary economic image offered to the modern citizen is not that of the producer but that of the consumer. As 'consumers', people are encouraged to shape their lives by the use of their purchasing power and to make sense of their existence by exercising their freedom to choose in a market in which they simultaneously purchase products and services, and conduct their own assembly, managing, and marketing (Rose 1990). Consumers are constituted as autonomous, self-regulating and self-actualizing individual actors seeking to maximize their 'quality of life'—in other words, to optimize the worth of their existence to themselves—by assembling a lifestyle or lifestyles, through personalized acts of choice in the marketplace. Thus, in contemporary consumer culture, freedom and independence emanate not from civil rights but from individual choices exercised in the market: 'The sovereignty that matters is not that of the king or the queen, the lord or the white man, but the sovereignty of the consumer in the marketplace' (Corner and Harvey 1991: 11).

As a number of commentators have argued, the development of contemporary consumer culture involves a substantive shift in modes of social regulation. This new mode of regulation distinguishes itself by the substitution of 'seduction' for 'repression', advertising for authority, and the endless creation of needs ('fashion') for norm imposition. What ties individuals to this social formation is their activity as consumers, their life organized around consumption (Bauman 1987: 168).

Within contemporary consumer culture, therefore, the character of the 'enterprising' consumer is placed at the center of the market-based universe. What counts as 'good' and 'virtuous' in this environment is judged by reference to the needs, desires, and projected aspirations of the 'sovereign consumer'. Success and failure in this market-based universe is, therefore, inextricably linked to the ability of producers to generate knowledge about the desires and aspirations of consumers and to translate this 'knowledge' into effective programs of intervention.

Through the mechanism of the 'customer', the relations between 'production' and 'consumption', between the inside and outside of the corporation and, most importantly perhaps, between work-based and consumption-based identities are progressively blurred. Not only are consumers more dependent upon the products and services generated by organizations for their own reproduction, materially and psychologically, but organizations, in turn, are increasingly structured around an image of the 'customer'. The presumed 'needs', 'desires', and 'aspirations' of customers are to be inscribed into organizational practices and technologies and the conduct of all organizational members is to be held accountable to that endeavor.

As I indicated earlier, to conform to the 'requirements of the customer' is to envisage a new type of governance and to imagine new ways for people to conduct themselves within the world of organizations as well as outside. For example, in reconstructing organizational life around the character of the 'customer', the 'worker' or 'manager' is reconceptualized as an individual actor in search of meaning, responsibility, a sense of personal achievement, and a maximized quality of life.

Work in the 'customer-saturated' organization is now construed as an activity through which people produce their identities. In effect, employees and managers are encouraged to relate to their work as consumers: work becomes an arena in which people exhibit an 'enterprising' and 'consuming' relationship to self, where they 'make a project of themselves', and where they develop a style of life that will maximize the worth of their existence to themselves. In other words, 'work' as an activity is re-imagined through the language of consumer culture. The 'culture of the customer' brooks no opposition between the mode of self-presentation required of people as consumers, and that required by employees and managers (du Gay and Salaman 1992). The relationship to self that the latter are expected to develop builds upon and extends the identity they are deemed to have as consumers. Both consumers and employees are represented as autonomous, calculating individuals in search of meaning and fulfillment, looking to 'add value' to themselves whether at work or at play. Whether formally located 'inside' or 'outside' the organizational arena, market-based forms of social regulation operate through the 'soul'—or 'subjectivity'—of individuals (Rose 1990; du Gay 1996).

This means, as Tom Peters (1992: 755) has pointed out, that 'life on the job is looking more like life off the job for a change ("For a change"? For the first time in a couple of hundred years more like it).' This has important repercussions for the ways in which organizations are viewed and view themselves. As the sociologist Charles Sabel (1992: 23–54) suggested:

Employees who are encouraged to think of themselves as entrepreneurs, to treat their employer as a market . . . are forced to manage resources and risks in ways that make it easier for them to imagine changing the conditions of their own lives . . . But this enhanced autonomy is simultaneously qualified by the same situation that produced it. Just as the firms form networks with one another and their environment in order to keep abreast of local knowledge, so do individuals secure their long-term employability through participation in neighborhood groups, hobby clubs, or other professional and social networks are likely to know when their current jobs are in danger, where new opportunities lie, and what skills are required in order to seize these opportunities. The more open corporate labor markets become, the greater the burden these networks will have to bear and the greater will be the economic compulsion to participate in the social activities they organize . . . Hence . . . it is becoming harder to say when one is working. Activities at work become preparation for turning the family into a family enterprise that absorbs all leisure; family and leisure activities become preconditions of employability. Anticipation of these possibilities undermines the distinctions between work, leisure and family.

MARKETS AND SOULS

With market-dependent consumption playing an enhanced role in the formation of consumer subjectivity and identity, the reproduction of the market requires the continual creation of new ways for consumers to be. In other words, as the economic folds seamlessly into the cultural, the battle for market share becomes articulated as a struggle for the *imagination of the consumer;* organizational success becomes increasingly dependent upon the ability to win over or more accurately to 'make up' the consumer. While this is obviously still a matter of 'numbers'—of 'logistical engineering', as it is sometimes known—it is also a matter of 'meaning', of interventions aimed at the expressive or symbolic dimensions of consumption practices.

In a truly relational manner, however, interventions aimed at the subjectivity of the sovereign consumer also have repercussions for the ways in which the work-based subject is constituted and regulated. 'Staying close to the customer' implies 'engineering the soul' of employees and managers to ensure that they acquire and exhibit particular 'enterprising' capacities and dispositions (du Gay 1996: 114–16). Through the medium of a variety of 'cultural' technologies and practices inscribed with the presuppositions of the 'enterprising self'—techniques for reducing dependency by reorganizing management structures ('delayering'); for eliciting individual accountability and responsibility through peer-review and appraisal schemes; and for developing 'interpersonal personal competencies' through training in Transaction Analysis or other such techniques—the internal world of the organization is reimagined. It is reconceived as a space in which customers' demands and desires will be satisfied, productivity enhanced, quality assured, innovation fostered, and flexibility guaranteed through the active involvement of the self-regulating and self-fulfilling impulses of all the organization's members.

If organizational success is premised upon the production of meaning for both consumers and producers, this suggests an increased significance for symbolic expertise. On the one hand, for example, the disciplines of marketing, design, and communication have played a crucial role in spearheading the progressive expansion of the market and in facilitating the growth of contemporary consumer culture. Underpinned by knowledge and techniques of subjectivity, symbolic expertise has played a vital role in the transmutation of goods and services into desires and needs and vice versa. In other words, symbolic expertise actively 'makes up' consumers.[6]

At the same time, however, symbolic expertise also makes a crucial contribution to the reflexive capabilities of organizations—such as their ability to continually learn new ways of operating in relation to perceived shifts in consumer behavior and demand—and hence to 'making up people' at work. Through their (claimed) intimate 'knowledge' of the customer, cultural intermediaries are able to affect the constitution of the internal world of the organization through 'translating' the consumer's 'search for expression and identity' into specific organizational images, practices, and market interventions. Thus, symbolic expertise produces meaning both for consumers and for organizations and their members at one and the same time.

In many respects, the dynamics of contemporary consumer culture and the emerging organizational rationalities that are both its medium and its outcome ensure an increasing importance for the symbolic expertise. In this sense, then, it is possible to suggest with Deleuze (1992: 6) that symbolic expertise has become the 'soul of the corporation', its 'nodal point' or 'reflexive core'.[7] Strategically located in 'production and consumption', as it were, the symbolic expertise of marketing, design, communication, and so on appears to possess a priority to mediate all other organizational 'functions', determining their place and their specific weight.[8]

NOTES

1 Deleuze is using the term 'marketing' to refer to more than one specific organizational specialism—meaning 'the marketing function'. In his usage, the term refers to all those creative practitioners dealing in the non-standardized manipulation of symbols—data, words, oral and visual representations.

2 Contemporary attempts to reinvent organizations appear to have thrown established hierarchies of professional expertise into some confusion. The uncertainties facing organizations in such 'interesting times' have ensured that, to a significant extent, professional advantage is 'up for grabs'.

3 While the term 'enterprise' is commonly used to refer to attempts by successive New Right administrations to create an 'enterprise culture' in Britain during the 1980s and 1990s, I have attempted to indicate on a number of occasions that the term has a much wider remit than this. I have suggested that 'enterprise' represents a profound shift in contemporary governmental rationality and that this governmental rationality informs the logic of the contemporary program of corporate restructuring in both public and private sectors. Rather than being 'yesterday's story', the triumph of the entrepreneur continues—witness, for example, the huge success of Osborne and Gaebler's text on 'Re-Inventing Government' subtitled 'How the Entrepreneurial Spirit is Transforming the Public Sector'.

4 According to the social theorist Frederic Jameson (1991), while 'market dependency' may in one sense represent the colonization of 'culture' by the economic, the resultant economic formation is distinctly 'aestheticized'. In other words, even as 'market dependency' effaces 'culture' as an autonomous sphere, it simultaneously positions artifice at the very heart of reality.

5 Gordon uses the term 'ethics' in a rather specialized way, one derived from the work of Michel Foucault. Foucault defines 'ethics' as the 'kind of relationship you ought to have with yourself, a "rapport a soi" that determines how the individual is supposed to constitute himself as a moral subject of his own actions' see Foucault (1984: 37).

6 For the role of design, advertising, and retailing in the construction of new forms of 'masculinity', see Nixon (1997b).

7 According to Deleuze (1992: 7), this development should not be greeted with joy. Instead, he writes 'we are taught that corporations have a soul, which is the most terrifying news in the world'.

8 For a discussion of the strategic importance of symbolic expertise for contemporary developments in two particular industries, retailing and the music business, see Negus (1993), du Gay and Negus (1994), du Gay (1996), and essays in du Gay (1997).

REFERENCES

Armstrong, P. (1989), 'Limits and Possibilities of HRM in an Age of Management Accountancy', in J. Storey (ed.), *New Perspectives in Human Resource Management* (London: Routledge).

Bauman, Z. (1987), *Legislators and Interpreters* (Cambridge: Polity Press).

Corner, J., and Harvey, S. (1991), 'Introduction', in J. Corner and S. Harvey (eds.), *Enterprise and Heritage: Crosscurrents of National Culture* (London: Routledge), 11.

Deleuze, G. (1992), 'Postscript of the Societies of Control', *October*, 59: 6.

du Gay, P. (1996), *Consumption and Identity at Work* (London: Sage).

—— (1997) (ed.), *Production of Culture/Cultures of Production* (London: Sage).

—— and Negus, K. (1994), 'The Changing Sites of Sound: Music Retailing and the Composition of Consumers', *Media, Culture and Society*, 16/3: 395–413.

—— and Salaman, G. (1992), 'The Cult[ure] of the Customer', *Journal of Management Studies*, 29: 5.

Foucault, M. (1984), 'On the Genealogy of Ethics: An Overview of Work in Progress', in P. Rabinow (ed.), *The Foucault Reader* (Harmondsworth: Penguin).

Gordon, C. (1987), 'The Soul of the Citizen', in S. Whimster and S. Lash (eds.), *Max Weber: Rationality and Modernity* (London: Allen & Unwin).

—— (1991), 'Governmental Rationality: An Introduction', in G. Burchell, C. Gordon, and P. Miller (eds.), *The Foucault Effect* (Brighton: Harvester Wheatsheaf).

Jameson, F. (1991), *Postmodernism, or the Cultural Logic of Late Capitalism* (London: Verso).

Kanter, R. (1989), *When Giants Learn to Dance: Mastering the Challenge of Strategy Management, and Careers in the 1990s* (New York: Simon & Schuster).

Keat, R. (1990), 'Introduction', in R. Keat and N. Abercrombie (eds.), *Enterprise Culture* (London: Routledge).

Miller, P., and O'Leary, T. (1993), 'Accounting Expertise and the Politics of the Product: Economic Citizenship and Modes of Corporate Governance', *Accounting, Organizations and Society*, 18: 2–3.

Negus, K. (1993), *Producing Pop: Culture and Conflict in the Popular Music Industry* (London: Edward Arnold).

Nixon, S. (1997a), 'Circulating Culture', in P. du Gay (ed.), *Production of Culture/ Cultures of Production* (London: Sage).

—— (1997b), *Hard Looks: Masculinities, Spectatorship and Contemporary Consumption* (London: UCL Press).

Osborne, D., and Gaebler, T. (1992), *Re-Inventing Government* (New York: Addison-Wesley).

Peters, T. (1992), *Liberation Management* (Basingstoke: Macmillan).

Rose, N. (1990), *Governing the Soul* (London: Routledge).

Sabel, C. (1992), 'Moebius Strip Organizations and Open Labour Markets: Some Consequences of the Re-Integration of Conception and Execution in a Volatile Economy', in P. Bourdieu and J. S. Coleman (eds.), *Social Theory for a Changing Society* (Boulder, Colo.: Westview Press), 23–54.

III

REPUTATION AS STRATEGY

6

The Road to Transparency: Reputation Management at Royal Dutch/Shell

Charles J. Fombrun and Violina P. Rindova

> Visionary companies display a powerful drive for progress that enables them to change and adapt without compromising their cherished core ideals.
>
> (Collins and Porras 1994: 9)

> A healthy living company will have members, both humans and other institutions, who subscribe to a set of common values and who believe that the goals of the company allow them and help them to achieve their own individual goals.
>
> (Arie de Geus 1997: 200)

In 1995 Royal Dutch/Shell—one of the world's three largest companies—faced two major crises. The first involved the proposed maritime sinking of an aging offshore drilling platform—the Brent Spar. Careful research conducted by Shell had supported sinking as the least environmentally damaging alternative for disposal of the rig. Nonetheless, Shell became the target of a Greenpeace 'action' that portrayed Shell as a greedy and irresponsible company whose support for sinking was motivated by purely economic reasoning—sinking happened to be the low cost alternative. Physical boarding of the inoperative Brent Spar by Greenpeace militants drew worldwide media coverage that sullied the Shell image, provoked massive boycotts of Shell stations in Germany, and ultimately forced the publicly humiliated company to back down in June 1995.

The second crisis of Shell's *annis horibilis* blossomed in the media in 1995 and involved Shell's operations in Nigeria. Under a joint venture contract with the Nigerian government, Shell extracted oil from reserves located in the Ogonilands.

We are grateful for the substantive contributions of many Shell employees to the results presented here, particularly Pauline van der Meer Mohr, Peter Robinson, Gary Steel, Tom Henderson, Charles Watson, Rob Dakors, Andrew Foulds, and Martin Bachmann. The work we report is very much shared with them.

Throughout 1995 Shell was accused of profiteering and political expediency for dealing with the ruling military junta of Nigeria that had taken power by force, and for forsaking the rights of the Ogoni people to a fair share of the oil profits generated from their lands. Violent confrontations at Shell operations in Nigeria drew vitriolic attacks from critics of multinational companies, most notably the outspoken Anita Roddick, founder of the Body Shop. In mid–1995 the military regime arrested Ken Saro Wiwa, the outspoken representative of the Ogoni people, for inciting insurgency. Media coverage painted a dark picture of Shell's non-involvement policy, and the crisis culminated in November 1995 with the trial, condemnation, and tragic execution of Mr Saro Wiwa.

In 1995 the market value of the Royal Dutch/Shell Group of companies fluctuated dramatically as investors reacted negatively to the two crises. Shell's managers recognized that the company's business results depended heavily on Shell's reputation, not only with the investment community, but also with the general public, the media, and even with activists. They concluded that reputation affected the Group's performance and competitive standing. As a result of their self-analysis, the firm launched a concerted effort to examine the global reputation of the Group, to delineate strategies for managing the Group's reputation, and to rebuild reputational capital with its key stakeholders.

This chapter describes Shell's efforts to learn about corporate reputations, their determinants and consequences, and how a company of its size ought to manage its own reputation. Consistent with the company's engineering culture, top managers at Shell took an analytical approach that combined systematic data gathering with model building in a process that closely parallels 'grounded theorizing' (Glaser and Strauss 1967). The process involved extensive data collection from both internal and external constituents, as well as active collaboration in theory building by Shell managers located in far-flung subsidiaries. Their efforts resulted in a deeper understanding of the relationship between corporate identity and reputation, and suggested the importance for companies like Shell to achieve 'transparency' of the firm to its outside publics. We capture here the essence of the unfolding process (Eisenhardt 1989) that induced Shell to become a more expressive and transparent organization, and describe some of the changes the company made to institutionalize its transparency and expressiveness, and thereby strengthen its reputation. Shell's experience is particularly conducive to developing a framework for understanding reputation management because it represents a rare and comprehensive effort to manage corporate reputation in the multicultural environment faced by global companies today.

THE CASE FOR REPUTATION MANAGEMENT

Corporate reputations are aggregate perceptions of outsiders about the salient characteristics of firms. They reflect the general esteem in which a firm is held by its multiple stakeholders (Fombrun 1996). Researchers in strategy, organizational theory, and organizational cognition have shown a growing interest in the role that corporate reputations play in relating organizations to their environments. They suggest two ways in which reputations matter. On the one hand, reputations are valuable: they have bottom-line effects on firms. On the other hand, reputations buffer firms from the immediate reactions of stakeholders in their environments when controversial events occur (Rindova and Fombrun 1999). Reputation management is, therefore, justified on both economic and strategic grounds.

Performance Benefits

Significant effort has been devoted to establishing both the drivers of corporate reputation and the consequences associated with positive organizational images. A mosaic of evidence confirms the financial gains that can result for companies with strong reputations. The evidence includes academic research on the financial benefits of good reputations, and the financial losses associated with reputational crises. Fombrun and Shanley (1990) reported positive impacts on reputation of prior financial performance, advertising, and charitable contributions, and negative impact of profit volatility and media visibility.

Findings from the research to date demonstrate that reputations are conferred (and taken away) by constituents. Investors reward firms with good reputations by bidding up the price at which the company's shares trade; customers willingly pay premium prices for their products; and employees enjoy and prefer to work for them. For instance, a study of one-year earnings forecasts of 303 companies made by financial analysts showed that their forecasts were most heavily explained by performance indicators, but were also influenced by the non-financial component of the company's reputation (Cordeiro and Sambharya 1997). Similarly, a study of ten portfolios of companies demonstrated that investors were willing to pay more for companies with higher reputations but comparable risk and return (Srivastava et al. 1997). Finally, annual surveys of students report that MBA students are invariably attracted to jobs in higher-reputation companies—that is, to companies that are larger and more visible in their industries.

Taken jointly, these studies support the idea that tangible financial benefits are associated with higher reputational standing—and vice versa. In systemic fashion, reputation not only accrues to better-performing companies, but also enables their performance. Stronger bottom-line performance comes about because better-regarded companies achieve 'first-choice' status with investors, customers, and employees. So actively managing reputation— although a costly activity that requires significant investments of time, energy, money, and commitment—is nothing less than enlightened self-interest (Fombrun 1996).

Behavioral Consequences

Various researchers have demonstrated that organization members experience events that have a negative effect on the organization's reputation also as being threatening to the organization's identity (Dutton and Dukerich 1991), such as affecting beliefs about what is core, distinctive, and enduring in their organizations (Albert and Whetten 1985). Since beliefs about organizational identity affect members' motivation and commitment, protecting and enhancing the organization's reputation affect its ability to manage its employees. Further, in their study of a public university's response to changes in higher education, Gioia and Thomas (1996) found that management's image for the institution influenced how they interpreted the changes in the environment and the strategic changes they made.

The management literature gives the impression that firms try to manipulate outsiders' perceptions (Goffman 1959; Schlenker 1980; Tedeschi 1981). They do so by selectively highlighting legitimating features of their firms: firms enhance their perceived legitimacy by providing explanations of company practices following good news, but offer excuses or justifications designed to attenuate corporate responsibility for controversial events and bad news (Salancik and Meindl 1984).

Elsbach (1994) and Elsbach and Sutton (1992) analyzed the statements provided by organizational spokespeople following widely publicized controversies and showed how those accounts affect a firm's perceived legitimacy or reputation. They found that spokespeople manipulate the arguments and evidence they present in order to influence outsiders' perceptions of their firms. Specifically, spokespeople try to provide explanations that are logical and credible. Though their accounts vary, the most effective appear to couple acknowledgment of responsibility with references to widely institutionalized organizational features.

Although these studies hint at how firms can influence audiences, less progress has been made in examining how firms proactively and systematically manage the perceptions and evaluations of their stakeholders. In another article, we have suggested that, in order to arrive at a complete account of how reputations emerge, a detailed analysis is required of the complex interactions that link firms to informational intermediaries and constituents (Fombrun and Rindova, forthcoming). In particular, we highlight three social processes from which reputations crystallize: (1) an *environmental shaping process* through which firms strategically target and influence constituents; (2) a *signal refraction process* through which intermediaries that specialize in assessing firms (e.g. journalists and financial analysts) convey interpretations to constituents; and (3) a *collective assessment process* that aggregates individual assessments of firms into reputational halos. There has been scant research that examines how these three processes actually operate.

To advance our understanding of how reputations develop, we focus here on the shaping process centered on a single firm. Consistent with qualitative case analysis methodology (Miles and Huberman 1984), we used as an orienting framework for exploring the shaping process the three-stage model of reputation building proposed by Fombrun (1996). Fombrun (1996) suggests that firms seeking to build reputation: (1) assess the current state of the company's reputation and that of its rivals; (2) analyze the desired future state of the company's reputation; and (3) articulate the projections that can move it from one configuration to the other. Through this framework we traced Shell's efforts to manage its reputation in response to the two controversial issues the company faced in 1995: Brent Spar and Nigeria. Following these crises, Shell's top managers recognized that the company's business results depended heavily on Shell's reputation with customers, the general public, the media, and the investment community. Fig. 6.1 shows a chart that was prepared by Shell's investor relations department in 1996. It describes the powerful effect that Shell's reputation was thought to have had on its financials. In response, in mid–1996, the firm launched a concerted effort to examine the Group's corporate reputation and to delineate strategies for rebuilding reputational capital with key stakeholders. We describe here Shell's efforts to understand the roots of its reputational crisis, and the steps the company took to develop a reputation management model and process for the Group.

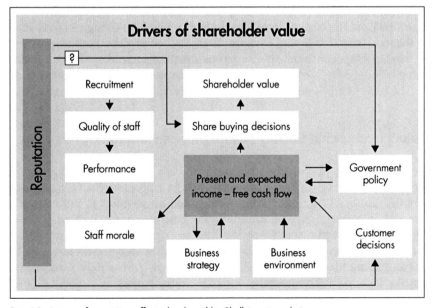

Fig. 6.1. A view of reputation effects developed by Shell investor relations

SHELL'S EXPERIENCE

Shell is an Anglo-Dutch multinational firm whose British founders began as sellers of oil for lamps in the Far East and whose Dutch founders imported kerosene from Sumatra. Shell was named after the seashells used as money in the Far East at the time. Since 1906, the merged company's primary business has been the production and marketing of oil products. Following the oil crisis of the 1970s, Shell diversified into more or less related domains including metals mining and nuclear power. By 1995 Shell operated as a loose confederation of over 3,000 highly decentralized operating companies in five core businesses: Exploration and Production, Oil Products, Gas and Coal, Chemicals, and Renewables. Structurally, the Shell Group is governed, not by a CEO, but by a consensually driven 'Committee of Managing Directors' (CMD) whose activities were then guided by Corr Herkstroter, the Group's official chairman. The assets of the Group put it among the world's top three companies, with revenues of over $100 billion, some 900,000 shareholders, operations in 144 countries, about 100,000 employees, another 700,000 contract employees, and annual profits of some $7 billion.

As discussed earlier, Shell faced two major crises in 1995 that precipitated introspection, analysis, and change. Here we describe this process: in particular, we examine two key projects that Shell initiated: (1) 'Assessing Society's Changing Expectations' and (2) 'Becoming WoMAC (The World's Most Admired Corporation)'. Ultimately, the projects induced ongoing changes, including a rethinking of the company's core values, redesigned systems for stakeholder management, and a global identity campaign. Shell's top executive, CMD Chairman Corr Herkstroter (1998), recently described the change as truly meriting the term 'transformation' because: 'Shell staff everywhere have responded to the need to adapt continuously to new business and societal challenges. A major theme is "openness"—to new ideas, about what we do, and to the ideas of others. The basis of this is our confidence in the strength of our own core values.'

Project I: Assessing Society's Changing Expectations

The crises of 1995 provoked considerable debate within Shell and an uneasy sense that the company had lost touch with its environment. To quote again from the Group's Chairman: 'We have devoted much effort to understanding how public expectations of international business are changing. This has involved widespread discussion with different strands of opinion around the world. And we have not been afraid to enter public debate where we believe we have something to say. Shell companies are increasingly working with community and environmental groups' (Herkstroter 1998).

Shell began its learning process about reputation management with data-gathering studies. For the first study in early 1996 Shell invited 101 senior-level opinion-leaders from more than fifty countries to participate in interviews and round tables about changing perceptions of the role of multinationals. Participants included politicians (14 percent), government agencies (19 percent), voluntary associations (28 percent), media representatives (9 percent), academics (12 percent), as well as businessmen (18 percent). The results were conclusive: expectations of companies were very high indeed, and would prove very difficult, if not impossible, to meet. Karen de Segundo (1997: 17–18), Shell's senior manager in charge of External Affairs for the Group, described the results and their effects on Shell in this way:

We found that people have much more confidence in the ability of companies than they do in governments. That confidence is rising and, along with it, so are the expectations of what companies, and multinationals in particular, can deliver . . . Here is an example. We found that many rational and intelligent people thought that it was a reasonable proposition that companies such as Shell should mediate to reduce tensions between different levels of government, or that they should take positions on social policy matters . . . Activities such as these are not within the normal, legitimate role of a business. Therefore we cannot meet such expectations. However, the fact is that they do exist . . . There is no doubt in our view that—to the extent that unfulfilled expectations persist—they detract from corporate reputation.

A second benchmark study focused on twenty-three peer companies from the USA, Australia, Japan, Germany, the UK, and the Netherlands. Participants included senior executives of these companies, who participated in confidential face-to-face interviews that focused on their views about the changing influence of stakeholders on their companies, and their effects on their corporate reputation management practices. The findings confirmed the view that societal expectations of multinationals have changed significantly in recent years and that companies now operate in a more demanding environment. Reasons given for this included: globalization of markets and the speed and ubiquity of communications; a drive towards enhanced health, safety, and ecological standards; empowered consumers; disenfranchised employees; decline in moral leadership by Church and State; and the rise of sophisticated pressure groups skilled at exploiting these trends.

A key finding of the peer company study was that most companies managed their corporate reputations in a fragmented fashion. They recommended closer involvement of the CEO in championing change; the development of improved stakeholder monitoring systems; closer relationships with stakeholders; a more centralized corporate communications function with CEO access. The study concluded: 'It appears that we are observing a paradigm shift in the way corporate reputation is won and how it might be managed.'

The study also compared Shell's relative position *vis-à-vis* the twenty-three benchmark companies on a composite score that captures responsiveness to a changing environment. Fig. 6.2 presents the results. These results suggested that, among peer companies, Shell was relatively proactive in responding to change, although not in a position of leadership.

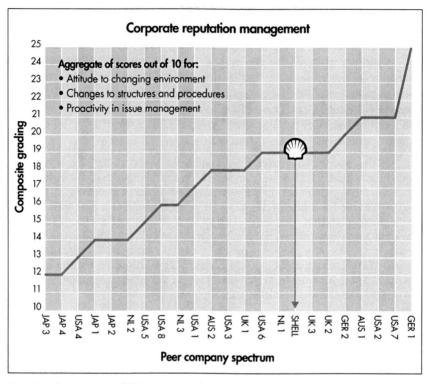

Fig. 6.2. Relative ranking of Shell against twenty-two peer companies

Project II: Becoming WoMAC (the World's Most Admired Corporation)

Having assessed the changing expectations of society, in August 1996 Shell invited a group of high-potential executives to tackle the questions: 'What gets a company admired? How can Shell become the world's most admired corporation?' The team consisted of seven executives from diverse parts of Shell, and an external consultant (the first author), who acted as an additional resource to the team. Between August 1996 and January 1997 the team met a dozen times on an episodic basis to explore its assigned questions. The unfolding process involved a combination of planning, data gathering, model building, and analysis. The work of the 'WoMAC team'—as the team came to be known—culminated in a report to Shell's CMD presented in January 1997 with specific recommendations for institutionalizing reputation management practices within Shell.

Understanding Various Aspects of Reputation Management

To gain in-depth understanding of various aspects of reputation management, the WoMAC team set out to address three questions: (1) how organizations who create reputational rankings evaluate firms; (2) what the financial value of corporate reputations is; and (3) what factors underlie Shell's reputation in different countries.

To answer the first question, a study compared ratings and rankings of firms from several sources, including publications such as *Fortune* and *Financial Times*, books like *100 Best Companies to Work for in America*, pressure groups such as the Council on Economic Priorities, and included Kinder, Lydenberg & Domini, and the Franklin Research & Development Corporation. Comparison of the lists they produce demonstrated that evaluators rank firms on very different criteria: firms that rate well with some evaluators do not always do so well with others.

To answer the second question, an event study of the Exxon Valdez oil spill of 1989 and its effect on market value for Exxon and the other oil majors was conducted. It was followed by the second event study of the effect of the 1995 crises on Shell's market value. Figs. 6.3 and 6.4 show the fluctuations in the cumulative excess market values of the oil majors in 1989 and 1995. Abnormal returns are computed following accepted financial practice. First, changes in market returns for a specific company are adjusted for changes in both the overall market and the oil index. Excess returns are then computed as departures from the five-year trend line of expected market returns. These daily excess returns are then cumulated over a particular time to identify period effects. Fig. 6.3 shows the impact that Valdez had in pulling down the excess returns of all the oil majors throughout 1989. Similarly, Fig. 6.4 demonstrates the negative influence of the unfolding Brent Spar and Nigerian controversies that Shell was involved with throughout the year, not only on Shell's returns, but also on the returns of the other oil majors. Industry-wide spillover is evident in both charts, indicating the high interdependence between the oil majors: a crisis for one is a loss for all; your reputation is partly your company's, partly your industry's.

To examine the third question—the drivers of reputation in different countries—the team commissioned market research with focus groups with students, executives, and the general public in Hong Kong, Indonesia, and Taiwan. The results confirmed the WoMAC team's basic hypothesis that, in different settings, the relative importance of stakeholders varies, and the factors that influence reputation are different. Shell would therefore have to recognize the diversity of local interests that influence its corporate reputation.

The State of the Art in Reputation Management

To examine the state of the art in reputation management by top companies around the world, the WoMAC team also commissioned a questionnaire

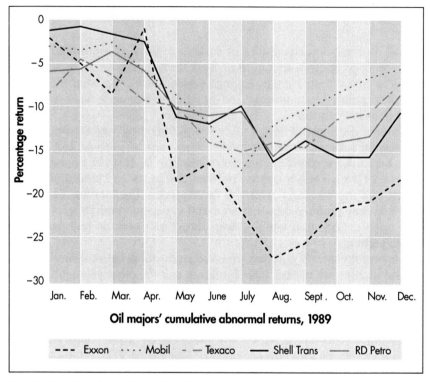

Oil majors' cumulative abnormal returns, 1989

--- Exxon ···· Mobil – — Texaco —— Shell Trans —— RD Petro

Fig. 6.3. The effects of the Valdez spill on Exxon and other oil majors, 1989

survey of CEOs of the 1,000 largest international companies in the USA and UK. A total of 139 usable responses were returned—a 14 percent response rate. The questionnaires were filled out by either the CEO or a member of the senior management team responsible for reputational matters. The responding companies were not significantly different from the larger sample in both size and reputational standing.

The purpose of the questionnaire was to examine how leading companies conceive and manage their reputation management practices based on three categories:

1. *constituent relationships*: how leading companies relate to their constituents; the standards against which they design their practices;
2. *reputation-building practices*: what kinds of strategies and systems leading companies rely on to build reputation and relate to their key constituents;
3. *organizational issues*: how companies organize themselves to manage reputation; do they have a reputation-building strategy, and who is responsible for it.

Individual items were designed to measure these practices, and summary scales were later developed. The results suggested that responding companies differed in the ways they interacted with stakeholders and the degree to which they pursued different reputation management practices. We further explored whether these differences could be traced to whether companies claimed to be pursuing a systematic reputation-building strategy or not. Specifically, we compared responses from companies that claimed to have a systematic reputation strategy against those that did not using standard analysis of variance techniques. The results confirmed that firms in both groups identify and communicate their core mission to constituents in similar ways, set their standards at similar levels, and have similar patterns of charitable activities in their communities. Having an overall reputation strategy, however, makes a significant difference in two aspects of firms' relationships with stakeholders: how they communicate and how they listen. Specifically, companies with an overall reputation strategy report using a broader scope of advertising themes, a broader variety of channels, and more varied representations of their operations. These companies try to impart to their stakeholders significantly more information, not only about their products, but also about a whole range of

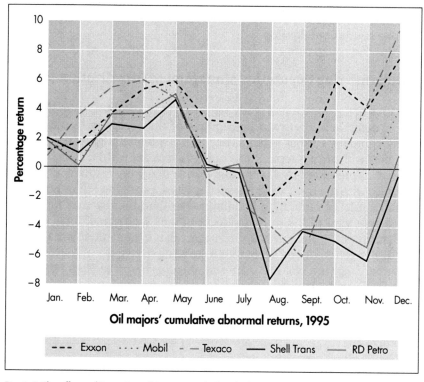

Fig. 6.4. The effects of Brent Spar/Nigeria on Shell and other oil majors, 1995

issues related to their operations, their identity, and their history (Fombrun and Rindova, forthcoming).

To companies following a systematic reputation strategy, stakeholder relationships appeared to be a two-way street: not only did they report working hard to impart knowledge about their firms to stakeholders, but they also reported working harder at understanding those stakeholders. They perceive stakeholders to have greater and more significant impact, and so have more systems in place to assess the concerns of those stakeholders.

Constructing a Systems Model

Based on the studies, WoMAC generated a systemic model that recognizes the interdependencies between the company, its stakeholders, and the bottom line. Following a cognitive elicitation process similar to Grinyer's (1992), the team brainstormed a list of factors that were thought to be either cause or consequence of reputation. These were verified against lists of factors generated by the studies on reputational rankings by social monitors. Following extensive debate, the team generated a model that represents reputation as a key element in various cycles that make the company 'first choice' with employees, customers, investors, and regulators. Fig. 6.5 shows the systemic model that the WoMAC team adopted as a guiding model for interpreting how corporate reputations develop.

Institutionalizing Reputation Management Organization-Wide

The results of the benchmark study suggested to the WoMAC team the importance of congruence between perceptions of the company by stakeholders and the company's inner reality. They also reinforced a growing sense that companies with strong reputations build them from within. Consistent with the research presented by Collins and Porras (1994) on visionary companies, companies with the most resilient reputations appeared to follow an identity-centered model of reputation building rather than the reactive, impression-management view of the world characteristic of Shell's traditional corporate communications. It led the team to suggest that systematic internal changes are critical to the company's reputation-building strategy.

In January 1997 the WoMAC team submitted its report to Shell's top officers in the CMD with detailed suggestions about institutionalizing reputation management at Shell. Key recommendations included:

1. integrate *the reputation management framework* into Shell's business processes;
2. identify Shell's *core purpose*;
3. adopt *everyday excellence* as a core value and give all Shell employees a stake in achieving it;

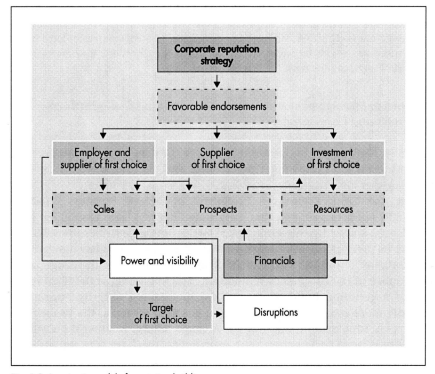

Fig. 6.5. A systemic model of reputation building

4. screen all Shell strategies in the corporate portfolio against key *reputation management responsibilities*;
5. adopt and implement the *reputation scorecard*, which appraises all management teams against rigorous criteria designed to support Shell's reputation;
6. publish a *statement of Shell's accountability to all stakeholders*;
7. conduct regular *benchmark surveys* of Shell's reputation against peer companies and with multiple stakeholders;
8. create a *reputation best practice capability* under the auspices of Shell's external affairs department.

A number of WoMAC's recommendations have been acted upon. According to CMD chair Corr Herkstroter:

We are responding to increasing public interest in Shell companies' activities by developing our reporting . . . The first Group health, safety and environment (HSE) report was issued last year—as well as separate reports for the main businesses. This year's Group report will include improvement targets against which future progress can be measured. In addition we will be presenting the contribution Shell companies make to economic, social and environmental progress in the new Shell Report. We are planning, as soon as practicable, to expand the scope to present a measured and verified annual report on the performance of Shell companies in fulfilling the responsibilities they committed themselves to in our business principles . . . Shell companies have become much more open, with far wider discussion about the directions they are taking . . . (www.shell.com, 20 June 1999)

Reputation Management Inside Out: Re-examining Shell's Business Principles and Core Purpose

Probably, Shell's most important response to the data from the two projects— 'Assessing Society's Changing Expectations' and 'Becoming WoMAC'—was to take a deeper look inside.

First, the Group revised its 'Statement of General Business Principles'. Originally published in 1976, that early statement had been among the first to be released and widely disseminated. The document describes the values and principles that guide Shell's activities. Within Shell it was widely interpreted as the company's 'contract with society'. The document explicitly recognized the importance of the company's reputation: 'The upholding of the Shell reputation is a common bond which can be maintained only by honesty and integrity in all activities. This reputation is a vital resource, the protection of which is of fundamental importance. A single failure, whether it be willful or due to misplaced zeal or short term expediency, can have very serious effects on the Group as a whole.' Following extensive internal and external consultation and all the reports that highlighted 'society's changing expectations' of multinational firms like Shell, key revisions were introduced in 1996 that included commitments to support fundamental human rights (a clear response to Shell's débâcle in Nigeria) and to contribute to sustainable development.

Second, Shell set out to examine its core purpose. As befits a company with a long history, Shell has a strong corporate culture, variously described as technical, scientific, analytical, able to get things done. A long-time executive at Shell describes the consistency and pervasiveness of Shell's recognizable core values in this way: 'During my Shell time, I was continually aware of the level of "membership" of everyone I met. I could encounter a salesman in East Africa or a depot foreman in North Pakistan and know of him—as he would know of me—that he was one of us, a Shell person whom I could trust' (de Geus 1997: 98).

The crises of 1995 had shown the incongruence between the firm's core values and societal values and perceptions outside the firm. For example, the firm was characterized in the press as 'patrician, slow-moving, fat, rich, bureaucratic, and closed' (Investors Chronicle, 24 Oct. 1997). Part of the reason for this incongruence was that the Shell Group appeared to have lost touch with its inner soul—what some called its 'beating heart'. Shell lacked a sense of self, an identity, to project to the outside world. Lacking this, the firm appeared opaque, mythical, and inimical to its observers.

It all added up to an image of Shell as a sort of giant phantom in a forest—difficult to see, with no specific contours, but with enormous, uncontrolled, undefined parts that might well do us harm. Moreover, it was a silent phantom. The multinational entity told no story about itself. Outsiders could only guess why it existed, what it did for a living . . . and how the world would be different if the company did not exist at all.   (de Geus 1997: 80)

To examine Shell's 'core purpose', the WoMAC team developed a systematic process based on Jim Collins's design (Collins and Porras 1994). The prototypical workshop involved a group of managers in a Shell subsidiary gathering to explore the company's identity through various exercises. The output of each workshop was expected to be that group's view of Shell's 'core purpose'. To guide their creativity, participants were shown short prototypical statements of core-purpose statements of top firms Hewlett-Packard, 3M, and Disney. Throughout 1997 and into 1998, a total of thirty-two workshops were held in twenty-four locations, involving 770 Shell participants from forty-eight countries. Typical statements that were generated by these groups include:

1. to work to make a difference in people's lives (Canada);
2. to keep people moving, improving the world (Malaysia);
3. to make people's lives easier now and in the future (China);
4. to unleash the world's energy resources to make the world run better (Nigeria);
5. to enhance people, companies, cultures, and countries (Australia).

Core-purpose statements were pooled around the world and presented to a meeting of Shell top managers from around the world. From close examination of those statements, introspection, and personal belief, the CMD crystallized Shell's core purpose as: 'Helping People Build a Better World'.

To express the theme to employees around the world, the WoMAC team commissioned a short film that would bring the theme to life. Developed by the firm of Maurice Saatchi, the film was shown on the first broadcast of the company's newly created internal network—Shell TV in March 1997. Thematically, it highlighted the evolving wonders of technological change as seen through the eyes of an infant.

In addition to this internal communication campaign, throughout 1998 Shell set in motion various initiatives that demonstrate a growing sense of accountability to its non-financial stakeholders. In support of its increased transparency, and increased awareness of purpose and principles, Shell released a report in Fall 1998 entitled 'Profits & Principles—Does There Have to Be a Choice?' The report highlights various steps Shell has taken to respond to stakeholder concerns about sustainable development and human rights. It also presents a road map of management systems under development for institutionalizing transparency and responsiveness, including accounting systems, standard setting, external verification, and continuous improvement. Fig. 6.6 summarizes these initiatives.

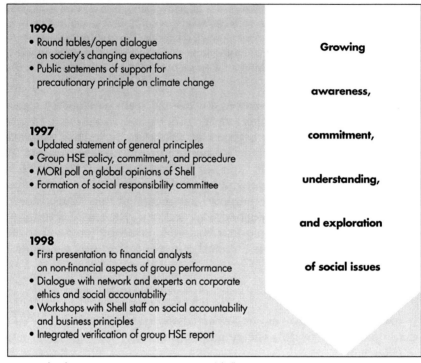

1996
- Round tables/open dialogue
  on society's changing expectations
- Public statements of support for
  precautionary principle on climate change

Growing

awareness,

1997
- Updated statement of general principles
- Group HSE policy, commitment, and procedure
- MORI poll on global opinions of Shell
- Formation of social responsibility committee

commitment,

understanding,

and exploration

1998
- First presentation to financial analysts
  on non-financial aspects of group performance
- Dialogue with network and experts on corporate
  ethics and social accountability
- Workshops with Shell staff on social accountability
  and business principles
- Integrated verification of group HSE report

of social issues

Fig. 6.6. The changing management systems at RD/Shell

REPUTATION MANAGEMENT: BUILDING EXPRESSIVENESS AND TRANSPARENCY

What did Shell learn from its experience? Clearly the 1995 crisis events and ensuing losses of reputation and market value precipitated a period of scrutiny within Shell and forced the company to re-examine its business model and historical values. In the process, Shell re-evaluated its business model in ways that incorporated stakeholder expectations. As a result of its revised understanding of the changing expectations of stakeholders, Shell developed a set of internal principles about its way of being and acting. Finally, Shell conveyed these changes to its stakeholders using a variety of communication devices. Fig. 6.7 presents the model of reputation management that emerged from the various initiatives of the WoMAC team. We propose that this model offers a generalizable process that other companies might follow.

Shell's experience suggests that well-targeted reputation management begins with a careful understanding of stakeholder expectations—the filters through which stakeholders process information about the firm. Understanding stakeholders' filters is important because stakeholders use the filtered information to form evaluative firms. We label this phase 'listening'. Listening involves attentive interacting with stakeholders, which enables the firm to understand the standards against which their actions will be evaluated. Through 'listening' the firm can also assemble the cognitive map of the world views espoused by its stakeholders and use the map as a guide in selecting its strategic positioning. Relying on focus groups and surveys in multiple countries and of multiple stakeholder groups, Shell made a sincere effort to really hear a variety of voices and to assemble as realistic a map of the expectations of its stakeholders as possible.

A company that is serious about building a strong reputation takes the input from the listening phase literally to heart—to the very heart and core of the firm's business activities. Shell re-examined both its 'business framework' and its core purpose. A firm's business framework incorporates its traditions, identity, and aspirations for the future (such as strategic performance objectives). We call this stage 'being', because here the firm relies on its history and strategy to define its distinctive way of conducting business. We also call it 'being' because it reflects concerted efforts to manage the firm's culture and identity, interweaving the firm's history, strategic goals, and relations with others. In doing so, the company balances the stable 'core' inertial elements of

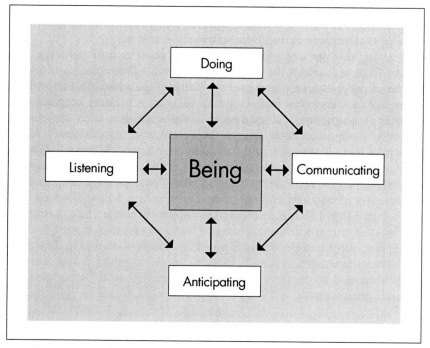

Fig. 6.7. A learning model for reputation management

the firm with those elements that require adaptation. The 'being' phase is a process of management of the organization's identity: it requires the firm to take stock of existing beliefs about 'who we are' and 'what we stand for' as an organization. Both the revision of the statement of the Group's business principles and its efforts to develop an identity statement are excellent examples of the sincere engagement in the 'being' phase of reputation management.

'Anticipating' extends 'listening' and 'being' into a plan of action: it involves selecting those stakeholder expectations that call for a change in fundamental organizational practices. This phase also addresses how organizational practices will change so that the firm's actions are consistent with stakeholder expectations. In that sense, it involves activating a new way of 'doing'. The principles of 'being' defined a set of relationships between Shell and its various stakeholders, including what set of expectations the Group would strive to meet and address.

Finally, Shell designed a number of communication items that communicated Shell's principles to stakeholders. We call this phase 'communicating'— it involves expressive interaction with stakeholders through which a firm conveys its position and the principles on which it will rely. Firms also take actions in accordance with these principles—actions that validate the content of their communications. The communications reflect the firm's identity, its way of 'being', while addressing the concerns of stakeholders. Communications address concerns by informing, explaining, framing, embellishing, or otherwise symbolically representing the firm's actions. Careful management of expectations and interpretations ensures that routine events in the life of large corporations do not turn into controversies and crisis.

We argue that by engaging in these processes a firm achieves *transparency—a state in which the internal identity of the firm reflects positively the expectations of key stakeholders and the beliefs of these stakeholders about the firm reflect accurately the internally held identity*. A primary mechanism for achieving 'transparency' is expressive communication with stakeholders: expressive communications seek to represent the organization's identity rather than to grab attention and favorable impressions. When a firm's interactions with stakeholders are based on the principles of 'transparency' and 'expressiveness', the favorability of stakeholders' impressions result from genuine meeting of interests and commonality of values. In the absence of this foundation, a firm's favorable reputation is likely to remain a temporary illusion that may crumble down under much lesser storms than the crises that hit Shell in 1995. Alternatively, acting from a foundation of mutual understanding based on transparency, a firm is likely to receive support from committed stakeholders and to preserve its reputational capital in the rougher seas of inevitable controversies.

CONCLUSION: PRACTICING REPUTATION MANAGEMENT

Companies are increasingly concerned about managing their reputations—the more or less favorable regard in which they are held by stakeholders. Good reputations help companies cope with growing competitiveness in global markets. Favorable reputations also minimize the threats from rising stakeholder activism and media coverage that force companies to operate in the public eye. 'Reputation management' describes an evolving set of practices that leading companies like Shell are developing to help them cope with the changing expectations of their many audiences, to manage the interpretations those audiences make, and to build favorable regard. In so doing, they are enhancing their ability to exploit a new source of competitive advantage that derives from cognitive assets—their reputational capital (Fombrun 1996).

Shell's experience shows that the environment can be represented by stakeholders' expectations. Therefore, stakeholder expectations should be routinely monitored to ensure that performance results are not jeopardized by shifting expectations. A corollary of this idea is that reputation management should be a cornerstone of strategic analysis because it addresses how firms position themselves in changing environments. It also follows that changes in strategy should be conceived and evaluated in terms of their possible reputational consequences.

The models of reputation management that Shell derived from its experience show that the management of organizational reputation is inextricably linked to the management of organizational identity. In order to influence 'how a firm wants to be perceived' it has to change 'who it believes itself to be'. In doing so, it also shifts from impression-management communications to expressive communications and achieves transparency, which stakeholders are likely to reward with a deeper sense of trust and commitment. Thus, the sustainability of a firm's reputation as an asset is also better ensured.

REFERENCES

Albert, S., and Whetten, D. A. (1985), 'Organizational Identity', in L. L. Cummings and B. M. Staw (eds.), *Research in Organizational Behavior, Volume 7* (Greenwich, Conn.: JAI Press), 263–95.

Brown, B. (1998), 'Do Stock Market Investors Reward Companies with Reputations for Social Performance?', *Corporate Reputation Review*, 1: 271–80.

Collins, J. C., and Porras, J. I. (1994), *Built to Last: Successful Habits of Visionary Companies* (New York: Harper Business).

Cordeiro, J., and Sambharya, R. B. (1997), 'Do Corporate Reputations Influence Security Analysis Earnings Forecasts?', *Corporate Reputation Review*, 1: 94–8.

de Geus, A. (1997), *The Living Company: Habits for Survival in a Turbulent Business Environment* (Boston: Harvard Business School Press).

de Segundo, K. (1997), 'Meeting Society's Changing Expectations', *Corporate Reputation Review*, 1: 16–19.

Dutton, J. E., and Dukerich, J. M. (1991), 'Keeping an Eye on the Mirror: Image and Identity in Organizational Adaptation', *Academy of Management Journal*, 34/3: 517–54.

Eisenhardt, K. (1989), 'Building Theories from Case Study Research', *Academy of Management Review*, 14: 532–50.

Elsbach, K. (1994), 'Managing Organizational Legitimacy in the California Cattle Industry: The Construction and Effectiveness of Verbal Accounts', *Administrative Science Quarterly*, 39: 57–88.

—— and Sutton, R. (1992), 'Acquiring Organizational Legitimacy through Illegitimate Actions: A Marriage of Institutional and Impression Management Theories', *Academy of Management Journal*, 35/4: 699–738.

Fombrun, C. J. (1996), *Reputation: Realizing Value from the Corporate Image* (Boston: Harvard Business School Press).

—— and Rindova, V. P. (forthcoming), 'Fanning the Flame: Corporate Reputations as Social Constructions of Performance', in J. Porac and M. Ventresca (eds.), *Constructing Markets and Industries* (Oxford: Oxford University Press).

—— and Shanley, M. (1990), 'What's in a Name? Reputation Building and Corporate Strategy', *Academy of Management Journal*, 33: 233–58.

Gioia, D., and Thomas, J. B. (1996), 'Identity, Image, and Issue Interpretation: Sensemaking during Strategic Change in Academia', *Administrative Science Quarterly*, 41: 370–403.

Glaser, J., and Strauss, A. (1967), *The Discovery of Grounded Theory* (Chicago: Aldine Publishing Co.).

Goffman, E. (1959), *The Presentation of Self in Everyday Life* (New York: Doubleday).

Grinyer, P. H. (1992), 'A Cognitive Approach to Facilitating Group Strategic Decision Taking: Analysis of Practice and a Theoretical Interpretation', *Knowledge and Policy*, 5: 26–49.

Herkstroter, Corr (1998), 'Royal Dutch Shell Annual Report'.

Miles, M., and Huberman, A. (1984), *Qualitative Data Analysis: A Sourcebook of New Methods* (Beverly Hills, Calif.: Sage).

Rindova, V., and Fombrun, C. (1999), 'Constructing Competitive Advantage: The Role of Firm-Constituent Interactions', *Strategic Management Journal*, 20: 691–710.

Salancik, G. R., and Meindl, J. (1984), 'Corporate Attributions as Strategic Illusions of Management Control', *Administrative Science Quarterly*, 29: 238–54.

Schlenker, B. R. (1980), *Impression Management* (Monterey, Calif.: Brooks/Cole Publishing Co.).

Srivastava, R. K., McInish, T. H., Wood, R. A., and Capraro, A. J. (1997), 'The Value of Corporate Reputation: Evidence from Equity Markets', *Corporate Reputation Review*, 1: 62–8.

Tedeschi, J. (1981) (ed.), *Impression Management Theory and Social Psychological Research* (New York: Academic Press).

7

Distorted Images and Reputation Repair

Janet M. Dukerich and Suzanne M. Carter

In the summer of 1999 officials of the Coca-Cola Company faced a potentially explosive situation; several people became ill after drinking the Coke brand, leading not only to the biggest recall in its 133-year history, but the forced closure of Coca-Cola plants in Europe for over a week. The incident has been described as a nightmare for the company, 'which has now discovered that the venerable Coke brand is vulnerable, not just to lapses in quality control that may have led to the contamination of its products but to the shifting perceptions and political sensitivities of its customers' (Cowell 1999). In such situations, members of the organization not only need to 'fix' the problem; they also need to attend to the perceptions that outsiders have of the organization—that is, they may need to engage in reputation repair. During that same summer, another organization, Smith & Wesson, a manufacturer of guns, also faced a potentially explosive situation. Similar to the lawsuits lodged against tobacco companies, gun manufacturers were beginning to be sued for producing a potentially 'dangerous' product. In a recent *New Yorker* article (Boyer 1999), Ed Shultz, the president of Smith & Wesson, described the changing situation: 'When I came to Smith & Wesson, there was virtually none of the stigma that you encounter today. The industry was a proud industry. We were in the mode of believing that we were doing things that were very important for preserving security and freedom and law and order and those kinds of things.' However, as a result of increasingly restrictive legislation in the USA (for example, the Brady Bill), and sensationalized accounts in the media of children leading assaults with an arsenal of guns, Shultz and his company 'unhappily found themselves cast in the Merchants of Death role' (Boyer 1999). These two examples differ in that, in the Smith & Wesson case, there was no precipitating action by the organization leading to any loss of public confidence as there was in the Coca-Cola case. Nonetheless, in both of these situations, managing the perceptions of critical stakeholders is the key to regaining the confidence of the public and other key stakeholders. Both organizations are faced with damage to their reputations and members of the organization need to decide what, if any, actions need to be done to repair that reputation.

In this chapter we focus on the factors that motivate members of the organization to engage in actions designed to repair a damaged corporate reputation. We also consider conditions where the amount of resources applied to reputation repair is either at an appropriate or inappropriate level. Much has been written on how organizations build and maintain a good reputation (Perrow 1961; Bromley 1993; Fombrun 1996), as well as the benefits to the organization of having such a favorable reputation (Milgrom and Roberts 1982; Fombrun and Shanley 1990; Hall 1993). But, while organizational members may always prefer to engage in behaviors that create good relations with key stakeholder groups (reputation building), ultimately there will be times when the organization is faced with a reputation-repair situation. These situations occur not only because of blunders by the organization (such as the Coca-Cola example given above) but also because of changes in perceptions by stakeholders and/or the media regarding the firm's choice of activities (such as the Smith & Wesson example). Because of this it is important to understand what types of circumstances may lead to improper or ineffective reputation repair.

We begin by describing corporate reputation and the reputation-repair process. We then argue that external stakeholders and organizational members may have conflicting images of the organization. In this chapter we differentiate between the reputation of the organization, which represents outsiders' views of the organization (Fombrun 1996), and the external image, which represents how organizational members think outsiders view the organization (Dutton and Dukerich 1991). We believe that sometimes a mismatch can occur between how outsiders see the organization (the reputation of the organization) and what organizational members believe the reputation to be (the external image), and that these mismatches may have a profound influence on the amount of resources organizational members allocate to repairing the reputation of their firm. Specifically, we suggest that at times members of organizations may either underreact or overreact to the unfavorable perceptions that outsiders have of the organization, due in part to the members' understanding of the organization's identity, and that these misperceptions of how outsiders actually see the organization can lead to inappropriate responses.

CORPORATE REPUTATION AND REPUTATION REPAIR

It is important to recognize that corporate reputations are based on perceptions, and it is those perceptions that drive reputational assessments, regardless of the reality of the situation. Thus, in terms of understanding how to manage reputations, it is less important whether the organization is in fact at fault when stakeholders send negative reputation signals than whether the stakeholders perceive the organization to be at fault. Reputations are assessed by stakeholders through both organizational activities and informational signals (Fombrun and Shanley 1990). The multiple audiences that organizations often attend to include, among others, local citizens, governmental regulators, stockholders, employees, pressure groups, and politicians. To complicate matters, each of these stakeholders may have diverse concerns, interests ,and goals, leading to multiple reputation assessments (Bromley 1993; Carter and Deephouse, 1999). These assessments are made public by the organization's stakeholders through a variety of outlets such as public forums, the media, opinion polls, and buyer purchasing behavior.

As stakeholders make these assessments public, organizational members use these cues in order to construct their understanding of how outsiders are perceiving their organization (Russ 1991; Hall 1993). The media play a large part in the dissemination of reputations. Thus, newspaper articles, daily radio or television news, as well as other printed material outlets, such as magazines or trade journals, may provide organizational members with cues as to how their stakeholders view the organization's reputation. For example, *Business Week* provides rankings of the Top Twenty Business Schools in terms of customer satisfaction levels. Also, since 1982, *Fortune* has provided information on the reputation of companies by publishing the results of an annual survey of corporate executives and industry experts regarding the reputations of over 300 of the largest *Fortune* 500 companies. Furthermore, real-time information regarding stock price and investor confidence is disseminated through the Internet as well as other media outlets, and can be used by organizational members to understand stakeholder perceptions. Industry experts often express their satisfaction or dissatisfaction with managerial decisions regarding strategic moves, downsizing, layoffs, or financial performance through television programs, the Internet, newsletters, and so on, that in turn lead to a recommendation for potential shareholders to buy, hold, or sell a company's stock.

Other reputation cues may be received directly by the organization rather than just presented in the media. Interest groups may communicate concerns directly to organizational members through such methods as letter-writing campaigns, picketing, phone calls, or other advertising mediums. As a case in point, the Southern Baptist Association made its concerns regarding Disney's decision to provide health benefits to same-sex partners known by publicly announcing a boycott of all products and services associated with the organization. Also, politicians or business leaders may publicly announce specific instances of concern or praise for local businesses.

Finally, organizational members may solicit information from external stakeholders regarding their reputations. For example, organizational members may gather reputation cues from stakeholders via community involvement. The ability of organizational members to directly communicate with their local community leaders and the public often helps them to understand the perceived implications of organizational actions on the community at large. In sum, there are numerous communication outlets that organizational members may attend to when determining how stakeholders assess the reputation of the organization.

Paralleling this information solicitation process, organizational members are continually attempting to influence the perceptions of their stakeholders. Corporate reputations, like individuals' reputations, can be managed both assertively and defensively (for discussions of applied impression management at the organizational level of analysis, see Gardner and Martinko 1988; Giacalone and Rosenfeld 1991; Rosenfeld *et al.* 1995). Organizational members can use reputation management actions to enhance an already well-established reputation (assertive), or to mitigate the effect of certain negative situations (defensive). Various strategies and signals are used to assertively manage corporate reputation, such as achieving equal opportunity employment, contributing to charity, developing non-polluting products, advertising, and creating philanthropic foundations. Defensive signals and activities include verbal accounts through press conferences, written accounts through press releases, and letters to shareholders, among others.

RESPONDING TO REPUTATIONAL CUES

In this chapter we focus specifically on the defensive actions taken in response to negative cues received from stakeholders of the organization (for example, a drop in the *Business Week* rankings, or a drop in the *Fortune's* Most Admired ranking) rather than assertive actions taken prior to stakeholder acknowledgment of a situation—these actions are termed reputation-repair behaviors. These reputation-repair behaviors can take many forms, ranging from simple denial of the problem to elaborate substantive changes to organizational policies and procedures. For example, organizational members may feel compelled to respond to attacks on their organization's reputation through such reputation-repair strategies as denials, evading responsibility, reducing the offensiveness of the act through explanations of behavior, or correcting the problem (Elsbach and Sutton 1992; Ginzel *et al.* 1993; Fombrun 1996).

Several communication devices and outlets are available to manage the organization's image through defensive actions such as annual reports, press releases, newsletters to shareholders, interviews in business publications, and press conferences (Russ 1991; Ginzel *et al.* 1993). The communications literature in particular has focused on the rhetoric that firms use as they attempt to influence outsiders' (as well as insiders') images of the organization (Cheney and Vibbert 1987; Cheney and Christensen, forthcoming). Numerous accounts exist detailing organizational responses to public relations crises, such as

NASA's difficulties with the Hubble Space Telescope (Kauffman 1997); Dow Corning's image-repair strategies in the breast implant crisis (Brinson and Benoit 1996); USAir's response to an aircraft crash in Pittsburgh (Benoit and Czerwinski 1997); and General Motors' response to negative press from Dateline NBC (Hearit 1996).

Of course, not all threats to the organization's reputation result in public relations crises. One might argue that organizational members receive negative information all the time, through consumer complaints or negative press. Individuals working in boundary-spanning positions (PR, Customer Service, Legal, and so on) will often receive both positive and sometimes extremely negative information about the organization. However, organizational members are unlikely to respond to any and every kind of damaging reputation cues. That is, not all of the negative information will serve as an impetus for trying to repair the reputation of the organization. Rather, certain types of reputation cues will be attended to more strongly than others. For example, some organizations include routines to log customer complaints and only attend to recurring ones. Other cues may not even be noticed by organizational members. Thus, an important question is, 'If indeed organizations do not respond to all negative reputation cues, when might reputation repair be more likely to occur?' We believe that organizational members are much more likely to respond to perceived attacks on the organization's character or identity (Albert and Whetten 1985) than other types of negative cues. As Ware and Linkugel (1973: 274) have suggested in their analysis of apologia: 'In life, an attack upon a person's character, upon his worth as a human being, does seem to demand a direct response. The questioning of a man's moral nature, motives, or reputation is qualitatively different from the challenging of his policies.'

We suggest that a parallel argument can be made about organizations. That is, when negative reputation cues are received, they are deemed much more salient when the negative information concerns the organization's identity. Specifically, when cues seem to damage what is central, distinctive, or enduring about the organization, organizational members may be much more likely to respond to these threats than if these negative cues are not aimed towards the organization's identity. For example, while faculty and administrators of some business schools may be extremely concerned about a drop in the *Business Week* rankings, faculty and administrators at other schools may demonstrate much less concern, focusing perhaps on how well they are rated on academic research, or public service to the surrounding community. In the Smith & Wesson example, the president noted, 'I'm depicted as a gunrunner, or as a trafficker in bad things.' This seemed in stark contrast to the image the organization had of itself as 'preserving security and freedom and law and order'. Thus, it is likely that engagement in reputation repair increases as the cues about the organization's reputation contain negative, identity-inconsistent attributes.

ATTENDING TO MULTIPLE STAKEHOLDERS

As previously mentioned, organizations often respond to a myriad of different stakeholders. But, because all stakeholders are not equally important in the eyes of organizational members, the organizational members, when receiving signals from their environment, look to particular stakeholder groups when making decisions regarding to whom they should pay attention. Mitchell, Agle, and Wood (1997) suggest that there are three primary attributes that lead to the salience of a stakeholder by management: power, legitimacy, and urgency. Powerful stakeholders include those that are in a position to carry out their will despite resistance. Legitimate stakeholders are those that have obtained 'a generalized perception or assumption [by others] that the actions of [the] entit[ies] are desirable, proper, or appropriate within some socially constructed systems of norms, values, beliefs, and definitions' (Suchman 1995: 574). Finally, urgent stakeholders are those that have convinced the organization that attending to a claim is both time sensitive and critical (that is, immediate action is called for). The salient groups consist of groups that contain all three of the attributes of power, legitimacy, and urgency. It follows then that these stakeholders will be recognized by management, and as a result are most likely to receive a response to their reputation cues.

On the other hand, if the stakeholders are not salient to organizational members, even when negative reputation cues are being sent to the organization, it is likely that the cues will be ignored or downplayed—at least in terms of a response aimed at external stakeholders of the organization. For example, it is more likely that organizational members would attend to a letter from a powerful and salient stakeholder in regard to product quality than if one letter were received from an obscure customer who was unlikely to provide repeat business for the organization. Thus, we propose that engagement in reputation repair increases as the cues about the organization's reputation are received from stakeholders whose salience is high (that is, meaning they have power, legitimacy, and urgency attributes).

We have just discussed the likelihood of reputation-repair behavior, depending on the type of negative reputation cues received and the types of sources who send them. In the following sections we introduce the concept of external image and suggest that this image has a direct effect on the likelihood that organizational members engage in reputation-repair behavior. We also note that organizational members may inaccurately assess reputation cues that are received and that distortions of these cues may lead to inappropriate reputation repair.

EXTERNAL IMAGE AND REPUTATION

In their article on how the Port Authority of New York & New Jersey responded to the issue of homelessness, Dutton and Dukerich (1991) argued that members of the organization developed an image of how outsiders perceived their organization (termed external image). They distinguished this image from corporate reputation to note that how insiders think outsiders see the organization may not be identical to how outsiders actually see the organization. We believe that it is this external image that directs reputation-repair behavior. Specifically, when organizational members believe that critical outside stakeholders see the organization in a negative, identity-inconsistent way, they are motivated to attend to the negative cues by engaging in reputation repair. However, as long as organizational members perceive the external image to be favorable, the receipt of subsequent negative reputation cues will be discounted or ignored. This is important, because the external image may not be an accurate portrayal as to how outsiders see the organization. Recognition of the critical role that the external image plays may help explain the seemingly inexplicable responses that organizational members make when negative reputation cues are received. While some organizations seem almost paranoid, blowing negative reputation cues out of proportion, others seem to be oblivious to the negative feedback that they receive.

We suggest that organizational members actively engage in a sense-making process when they encounter cues about the firm's reputation and that, specifically, these cues are filtered through an organizational identity lens. When reputation cues are sent by various external stakeholders, the identity of the organization influences which cues are attended to and how these cues are interpreted. We expect that organizational members pay close attention to cues that concern the distinctive attributes of the organization, whereas information not directly applicable to the identity of the organization might be deemed less important. Thus, identity may have the effect of distorting reputation cues, leading to an external image of the organization that is not consistent with the true reputation of the firm. Since it is the external image of the organization, and not the actual reputation of the organization, that encourages response by organizational members, engagement in reputation repair is most likely to increase as the external image is seen as negative and identity-inconsistent and when cues are received from salient stakeholders, regardless of the organization's true reputation. Fig. 7.1 depicts the relationships between corporate reputation, organizational identity, and external image.

As can be seen in the figure, there are reciprocal relationships between organizational identity, the beliefs that outsiders have about the organization (corporate reputation), and the beliefs that organizational members have about outsiders' perceptions (external image). Organizational identity not only influences how organizational members attend to and interpret reputational cues sent by stakeholders; identity constrains what are deemed to be

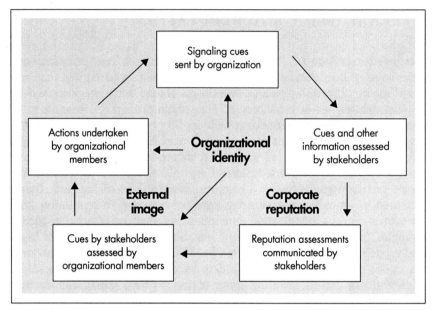

Fig. 7.1. The interrelationship between corporate reputation, image, and identity

legitimate responses to these cues. Organizational actions in turn influence subsequent assessments by outsiders of the reputation of the organization.

MISALLOCATION OF RESOURCES TOWARDS MANAGING CORPORATE REPUTATION

Given the above arguments, it is possible to speculate on situations where organizational members may misallocate resources towards managing the corporate reputation. Fig. 7.2 specifies the misallocation possibilities by organizational members. As the figure indicates, there are two instances in which an appropriate allocation of resources is likely to occur. Both of these cases are when the corporate reputation is accurately assessed, and thus the resultant external image is an accurate representation of the corporate reputation of the firm. When both are favorable—that is, the reputation of the firm is positive and organizational members' external image is positive as well—we argue that organizational members are in a good position to allocate resources appropriately towards maintaining or enhancing the already well-established reputation, or perhaps to allocate those resources towards other areas of the organization, such as product development and improvement (which could ultimately enhance the reputation of the firm). On the other hand, when the organization suffers a serious decline in reputation and the members of the organization accurately perceive the loss of faith by their key stakeholders, we predict that resources will be channeled towards dealing with the problem and ultimately repairing the reputation. We cannot predict whether these reputation-repair activities will be successful or not, but we believe that in this situation organizational members are at least allocating resources towards reputation repair in a more appropriate way than in the situations described below.

The area of misidentification lies in the situations where organizational members are unable to properly assess the organization's true reputation as seen by outside stakeholders. There is a possibility that organizational members will either allocate an inordinate amount of resources towards repairing the corporate reputation because they have magnified the negativity of the reputation cues, or they will allocate an insufficient amount of resources towards repairing the corporate reputation because they have minimized the negativity of these cues.

Magnification of Negative Cues and Inordinate Allocation of Resources

One error in the allocation of resources is when members of the organization spend an inordinate amount of time and money trying to repair a reputation that really is not so negative as they believe it to be. Consistent with our previous arguments, we expect that organizational members will greatly attend to

		External image (by insiders)	
		Unfavorable	Favorable
Corporate reputation (by outsiders)	Favorable	**Mismatched** Inordinate allocation of resources to defending reputation	**Matched** Appropriate allocation of resources to maintaining or enhancing reputation or to other interests
	Unfavorable	**Matched** Appropriate allocation of resources to defending reputation	**Mismatched** Insufficient allocation of resources to defending reputation

Fig. 7.2. Resource utilization as a function of matches and mismatches between external image and corporate reputation

reputation cues that threaten the core identity of the organization, magnifying the negativity of these cues and the expected response requirements. For instance, imagine a firm whose identity contains the attribute 'environmentally conscientious'. An overreaction may occur if organizational members believe that a newspaper article's portrayal of the organization as a polluter is much more negative than outsiders believe. In such a case, members of the organization may believe that the corporate reputation has been badly damaged and actions should be taken to reinstate the organization's good name, even though the newspaper article's portrayal may have been disregarded by the majority of the organization's stakeholders because these stakeholders have a strong belief in the organization's dedication to the environment. Nonetheless, in this situation, an aggressive marketing campaign may be engaged to counteract the imagined 'slights' to the organization's reputation (Fombrun 1996). Such actions may backfire for the organization, as outsiders begin to wonder why the organization is 'protesting too much' (Ashforth and Gibbs 1990).

Indeed, when organizations defend their legitimacy, these activities tend to stand out from the regular management of reputation because of their reactive and intense nature (Ashforth and Gibbs 1990). In the 1980s Procter & Gamble began to face rumors that its corporate logo symbol, 'man in the moon', was a satanic symbol and the mark of the devil. After several years of minimal response, Procter & Gamble took a huge risk and went on the offensive. The company filed suit against seven people for spreading 'false and malicious' rumors, risking a public uproar over its very highly publicized actions (Salmans 1982). Although these lawsuits seemed to curb the threat temporarily, three years later these rumors still haunted the company. In 1985 Procter & Gamble announced that it was going to remove the corporate logo from its products. A spokesperson for the firm denied that the rumors had cost the company 'hundreds of thousands of dollars' but added that the company would 'continue to fight the situation on all fronts' (Salmans 1985). While the initial response of Proctor & Gamble may have been minimal, the ultimate response could almost be characterized as overzealous, and the majority of stakeholders may have had little to say against the corporate logo. Perhaps the identity-threatening nature of the claims encouraged Proctor & Gamble officials to allocate all resources deemed necessary to squelch the rumors.

The magnification of negative reputation cues may also arise if the organization has historically had a poor reputation but that reputation has recently improved. The previously negative reputation may have led organizational members to develop organizational routines (Ginzel *et al.* 1993) that allocate what might now be considered by stakeholders to be an inordinate amount of resources to managing the corporate reputation. Thus, we propose that a magnified unfavorable image leads to an inordinate allocation of resources devoted towards repairing the organization's reputation. The result of this misallocation may be not only a loss of financial or other resources, but also a further damage to the organization's reputation in the eyes of stakeholders.

Minimization of Negative Cues and Insufficient Allocation of Resources

When organizational members fail to see how unfavorable the reputation of their organization actually is in the minds of their stakeholders, they may not react in an appropriate manner either. Organizational members may choose to ignore or indeed may not even notice corporate reputation cues that do not directly threaten the organization's core identity. In this case, the filtering of reputation cues through the organization's identity is likely to result in a minimization of the perceived negativity of the information. In such a situation, organizational members may not allocate an appropriate amount of resources towards managing the organization's reputation. Dow Corning has been given as an example of a firm that did not attend to the negative assessments that outsiders had made during the breast implant issue. Indeed, 'most of management saw the implant issue as a scientific issue, not one of communications' (quote from 1996 Carmichael interview, as reported by Argenti 1997). In this case, managers in Dow may have believed their firm's external image was not as unfavorable as outsiders actually perceived it to be. This inattention or discounting of the negative cues contributed to the public relations crisis described by Brinson and Benoit (1996) and Argenti (1998), among others.

Similarly, reputation cues received by organizational members from non-salient stakeholders may likewise be of less concern to the organizational members. When organizational members see negative cues from stakeholders that are not considered to be important to the firm as a whole, it is likely that reputation-repair behavior will not be initiated by the organization. Until the reputation cues come from credible stakeholders, no repair behavior will be seen as necessary. Thus, non-salient stakeholders may not be able to elicit a response from organizational members. This lack of action on the part of organizational members may be interpreted negatively by external stakeholders, thinking the organization is ignoring negative information or hoping it will all blow over. If these stakeholders are indeed peripheral to the organization, it is possible that a minimization of the negativity of the reputation cues by organizational members is completely appropriate. However, if organizational members fail to recognize key attributes of the stakeholders that may make them more threatening than otherwise determined, then this minimization or discounting of the cues could be detrimental to the organization. Consequently, a lack of attention to the negative reputation cues by organizational members may erode the organization's legitimacy and reputation as well.

Mitchell, Agle, and Wood (1997) provide an example of this type of situation. In 1993 stockholders from several *Fortune* 500 companies, including IBM, General Motors, Kodak, Westinghouse, and American Express, after suffering extensive stock valuation losses, expressed concerns that management was not attending to their legitimate interests or their needs as 'definitive' stakeholders (that is, those with power, legitimacy, and urgency). Because top managers did not sufficiently address these claims, many of them were subsequently removed from the companies. As Mitchell, Agle, and Wood (1997: 878) note, this demonstrates 'the importance of an accurate perception of power, legitimacy, and urgency; the necessity of acknowledgement and action that salience implies; and, more specifically, the consequences of the misperception of or inattention to the claims of definitive stakeholders'.

A minimization of negative reputation cues, because the cues either are perceived as peripheral to the identity, and/or come from non-salient stakeholders, can result in an external image that is not as unfavorable as the actual reputation. As a result, organizational members may not provide adequate time or resources towards repairing the reputation of the firm. For example, in 1994 IDB Communications in Los Angeles decided to allow its auditor, Deloitte & Touche, to resign because of a disagreement. While apparently IDB considered this a matter not worthy of external signaling attention, the FTC, the company's investors, and the media disagreed. After watching its stock price halve in the next several months, the company was sold at a rock-bottom price to one of its competitors (*Chief Executive* 1995). This demonstrates IDB's lack of understanding about the criticality of certain stakeholders. We suggest that, in general, a minimized unfavorable external image will lead to an insufficient allocation of resources devoted to repairing the organization's reputation, and will result in a detrimental effect on the organization's reputation.

IMPLICATIONS FOR MANAGERIAL BEHAVIOR

In this chapter we have proposed that organizations attend to some, but not all, negative reputation cues sent by their various stakeholders. We have suggested that there are two critical components that determine whether reputation-repair behavior is initiated by the organization—the degree to which negative reputation cues are identity inconsistent, and the salience of the stakeholders who are sending the negative reputation cues. We predicted that, when organizational members do not accurately assess the organization's true reputation, the reputation-repair behavior engaged in by the organization will likely result in a misallocation of the firm's resources.

The existence of inaccurate perceptions of corporate reputation has many implications for organizations. If, indeed, the organization's identity acts as a lens, distorting true reputation cues, a misallocation of resources for managing the reputation of the firm may result. The academic literature and the popular press are full of examples of firms, such as Exxon or BeechNut, that have ignored serious damages to their reputation, resulting in disastrous effects. The spectacular public relations crises that firms face when underestimating their constituencies' negative perceptions may lead researchers and practitioners to believe that minimization of an unfavorable external image is a more prevalent (and serious) problem. However, the opposite effect—overreacting to negative reputation cues—may be equally as damaging to the organization's effectiveness. Magnification of negative reputation cues may, over time, have an insidious effect that results in a redirection of corporate resources away from more appropriate or even more important elements, such as product development. Organizations that have a strong commitment to maintaining a good reputation, and thus feel this is part of their overall identity, may be the very ones that are most likely to overreact and allocate too much of the organization's resources to responding to the negative reputation cues. Such responses may ultimately damage the organization, as stakeholders come to believe that there must indeed be something wrong with the organization (where there's smoke there must be fire). Thus, it is imperative that organizations begin to understand how they may misperceive others' views of them. An accurate perception of the corporate reputation seems to be an important element to an effective response by the organization during reputation-repair circumstances.

How can corporate reputation misperceptions by organizational members be avoided? First, it is imperative that the organization has procedures in place to continually monitor the opinions of external stakeholders. By doing so, this will allow the organizational members to be better able to judge public reactions to organizational actions and behavior and thus be better prepared when reputation repair becomes necessary. Conducting both formal and informal surveys of key stakeholder groups such as customers and suppliers will further allow organizational members to stay abreast of current assessments of the organization's reputation. It is also critical that organizational members fully understand the impact of different stakeholder groups on organizational effectiveness. Recognizing which group of stakeholders is most likely to have the legitimacy, motivation, and power to sway other stakeholders regarding key reputation-threatening situations will help organizational members to more accurately and appropriately attend to reputation-repair circumstances as they arise. Finally, just being aware of the impact that an organization's identity may have on assessing corporate reputation could help organizational members to more accurately judge reputational assessment cues from key stakeholders.

To some degree we have painted a fairly simplistic picture, focusing on the mismatches that may exist between a single identity, a single image, and a single reputation. Obviously, organizations can have multiple identities, images, and reputations, depending on the particular stakeholder groups. It is important to consider the varying perceptions of multiple stakeholders when examining an organization's reputation. The tobacco industry offers an excellent example regarding how multiple reputations and stakeholder perceptions may affect an organization's reputation-repair strategy. Cigarette manufacturers have several very distinct stakeholders, including the government, the consumer, and the American Cancer Society, among many others. It is quite apparent that each of these stakeholders has very different concerns and views of these manufacturers. Each of these stakeholders places different demands and sends different signals to the companies. Consumers may demand lower-priced cigarettes, while the government at the same time is demanding higher taxes. Additionally, advocate groups such as the American Cancer Society may be fighting to eliminate the legality of cigarettes entirely. It is impossible for the organizations within the tobacco industry to meet the demands of all of these stakeholders. Thus, at any one point in time, it may be necessary to engage in different reputation-repair strategies *vis-à-vis* these different stakeholder groups.

It is also important to note that not all organizational members may react identically to negative reputation cues received by stakeholders. Some organizational members may feel a greater identification with the organization, which may ultimately increase the attention that they pay to organizational actions (Dutton *et al.* 1994). Additionally, some organizational members may have different views as to which stakeholders are particularly critical to the organization's success. For example, marketing personnel may be more likely to attend to the cues received from customers than would accounting personnel. However, in each of these instances, organizational members will react to these cues through their own understanding of the organization's identity, and this reaction is likely to affect organizational actions.

CONCLUSION

Just as individuals would rather not have to defend their own reputations, organizational members would gladly choose to never be in a position requiring them to defend their organization's reputation. Enhancing an already favorable reputation is a much easier task than trying to defend a faltering reputation. But there are times when repairing a reputation is an essential task. Understanding how and when to do so is imperative for the successful management of corporate reputation. Moreover, taking the appropriate reputation-repair steps can help to build an organization's reputation back to its previous level, and perhaps even higher. To do this effectively, we believe that it is critical for organizational members to understand the interrelationships between the organizational identity(ies), corporate reputation(s), and external image(s). Specifically, identity-inconsistent reputation threats influence organizational actions. Furthermore, the identity of the organization serves as a lens that may distort, through magnification or minimization, the cues sent to organizational members by stakeholders. This is likely to affect how organizational members choose to allocate resources towards managing the corporate reputation. By focusing on the concept of external image and its relationship to corporate reputation, the complexities of the relationship between identity and reputation may be better understood.

REFERENCES

Albert, S., and Whetten, D. A. (1985), 'Organizational Identity', in L. L. Cummings and B. M. Staw (eds.), *Research in Organizational Behavior, Volume 7* (Greenwich, Conn.: JAI Press), 7: 263–95.

Argenti, P. (1997), 'Dow Corning's Breast Implant Controversy: Managing Reputation in the Face of "Junk Science"', *Corporate Reputation Review*, 1/1–2: 126–31.

—— (1998), 'Corporate Communication Strategy: Applying Theory to Practice at Dow Corning', *Corporate Reputation Review*, 3: 234–49.

Ashforth, B. E., and Gibbs, B. (1990), 'The Double-Edge of Organizational Legitimation', *Organization Science*, 1/2: 177–94.

Benoit, W., and Czerwinski, A. (1997), 'A Critical Analysis of USAir's Image Repair Discourse', *Business Communication Quarterly*, 60/3: 38–57.

Boyer, P. J. (1999), 'Big Guns', *New Yorker*, 17 May, 54–67.

Brinson, S., and Benoit, W. (1996), 'Dow Corning's Image Repair Strategies in the Breast Implant Crisis', *Communication Quarterly*, 44/1: 29–41.

Bromley, D. B. (1993), *Reputation, Image, and Impression Management* (Chichester, England: John Wiley & Sons).

Carter, S., and Deephouse, D. (1999), 'Tough Talk and Soothing Speech: Managing Multiple Reputations', *Corporate Reputation Review*, 2/4: 308–32.

Cheney, G., and Christensen, L. (forthcoming), 'Identity at Issue: Linkages between "Internal" and "External" Organization Communication', in F. M. Jablin and L. L. Putnam (eds.), *New Handbook of Organizational Communication* (Thousand Oaks, Calif.: Sage).

—— and Vibbert, S. (1987), 'Corporate Discourse: Public Relations and Issue Management', in F. Jablin, L. L. Putnam, L. H. Porter, and K. H. Roberts (eds.), *Handbook of Organizational Communication: An Interdisciplinary Perspective* (Newbury Park, Calif.: Sage), 165–94.

Chief Executive (1995), 'Under Scrutiny', Jan.: 2–7.

Cowell, A. (1999), 'The Coke Stomach Ache Heard Round the World', *New York Times*, 25 June .

Dutton, J. E., and Dukerich, J. M. (1991), 'Keeping an Eye on the Mirror: Image and Identity in Organizational Adaptation', *Academy of Management Journal*, 34/3: 517–54.

—— —— and Harquail, C. V. (1994), 'Organizational Images and Member Identification', *Administrative Science Quarterly*, 39: 239–63.

Elsbach, K., and Sutton, R. (1992), 'Acquiring Organizational Legitimacy through Illegitimate Actions: A Marriage of Institutional and Impression Management Theories', *Academy of Management Journal*, 35/4: 699–738.

Fombrun, C. J. (1996), *Reputation: Realizing Value from the Corporate Image* (Boston: Harvard Business School Press).

—— and Shanley, M. (1990), 'What's in a Name? Reputation Building and Corporate Strategy', *Academy of Management Journal*, 33/2: 233–58.

Gardner, W., and Martinko, M. (1988), 'Impression Management in Organizations', *Journal of Management*, 14/2: 321–38.

Giacalone, R., and Rosenfeld, P. (1991), *Applied Impression Management: How Image-Making Affects Managerial Decisions* (Newbury Park, Calif.: Sage).

Ginzel, L., Kramer, R., and Sutton, R. (1993). 'Organizational Impression Management as a Reciprocal Influence Process: The Neglected Role of the Organizational Audience', in L. L. Cummings and B. Staw (eds.), *Research in Organizational Behavior* (Greenwich, Conn.: JAI Press), 15: 227–66.

Hall, R. (1993), 'A Framework Linking Intangible Resources and Capabilities to Sustainable Competitive Advantage', *Strategic Management Journal*, 14: 607–18.

Hearit, K. (1996), 'The Use of Counter-Attack in Apologetic Public Relations Crises: The Case of General Motors and Dateline NBC', *Public Relations Review*, 22/3: 233–48.

Kauffman, J. (1997), 'NASA in Crisis: The Space Agency's Public Relations Efforts Regarding the Hubble Space Telescope', *Public Relations Review*, 23/1: 1–10.

Milgrom, P., and Roberts, J. (1982), 'Predation, Reputation, and Entry Deterrence', *Journal of Economic Theory*, 27: 280–312.

Mitchell, R. K., Agle, B. R., and Wood, D. J. (1997), 'Toward a Theory of Stakeholder Identification and Salience: Defining the Principle of Who and What Really Counts', *Academy of Management Review*, 22/4: 853–86.

Perrow, C. (1961), 'Organizational Prestige: Some Functions and Dysfunctions', *American Journal of Sociology*, 61: 373–91.

Rosenfeld, P., Giacalone, R., and Riordan, C. (1995), *Impression Management in Organizations* (New York: Routledge).

Russ, G. (1991), 'Symbolic Communication and Image Management in Organizations', in R. Giacalone and P. Rosenfeld (eds.), *Applied Impression Management: How Image-Making Affects Managerial Decisions* (Newbury Park, Calif.: Sage), 219–40.

Salmans, S. (1982), 'Procter & Gamble's Battle with Rumors', *New York Times*, 22 July.

—— (1985), 'Procter & Gamble Drops Logo: Cites Satan Rumor', *New York Times*, 25 April.

Suchman, M. (1995), 'Managing Legitimacy: Strategic and Institutional Approaches', *Academy of Management Review*, 20/3: 571–610.

Ware, B., and Linkugel, W. (1973), 'They Spoke in Defense of Themselves: On the Generic Criticism of Apologia', *Quarterly Journal of Speech*, 59: 273–83.

IV

ORGANIZATIONS AS BRANDS

8

Building and Managing Corporate Brand Equity

Kevin Lane Keller

This chapter examines issues in building and managing corporate brand equity. Its purpose is to provide language, concepts, and guidelines that will improve the understanding of corporate brand equity management. Essentially, all firms have the opportunity to build corporate brand equity if they so choose. An increasing number of firms are employing their corporate brand as a strategic marketing weapon in the marketplace to improve their financial performance (Roberts and Dowling 1998). The discussion in this chapter will highlight some academic progress in this area, as well as suggest industry best practice.

Corporate brand equity can be defined as *the differential response by consumers, customers, employees, other firms, or any relevant constituency to the words, actions, communications, products or services provided by an identified corporate brand entity.* In other words, positive corporate brand equity occurs when a relevant constituent responds more favorably to a corporate ad campaign, a corporate-branded product or service, a corporate-issued PR release, or similar than if the same offering were to be attributed to an unknown or fictitious company.

Corporate brand equity occurs when relevant constituents hold strong, favorable, and unique associations about the corporate brand in memory. As will be developed below, a corporate brand is distinct from a product brand in that it can encompass a much wider range of associations. A corporate brand thus is a powerful means for firms to express themselves in a way that is not tied into their specific products or services.

The chapter is organized as follows. We begin by providing a corporate-wide perspective on branding by introducing the concept of the brand

This chapter is based on Chapter 11 of Kevin Lane Keller, *Strategic Brand Management: Building, Measuring and Managing Brand Equity* (Upper Saddle River, NJ: Prentice Hall, 1998).

hierarchy. We next discuss the role of the corporate brand and describe the various corporate image dimensions. Finally, we consider issues in designing and implementing a brand strategy in terms of brand hierarchies and supporting marketing programs.

BRAND HIERARCHY

To put a corporate brand in perspective, a useful concept is the brand hierarchy. In this section, we review the rationale, theory, and practice behind this concept.

Definitions

In many cases, a firm may want to make connections across products and brands to show consumers how these products and brands may be related. As a result, brand names of products are typically not restricted to one name but often consist of a combination of multiple brand-name elements. For example, a Toyota Camry XLE automobile consists of three different brand-name elements, 'Toyota', 'Camry', and 'XLE'. Some of these brand-name elements may be shared by many different products; other brand-name elements are limited to a more restricted range of products. For example, whereas Toyota uses its corporate name to brand many of its products, Camry designates a certain type of car (one that is at the high end of the full-size family car price point and quality level); and XLE identifies a particular version of Camry (the 'top-of-the-line' version with many special features such as a leather trim package, high-end audio system, side-impact air bags, and so on).

A *brand hierarchy* reveals an explicit ordering of brand elements by displaying the number and nature of common and distinctive brand elements across the firm's products (Farquhar 1989). By capturing the potential branding relationships among the different products sold by the firm, a brand hierarchy is a useful means to graphically portray a firm's branding strategy. By providing a complete and vivid picture of how a branding strategy comes across to consumers or to other firms, a brand hierarchy is a useful diagnostic tool.

Specifically, a brand hierarchy is based on the realization that a product can be branded in different ways depending on how many new and existing brand elements are used and how they are combined for any one product. Because certain brand elements are used to make more than one brand, a hierarchy can be constructed to represent how (if at all) products are nested with other products because of their common brand elements. Some brand elements may be shared by many products (e.g. Ford); other brand elements may be unique to a certain set of products (e.g. F-Series trucks); and so on.

As with any hierarchy, moving from the top level to the bottom level of the hierarchy typically involves more entries at each succeeding level or, in this case, more brands. There are different ways to define brand elements and levels of the hierarchy. Perhaps the simplest representation of possible brand elements and thus potential levels of a brand hierarchy—from top to bottom—might be:

1. Corporate (or company) brand;
2. family brand;
3. individual brand;
4. modifier (designating item or model).

The highest level of the hierarchy technically always involves one brand—the *corporate or company brand*. For legal reasons, the company or corporate brand is almost always present somewhere on the product or package, although it may be the case that the name of a company subsidiary may appear instead of the corporate name. For example, although Toyota adopted a branding strategy that used its corporate name combined with individual brand names and modifiers for most of its cars and trucks, it chose to brand its top-of-the-line cars as Lexus, deliberately avoiding using the Toyota name. For some firms, the corporate brand is virtually the only brand used (as, for example, with Motorola and General Electric). Some other firms combine their corporate brand name with family brands or individual brands (for example, conglomerate Siemens varied electrical engineering and electronics business units are branded with descriptive modifiers such as Siemens Transportation Systems). Finally, in some other cases, the company name is virtually invisible and, although technically part of the hierarchy, receives virtually no attention in the marketing program (for example, Black & Decker does not use its name on its high-end DeWalt professional power tools).

Although corporate brands are the focus of this chapter, it is useful to review other levels of the hierarchy too. At the next lower level, a *family brand* is defined as a brand that is used in more than one product category but is not necessarily the name of the company or corporation itself. For example, ConAgra's Healthy Choice family brand is used to sell a wide spectrum of food products, including frozen microwave entrées, packaged cheeses, packaged meats, sauces, and ice cream. Other family brands boasting over a billion dollars in annual sales include General Mills' Betty Crocker cakes and desserts and Nabisco's SnackWell's foods. Most firms typically support only a handful of family brands. If the corporate brand is applied to a range of products, then it functions as a family brand too, and the two levels collapse to one for those products.

An *individual brand*, on the other hand, is defined as a brand that has been restricted to essentially one product category, although it may be used for several different product types within the category. For example, in the 'salty-snack' product class, Frito-Lay offers Fritos corn chips, Doritos tortilla chips, Lays and Ruffles potato chips, and Rold Gold pretzels. Each brand has a dominant position in its respective product category within the broader salty-snack product class. A *modifier* is a means to designate a specific item or model type or particular version or configuration of the product. Thus, many of Frito-Lay's snacks come in both full-flavor and low-fat 'Better for You' forms. Similarly, Visa offers 'classic', 'gold', 'platinum', and 'signature' versions of its credit card. Yoplait yogurt comes in 'light', 'custard style', or 'original' flavors.

Building Corporate Brand Equity

For simplicity, we refer to a corporate and company brand interchangeably, recognizing that consumers may not necessarily draw a distinction between the two (that is, that corporations are potentially more encompassing and may subsume multiple companies). A corporate image *can be thought of as the associations in the consumer's memory to the company or corporation making the product or providing the service as a whole.* Corporate image is a particularly relevant concern when the corporate or company brand plays a prominent role in the branding strategy adopted.

More generally, some marketing experts believe that a factor increasing in importance in consumer purchase decisions is consumer perceptions of a firm's whole role in society, including how a firm treats its employees, shareholders, local neighbors, and others. As Procter & Gamble's one-time CEO Ed Artz remarked, 'Consumers now want to know about the company, not just the products' (Swasy 1991). Similarly, as Laurel Cutler, vice-chairman of the large New York City advertising agency FCB/Leber Katz Partners, was quoted: 'The only sustainable competitive advantage any business has is its reputation' (Caminit 1995). Finally, in a business-to-business setting, Opinion Research announced the results of a survey of 3,000 executives that indicated that 'knowing a company very well' was a key reason to award new business.

A realization that consumers may be interested in issues beyond product characteristics and associations has prompted much marketing activity to establish the proper corporate image. A corporate image will depend on a number of factors, such as: (1) the products a company makes, (2) the actions it takes, and (3) the manner with which it communicates to consumers. As Ralph Larson, CEO at Johnson & Johnson, observes, 'Reputations reflect behavior you exhibit day in and day out through a hundred small things. The way you manage your reputation is by always thinking and trying to do the right thing every day.'

In establishing a corporate image, a corporate brand may evoke associations wholly different from an individual brand, which is only identified with a certain product or limited set of products. For example, a corporate brand name may be more likely to evoke associations of common products and their shared attributes or benefits; people and relationships; programs and values; and corporate credibility. Any contact that a customer or any other constituent has with the firm, directly or indirectly, may affect the existence or strength of the associations. Nevertheless, these associations ideally should be shaped as the result of very carefully designed and executed marketing programs by the firm. The essence of good marketing is the ability to influence consumer's perceptions, preferences, and behaviors in a manner that provides maximum benefits to the firm through optimal product, communication, distribution, pricing strategies, and so on.

Corporate Image Dimensions

In this section we highlight some of the different types of associations that are likely to be linked to a corporate brand and which can potentially have an impact on brand equity (see Box 8.1). Excellent reviews of corporate images are also available, such as Dowling (1994) and Gregory (1991).

Box 8.1. Important corporate image associations

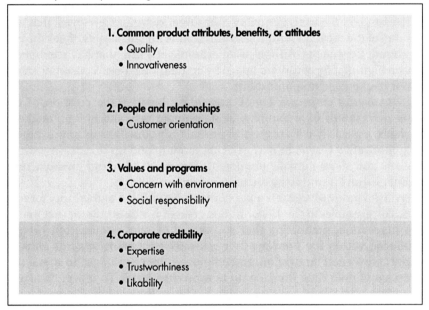

1. **Common product attributes, benefits, or attitudes**
   - Quality
   - Innovativeness

2. **People and relationships**
   - Customer orientation

3. **Values and programs**
   - Concern with environment
   - Social responsibility

4. **Corporate credibility**
   - Expertise
   - Trustworthiness
   - Likability

Common Product Attributes, Benefits, or Attitudes

As with individual brands, a corporate or company brand may evoke product-related or non-product-related attribute or benefit associations as well as attitude associations. Thus, a corporate brand may evoke a strong association with consumers to a product attribute (e.g. Hershey with 'chocolate'), type of user (e.g. Marlboro with 'rugged, independent or masculine individuals'), usage situation (e.g. Miller Genuine Draft with 'Miller Time'), or overall evaluation or attitude (e.g. Sony with 'quality').

If a corporate brand is linked to products across diverse categories, then some of its strongest associations are likely to be those intangible attributes, abstract benefits, or attitudes that span each of the different product categories. For example, companies may be associated with products or services that solve particular problems (e.g. Black & Decker), bring excitement and fun to certain activities (e.g. Nintendo), be built with the highest quality standards (e.g. Motorola), contain advanced or innovative features (e.g. Rubbermaid), or represent market leadership (e.g. Hertz). Two specific product-related corporate image associations—high quality and innovation—deserve special attention.

A *high-quality corporate image association* involves the creation of consumer perceptions that a company makes products of the highest quality. A number of different organizations rate products (e.g. J. D. Powers, *Consumer Reports*, and various trade publications that conduct laboratory tests and consumer surveys to evaluate automobiles) and companies (e.g. the Malcolm Baldridge award given to US companies that excel in performance and competitiveness) on the basis of quality. Consumer surveys often reveal that quality is one of the most important decision factors for consumers, if not the most important. Continental Airlines is an example of a firm that has attempted to create a high-quality corporate image by emphasizing these consumer surveys in their marketing communications.

An *innovative corporate image association* involves the creation of consumer perceptions of a company as developing new and unique marketing programs, especially with respect to product introductions or improvements. Being innovative is seen in part as being modern and up to date, investing in research and development, employing the most advanced manufacturing capabilities, and introducing the newest product features.

Perceived innovativeness is a key competitive weapon and priority for many firms. For example, in the USA, 3M has created a strong culture that emphasizes innovation, mandating that 30 percent of sales comes from products introduced within the previous four years. The company rewards entrepreneurial activity and innovation, and employees are encouraged to spend up to 15 percent of their time thinking up new product ideas. To reflect this corporate philosophy, the advertising slogan has been 'Innovation working for you'. 3M's branding strategy uses its corporate name to endorse a diverse range of products (e.g. overhead projectors, cameras, medical adhesives, and Post-It notes). Similarly, 3M's strong Scotch family brand has also been used on a whole host of products, including videocassettes, photographic films, and fabric protectors.

People and Relationships

Corporate image associations may reflect characteristics of the employees of the company. Although this is a natural positioning strategy for service firms such as airlines (e.g. Delta), rental cars (e.g. Avis), and hotels (e.g. Doubletree), manufacturing firms such as DuPont, Philips, and others have also focused attention on their employees in communication programs. General Motors created an entire car division, Saturn, which advertises itself as a 'Different Kind of Car Company' in an attempt to build unique relationships with consumers. All of these various marketing efforts can be seen as means to try to humanize employees and signal to customers their enhanced importance to the firm. Retail stores also derive much brand equity from employees within the organization. For example, growing from its origins as a small shoe store, Seattle-based Nordstrom became one of the nation's leading fashion specialty stores through a commitment to quality, value, selection, and, especially, service. The company is legendary for its 'personalized touch' and willingness to go to extraordinary lengths to satisfy customers. The success of the company's brand equity is due in large part to the efforts of salespeople and the relationships they have with consumers.

Thus, a *customer-focused corporate image association* involves the creation of consumer perceptions of a company as responsive to and caring about its customers. In such cases, consumers believe that 'their voice will be heard' and that the company is not attempting to be exploitative. Thus, a company seen as customer-focused is likely to be described as 'listening' to customers and having their best interests in mind. Often this philosophy is reflected all through the marketing program and communicated through advertising, such as with Gateway computer's 'Your:)Ware'.

Values and Programs

Corporate image associations may reflect values and programs of the company that do not always relate directly to the products that it sells. In many cases, these efforts are publicized through marketing communication campaigns. Firms can run corporate image ad campaigns as a means to describe to consumers, employees, and others the philosophy and actions of the company with respect to organizational, social, political, or economic issues. For example, a focus of many recent corporate advertising campaigns has been on company programs and activities designed to address environmental issues and communicate social responsibility, which we highlight next.

An *environmentally concerned corporate image association* involves the creation of consumer perceptions of a company as developing marketing programs to protect or improve the environment and make more effective use of scarce natural resources (*Journal of Advertising* 1995). Concern for the environment is a growing social trend that is reflected in attitudes and behavior of both consumers and corporations (Alwitt and Pitts 1996; Menon and Menon 1997). For example, one survey found that 83 percent of American consumers said they prefer to buy environmentally safe products (Dagnoli 1991). Another survey found that 23 percent of American consumers now claim to make purchases based on environmental considerations (Joseph 1991).

At the same time, a number of studies have concluded that consumers as a whole may not be willing to actually pay a premium for environmental benefits, although there may be certain market segments that will. Most consumers appear unwilling to give up the benefits of other options to choose green products. For example, some consumers dislike the performance, appearance, or texture of recycled paper and household products. Similarly, some consumers are unwilling to give up the convenience of disposable products, such as diapers.

Nevertheless, on the corporate side, successful 'green-marketing' initiatives have been undertaken with environmental overtones. For example, Chevron's highly visible 'People Do' ad campaign attempted to transform consumers' negative perceptions of oil companies and their effect on the environment by describing specific Chevron programs designed to save wildlife, preserve seashores, and so on (Winters 1988).

A *socially responsible corporate image association* involves creation of consumer perceptions of a company as contributing to community programs, supporting artistic and social activities, and generally attempting to improve the welfare of society as a whole (Cunningham and Berger 1997). The 1980s saw the advent of 'cause-related marketing'. Formally, *cause-related marketing* has been defined by Varadarajan and Menon (1988) as 'the process of formulating and implementing marketing activities that are characterized by an offer from the firm to contribute a specified amount to a designated cause when customers engage in revenue-providing exchanges that satisfy organizational and individual objectives'. They note that the distinctive feature of cause-related marketing is the firm's contribution to a designated cause being linked to customers engaging in revenue-producing transactions with the firm.

One major research study that tracked consumer reactions to cause marketing reported the following findings based on a US representative sample (1999 Cone/Roper Cause Related Trends Report): (1) 83 percent of Americans had a more positive image of companies that supported a cause they cared about; (2) 74 percent accepted cause programs as a business practice; (3) 66 percent reported greater trust in those companies aligned with a social issue; and (4) roughly two-thirds said, when price and quality were equal, that they would switch brands or retailers to one associated with a good cause. Additional findings revealed that employees were prouder at and felt more loyalty to companies with cause-related marketing programs.

Cause marketing comes in many forms. Notable programs include American Express's 'Charge against Hunger', Avon's 'Breast Cancer Awareness Crusade', and WalMart's 'Good Works' program. Some firms have used cause marketing very strategically to gain a marketing advantage (for example, the Body Shop, which has adopted cause-related marketing as the essence of its brand positioning, Timberland, Working Assets, and so on). Ben & Jerry's is another firm that has created a strong association as a 'do-gooder' through various products and programs—such as its rainforest crunch ice cream—and by donating 7.5 percent of pre-tax profits to various social causes (from anti-nuclear campaigns to gay rights).

As with green marketing, which can be seen as closely related to cause marketing, the danger is that the promotional efforts behind a cause-marketing program could backfire if cynical consumers question the link between the product and the cause and see the firm as being self-serving and exploitative as a result. The hope is that cause marketing strikes a chord with consumers and employees, improving the image of the company and energizing these constituents to act (Drumwright 1996). With near-parity products, some marketers feel a strongly held point-of-difference on the basis of community involvement and concern may in some cases be the best way—and perhaps the only way—to uniquely position a product.

Perhaps the most important benefit of cause-related marketing is that, by humanizing the firm, consumers may develop a strong, unique bond with the firm that transcends normal marketplace transactions. A dramatic illustration of such benefits is with McDonald's, whose franchises have long been required to stay close to local communities and whose Ronald McDonald Houses for sick children are a concrete symbol of their 'do-good' efforts. When whole blocks of businesses were burned and looted in the South Central Los Angeles riots of 1992, one McDonald's executive observed, 'We literally had people standing in front of some restaurants saying, "No, don't throw rocks through this window—these are the good guys."' When the dust cleared, all sixty McDonald's restaurants in South Central had been spared.

Corporate Credibility

Besides all the associations noted above, consumers may form more abstract beliefs about the company, including perceptions of the personality of a corporate brand. For example, one major utility company was described by customers as 'male, 35–40 years old, middle class, married with children, wearing a flannel shirt and khaki pants, who would be reliable, competent, professional, intelligent, honest, ethical and business-oriented'. On the downside, the company was also described by these same customers as 'distant, impersonal, and self-focused', suggesting an important area for improvement in its corporate brand image.

A particularly important set of abstract associations to a corporate brand is corporate credibility (Keller and Aaker 1992). *Corporate credibility* refers to the extent to which consumers believe that a firm can design and deliver products and services that satisfy customer needs and wants. Thus, corporate credibility relates to the reputation that the firm has achieved in the marketplace.

Corporate credibility, in turn, depends on three factors:

1. *corporate expertise*—the extent to which a company is seen as able to make and sell its products or conduct its services competently;

2. *corporate trustworthiness*—the extent to which a company is seen as motivated to be honest, dependable, and sensitive to customer needs;
3. *corporate likability*—the extent to which a company is seen as likable, attractive, prestigious, dynamic, etc.

In terms of consequences, a number of other characteristics can also be related to these three dimensions, such as success, leadership, and so on. Creating a firm with a strong and credible reputation may offer benefits beyond the consumer response in the marketplace. A highly credible company may also be treated more favorably by other external constituencies, such as government or legal officials. It also may be possible to attract better-qualified employees as a result. Consulting firms such as Andersen Consulting use their industry leadership position and credibility to target top college graduates.

A highly credible company may also help to motivate existing employees to be more productive and loyal. As one Shell Oil employee remarked as part of some internal corporate identity research, 'If you're really proud of where you work, I think you put a little more thought into what you did to help get them there.' A strong corporate reputation can help a firm survive a brand crisis and avert public outrage that could potentially depress sales, encourage unionism, or block expansion plans. As Harvard's Steve Greyser notes, 'Corporate reputation . . . can serve as a capital account of favorable attitudes to help buffer corporate trouble.'

Keller and Aaker (1998) experimentally showed how different corporate image strategies—being innovative, environmentally concerned, or community involved—can differentially affect corporate credibility and strategically benefit the firm by increasing the acceptance of brand extensions as a result (see also Goldberg and Hartwick 1990). Specifically, they showed how environmentally concerned and community-involved corporate images affected perceptions of corporate trustworthiness and likability but not corporate expertise. Interestingly, an innovative corporate image was seen not only as expert but also as trustworthy and likable. Because only an innovative corporate image affected perceptions of corporate expertise, however, it was the only image type to affect perceptions of the fit and quality of a proposed extension. The other two image types, although perhaps useful in other contexts, were not as much of an asset in facilitating new product acceptance.

Summary

In short, all types of associations that transcend physical product characteristics may become linked to a corporate brand (Brown and Dacin 1997; Brown 1998). These intangible associations may provide valuable sources of brand equity and serve as critical points-of-parity or points-of-difference in terms of positioning with respect to competitive offers. Companies also have a number of means—indirect or direct—of creating these associations. In doing so, it is important that companies 'talk the talk *and* walk the walk' by communicating to consumers as well as backing up their claims with concrete programs that consumers can easily understand or even experience.

DESIGNING A BRANDING STRATEGY

Keller (1999) provides a detailed review of how to design and implement a branding strategy. Given the different possible levels of a branding hierarchy, a firm has a number of branding options available to it, depending on how each level is employed, if at all. There is no uniform agreement as to one type of branding strategy that should be adopted by all firms for all products (LaForet and Saunders 1994). Even within any one firm, different branding strategies may be adopted for different products. For example, although Miller has used its name across its different types of beer over the years with various sub-brands (e.g. Miller High Life, Miller Lite, and Miller Genuine Draft), it carefully branded its no-alcohol beer substitute as Sharp's with no overt Miller identification.

Thus, it is important to note that *the brand hierarchy may not be symmetric.* Because of considerations related to corporate objectives, consumer behavior, or competitive activity, there may sometimes be significant deviations in branding strategy and the way in which the brand hierarchy is organized for different products or for different markets. Brand elements may receive more or less emphasis, or not be present at all, depending on the particular products and markets involved. For example, in appealing to an organizational market segment where the DuPont brand name may be more valuable, it receives more emphasis than associated sub-brands. In appealing to a consumer market segment, a sub-brand such as Dacron may be more meaningful and thus receive relatively more emphasis.

How does a firm use different levels of the brand hierarchy to build brand equity? Brand elements at each level of the hierarchy may contribute to brand equity through their ability to create awareness and foster strong, unique, and favorable brand associations for products. Therefore, the challenge in setting up the brand hierarchy and arriving at a branding strategy is:

1. to design the proper brand hierarchy in terms of the number and nature of brand elements to use at each level;
2. to design the optimal supporting marketing program in terms of creating the desired amount of brand awareness and type of brand associations at each level.

A number of specific issues arise in designing and implementing a branding strategy with respect to these two areas, some of which we discuss next.

Designing the Brand Hierarchy

Designing a brand hierarchy involves decisions related to:

1. the number of levels of the hierarchy to use in general;
2. how brand elements from different levels of the hierarchy are combined, if at all, for any one particular product;
3. how any one brand element is linked, if at all, to multiple products;
4. how brand elements are organized at any one level of the hierarchy.

Number of Levels of the Brand Hierarchy

The first decision to make in defining a branding strategy is, broadly, which level or levels of the branding hierarchy should be used. In general, most firms choose to use more than one level for two main reasons. Each successive branding level that is used allows the firm to communicate additional, specific information about its products. Thus, developing brands at lower levels of the hierarchy allows the firm flexibility in communicating the uniqueness of its products. At the same time, developing brands at higher levels of the hierarchy such that the brand is applied across multiple products is obviously an economical means of communicating common or shared information and providing synergy across the company's operations, both internally and externally.

The practice of combining an existing brand with a new brand to brand a product is called *sub-branding*, as the subordinate brand is a means of modifying the superordinate brand. Sub-branding often combines brands from different levels of the hierarchy, such as the company or family brand name with individual brands and even model types. Extending our earlier example, Camry can be seen as a sub-brand of Toyota with XLE as a second-level sub-brand to further modify the meaning of the product. As suggested above, a sub-brand, or hybrid branding, strategy offers two potential benefits in that it can both:

1. facilitate access to associations and attitudes to the company or family brand as a whole and, at the same time,
2. allow for the creation of specific brand beliefs.

Using the Toyota name allows access to global associations that consumers may have towards the company, which include reliability, dependability, and high quality. Introducing different sub-brands—Celica, Corolla, Avalon, RAV4, Tacoma, etc.—allows Toyota to develop distinct brand images at the same time.

Sub-branding creates a stronger connection to the company or family brand and all the associations that come along with that. At the same time, developing sub-brands allows for the creation of brand-specific beliefs. This more detailed information can help customers better understand how products vary and which particular product may be the right one for them. Sub-brands also help to organize selling efforts, so that salespeople and retailers have a clear picture as to how the product line is organized and how it might best be sold. For example, one of the main advantages to Nike of continually creating sub-brands in its basketball line (e.g. Air Jordan, Flight, Force, and so on) has been to generate retail interest and enthusiasm.

In general, the desired number of levels of the brand hierarchy depends on the complexity of the product line or product mix associated with a brand and thus the combination of shared and separate brand associations that the company would like to link to any one product in its product line or mix. With relatively simple, low-involvement products—such as light bulbs, batteries, and chewing gum—the branding strategy often consists of an individual or perhaps family brand combined with modifiers that describe differences in product features. For example, with a fairly simple product such as light bulbs, GE has two main brands (Soft White and Enrich) combined with functionality (3-way, Super, Miser, etc.) and performance (40, 60, 100, etc. watts) designations. With a complex set of products—such as cars, computers, or other durable goods—more levels of the hierarchy may be necessary. Regardless of the complexity involved, it is difficult to brand a product with more than three levels of brand names without overwhelming or confusing consumers. In such cases, a better approach might be to introduce multiple brands at the same level (e.g. multiple family brands) and expand the depth of the brand portfolio.

Combining Brand Elements from Different Levels

If multiple brand elements from different levels of the brand hierarchy are combined to brand new products, it is necessary to decide how much emphasis should be given to each brand element. For example, if a sub-brand strategy is adopted, how much prominence should individual brands be given at the expense of the corporate or family brand?

When multiple brands are used, each brand element can vary in the relative emphasis it receives in the combined brand. The *prominence* of a brand element refers to its relative visibility as compared to other brand elements. For example, the prominence of a brand-name element depends on several factors, such as its order, size, and appearance, as well as its semantic associations. A brand name should generally be more prominent when it appears first, is larger, and looks more distinctive than the other elements. For example, assume Tropicana has adopted a sub-branding strategy to introduce a new sodium-free orange juice, combining its corporate family brand name with a new individual brand name (e.g. 'Sunburst'). The Tropicana name could be made more prominent by placing it first and making it bigger, an example of which would be TROPICANA *Sunburst*. On the other hand, the individual brand could be made more prominent by placing it first and making it larger: SUNBURST by *Tropicana*.

The relative prominence of the brand elements determines which element(s) becomes the primary one(s) and which element(s) becomes the secondary one(s). In general, primary brand elements should be chosen to convey the main product positioning and points-of-difference. Secondary brand elements are often chosen in more of a supporting role to convey a more restricted set of associations such as points-of-parity or perhaps an additional point-of-difference. A secondary brand element may also facilitate awareness. Thus, with the Canon Rebel 35mm camera, the primary brand element is the Rebel name, which reinforces the youthful, active lifestyle that makes up the desired user and usage imagery for the camera. The Canon name, on the other hand, is more of a secondary brand element, which ideally would convey credibility, quality, and professionalism.

The relative prominence of the individual brand compared to the corporate brand should affect perceptions of product distance and the type of image created for the new product. If the corporate or family brand is made more prominent, then its associations are more likely to dominate. If the individual brand is made more prominent, on the other hand, then it should be easier to create a more distinctive brand image. In this case, the corporate or family brand is signaling to consumers that the new product is not as closely related to the other products that share that name. As a result, consumers should be less likely to transfer corporate or family brand associations. At the same time, the success or failure of the new product should, because of the greater perceived distance involved, be less likely to affect the image of the corporate or family brand. With a more prominent corporate or family brand, however, feedback effects are probably more likely to be evident.

To illustrate how relative prominence can affect the resulting image of a product, assume in the Tropicana Sunburst example above that Tropicana was the more prominent brand element as compared to Sunburst. By making the corporate and family brand prominent, the new product would take on many of the associations that would be in common with other Tropicana-branded products (e.g. orange juice). If the Sunburst brand were more prominent, however, then the new product would most likely take on a much more distinct positioning. In this case, the Topicana name would function more for awareness and perhaps only transfer broader, more abstract associations such as perceived quality or brand personality.

Finally, in some cases, the brand elements may not be explicitly linked at all. A *brand endorsement strategy* is when a brand element appears on the package, signage, or product appearance in some way but is not directly included as part of the brand name. Often this distinct brand element is the corporate brand name or logo. For example, General Mills places its 'Big G' logo on its cereal packages but retains distinct brand names such as Cheerios, Wheaties, and so on. As noted above, Kellogg's, on the other hand, adopts a sub-brand strategy with its cereals that combines the corporate name with individual brands, which include Kellogg's Corn Flakes, Kellogg's Special K, and so on. The brand endorsement strategy presumably establishes the maximum distance between the corporate or family brand and the individual brands, suggesting that it would yield the smallest transfer of brand associations to the new product but, at the same time, minimize the likelihood of any negative feedback effects.

Linking Brand Elements to Multiple Products

The previous discussion highlighted how different brand elements may be applied to a particular product (that is, 'vertical' aspects of the brand hierarchy). Next, we consider how any one brand element can be linked to multiple products (that is, 'horizontal' aspects of the brand hierarchy). There are many different ways to connect a brand element to multiple products. The simplest way is literally to use the brand element 'as is' across the different products involved. Other possibilities can be created by adapting the brand, or some part of it, in some fashion to make the connection. For example, a common prefix or suffix of a brand name may be adapted to different products. Hewlett-Packard capitalized on its highly successful LaserJet computer printers to introduce a number of new products using the 'Jet' suffix, including the DeskJet, PaintJet, ThinkJet, and OfficeJet printers. Sony has designated its portable audio equipment with a 'Man' suffix, resulting in Walkman personal stereos and Discman portable CD players. McDonald's has used its 'Mc' prefix to introduce a number of products, such as Chicken McNuggets, Egg McMuffin, and the McRib sandwich. Initials can sometimes be used if multiple names make up the brand name, as is the case with a designer name such as Donna Karan's DKNY brand, Calvin Klein's CK brand, and Ralph Lauren's Double RL brand. A relationship between a brand and multiple products can also be made with common symbols. For example, corporate brands often place their corporate logo more prominently on their products than their name (e.g. Nabisco), creating a strong brand endorsement strategy.

Organizing Brand Elements at any One Level of the Brand Hierarchy

Often it is desirable to have a logical ordering among brands in a product line to communicate how the different brands are related and to simplify consumer decision-making. The relative ordering may be communicated to consumers though colors (for example, American Express offers Green, Gold, and Platinum Cards), numbers (for example, BMW offers their 3, 5, and 7 series cars), or other means. Such a branding strategy is especially important in developing brand migration strategies as to how customers should switch among the brands offered by the company, if at all, over their lifetime.

Another 'horizontal' brand hierarchy issue concerns the relative emphasis received by different products making up any level of the brand hierarchy. If a corporate or family brand is associated with multiple products, which product should be the core or 'flagship' product? What should represent 'the brand' to consumers? Which product do consumers think best represents or embodies the brand? Understanding these brand 'drivers' is important in identifying sources of brand equity and therefore how to best fortify and leverage the brand.

Designing Supporting Marketing Programs

At the same time that the broad parameters of the brand hierarchy are put into place as to how brand elements relate to particular products, decisions also have to be made as to how to design the supporting marketing program in a way that best reflects the desired content and structure of the brand hierarchy. In doing so, decisions have to be made concerning: (1) the planned or desired image at each brand hierarchy level; and (2) any necessary adjustments that should be made to the marketing program to support the new image.

Desired Awareness and Image at Each Hierarchy Level

Once multiple brand levels are chosen, the question becomes, how much awareness and what types of associations are to be created for brand elements at each level? Achieving the desired level of awareness and strength, favorability, and uniqueness of brand associations may take some time and involve a considerable change in consumer perceptions. Marketing programs must be carefully designed, implemented, and evaluated. Assuming some type of sub-branding strategy is adopted involving two or more brand levels, two general principles—relevance and differentiation—should guide the brand knowledge creation process at each level.

The first principle, relevance, is based on the advantages of efficiency and economy. In general, it is desirable to create associations that are relevant to as many brands nested at the level below as possible, *especially at the corporate or family brand level*. The more an association has some value in the marketing of products sold by the firm, then the more efficient and economical it is to consolidate this meaning into one brand that becomes linked to all these products. For example, Nike's slogan ('Just Do It') reinforces a key point-of-difference for the brand—performance—that is relevant to virtually all the products they sell. The more abstract meaning the association has, in general, the more likely it is to be relevant in different product settings. Thus, benefit associations are likely to be extremely advantageous associations because they can potentially 'cut across' so many product categories.

The second principle, differentiation, is based on the disadvantages of redundancy. In general, it is desirable to distinguish brands at the same level as much as possible. If two brands cannot be easily distinguished, then it may be difficult for retailers or other channel members to justify supporting both brands. It may also be confusing for consumers to have to choose between them. For example, Tropicana's orange juice sub-brands have included their flagship Pure Premium (which comes in several flavors including Ruby Red Orange) as well as Grovestand ('The Taste of Fresh Squeezed') and Season's Best (100 percent pure orange juice from concentrate with vitamins added) extensions, which also come in different varieties and packaging. Certainly, on the basis of the names and positionings, there would seem to be the potential for consumer confusion as to how the different varieties of juice differ and which Tropicana juice is the right product for each prospective purchaser.

Although the principle of differentiation is especially important at the individual brand or modifier levels, it is also valid at the family brand level. For example, one of the criticisms of marketing at General Motors is that it has failed to adequately distinguish its family brands of automobiles. Similarly, Ford Motor Co. has faced similar problems with its Mercury family brand, prompting the second largest US car-maker to embark on the largest advertising and promotional campaign, 'Imagine Yourself in a Mercury'.

Adjustments to the Marketing Program

As noted above, a corporate image will depend on a company's products, actions, and the manner in which it communicates to consumers. If a sub-brand strategy is adopted, it often makes sense to create a marketing communication campaign at the corporate, company, or family brand levels to complement more product-specific or individual brand marketing communication campaigns. As part of this 'higher-level' campaign, companies may employ the full range of marketing communication options, including advertising, public relations, promotions, and sponsorship. Two potentially useful marketing communication strategies to build brand equity at the corporate brand or family brand level are discussed here.

Corporate image campaigns are designed to create associations to the corporate brand as a whole and, consequently, tend to ignore or downplay individual products or sub-brands in the process (for a review of current and past practices, see Schumann *et al.* 1991). As would be expected, some of the biggest spenders on these kinds of campaigns are those well-known firms that prominently use their company or corporate name in their branding strategies, including GE, Toyota, British Telecom, IBM, Novartis, Microsoft, Deutsche Bank, etc. More firms are now running these types of non-product-specific ads—especially retail and service brands that commonly use their corporate name—in part due to the fact that so many products have become linked to their family or corporate brands over time through brand extensions, and so on.

Corporate image campaigns have been criticized by some in the past as an ego-stroking waste of time. To maximize the probability of success, objectives of a corporate image campaign must be clearly defined *and* results must be carefully measured against these objectives (Bender *et al.* 1996; Ind 1998; van Riel *et al.* 1998). There can be a number of different possible objectives in a corporate brand campaign (Biehal and Shenin 1998):

1. to build awareness of the company and the nature of its business;
2. to create favorable attitudes and perceptions of company credibility;
3. to link beliefs that can be leveraged by product-specific advertising;
4. to make a favorable impression on the financial community;
5. to motivate present employees and attract better recruits;
6. to influence public opinion on issues.

In terms of building customer-based brand equity, the first three objectives are particularly critical, because they will determine the extent to which a corporate image campaign can enhance awareness and create a more positive image of the corporate brand that will influence customer evaluations and increase the equity associated with individual products and any related sub-brands. In certain cases, however, the latter three objectives can take on greater importance (see e.g. Gilly and Wolfinbarger 1996).

Because the first three objectives are the ones most directly related to building customer-based brand equity, we highlight notable examples for each.

1. *To build awareness of the company and the nature of its business.* Fortune Brands ran an extensive print ad campaign to shed its older image as a tobacco company and to highlight consumer products that it had acquired over the years, such as Jim Beam bourbon, Foot-Joy golf shoes, Titleist golf balls, Master Lock locks, Swingline staplers, and Moen faucets. Similarly, Honeywell has advertised to correct the widespread—but incorrect—belief that it is still a 'computer company'.

2. *To create favorable attitudes and perceptions of company credibility.* Johnson & Johnson recently launched an ad campaign to promote the trustworthiness of the corporate brand. The commercials featured many 'warm and fuzzy' shots of families. Johnson & Johnson products were not emphasized, although their baby powder, Band-Aids, and Reach toothbrush products were shown in passing. The ad concluded with the words: 'Over the years, Johnson & Johnson has taken care of more families than anyone else.'

3. *To link beliefs that can be leveraged by product-specific advertising.* Since the 1930s the 'Better Things for Better Living' slogan has helped to win brand recognition among DuPont's business customers and consumers alike. In 1999 DuPont decided to abandon this slogan and launched a new corporate image with the introduction of its 'Miracles of Science' campaign. According to one DuPont marketing executive, the new campaign 'sets the record straight on what kind of company we are and what we are becoming'—that is, it emphasizes DuPont's use of pure scientific research to engender new-age products that have even wider applications than the company's previous product portfolio.

Thus, corporate image campaigns focus on characteristics or aspects of the brand as a whole. These broader image campaigns may also be employed at the family brand level.

A second marketing communication strategy to build brand equity at the corporate brand or family brand level is with brand line campaigns. *Brand line campaigns* emphasize the breadth of products associated with the brand. Unlike a corporate image campaign that presents the brand in abstract terms with perhaps few, if any, references to specific products, brand line campaigns refer to the range of products associated with a brand line. For example, in the summer of 1998 Kraft launched a $50 million brand campaign that showcased its Kool-Aid, Philadelphia cream cheese, Post cereal, and Tombstone frozen pizza brands into single television spots and Sunday circulars. By showing consumers the different uses or benefits of the multiple products offered by a brand, brand line ads may be particularly useful in building brand awareness, clarifying brand meaning, and suggesting additional usage applications.

CLOSING REMARKS

Summary

This chapter has reviewed some key issues in building and managing corporate brand equity. Particular emphasis has been placed on how to design and implement a corporate branding strategy. The above discussion can be summarized in terms of five key points:

1. A strong corporate brand can provide a number of marketing advantages. A strong corporate brand allows a firm to express itself in terms of 'who it is' and 'what it is about' and therefore provides a means to transcend the types of associations found for products alone.
2. Corporate brand associations that exist in the minds of customers come in all forms. Broadly, corporate brand associations can be classified in terms of common product attributes, benefits, or attitudes; people and relationships; values and programs; and corporate credibility.
3. A corporate brand must be integrated with product brands in terms of a brand hierarchy.
4. A brand hierarchy should be constructed on the basis of principles of relevance and differentiation and other 'vertical' and 'horizontal' considerations.
5. Even corporate brands have boundaries and should not be extended to all products sold by a firm.

Implications

Adopting a corporate branding strategy has broader implications that go beyond the specific recommendations outlined above. Most importantly, developing a corporate brand requires that marketers blend bottom-up versus top-down brand management and internal versus external brand management.

Bottom-up brand management requires marketing managers primarily to direct their marketing activities to maximize brand equity for individual products for particular markets—with relatively little regard for other brands and products sold by the firm or for other markets in which their brands and products may be sold. Although such close, detailed brand supervision can be advantageous, creating brand equity for every different possible product and market in this way can be an expensive and difficult process and, most importantly, ignores possible synergies that may be obtainable.

Top-down brand management, on the other hand, involves marketing activities that capture the 'big picture' and recognize the possible synergies across products and markets to brand products accordingly. Such a top-down approach would seek to find common products and markets that could share marketing programs and activities for brands and only develop separate brands and marketing programs and activities as dictated by the consumer or competitive environment. Unfortunately, if left unmanaged, firms tend to follow the bottom-up approach, resulting in many brands being marketed inconsistently and incompatibly. Managing brands in a top-down fashion requires centralized and coordinated marketing guidance and actions from high-level marketing supervisors. Particular attention would be paid on how to best develop and leverage the corporate brand.

External brand management involves understanding the needs, wants, and desires of consumers to create marketing programs for brands that fulfill and even surpass consumer expectations. With these marketing programs, consumers would have a clear picture of what the brand represents and why it is special. Consumers would then view the brand as a 'trusted friend' and value its dependability and superiority. With external brand management, marketers engage in dialogue with consumers, listening to their product joys and frustrations, and establishing a rapport and relationship that would transcend mere commercial exchanges. Marketers would develop a deep understanding of what makes their brand successful, retaining enduring core elements while modifying peripheral elements that fail to add value or unnecessarily absorb costs.

Internal brand management, on the other hand, involves activities that ensure that employees and marketing partners appreciate and understand basic branding notions, and how they can impact and help—or hurt—the equity of brands. For example, the company view of brand equity can be formalized into 'brand equity charters' that chronicle the company's general philosophy with respect to brand equity, highlight relevant brand research, outline guidelines for brand strategies and tactics, and document proper treatment of the brand. Brand equity reports can be distributed to management on a regular basis (monthly, quarterly, or annually) to provide descriptive information as to *what* is happening with a brand as well as diagnostic information as to *why* it is happening.

Internal brand management involves assigning corporate-level managers who are responsible for overseeing the implementation of the brand equity charter and brand equity reports to ensure, as far as possible, that product and marketing actions across divisions and geographical boundaries are enacted in such a way as to reflect the spirit of the charter and the substance of the report, so as to maximize the long-term equity of the brand. Internal brand management is critical for a corporate brand, where every employee directly or indirectly can impact on brand equity. Internal brand management also helps to ensure that external brand management is properly carried out.

Both pairs of brand management activities can be complementary and mutually reinforcing. Successful corporate brands will be those that effectively blend top-down versus bottom-up and internal versus external brand management activities. Ignoring one or more of these dimensions can put the brands of a firm in peril, especially in terms of corporate brands, where top-down and internal brand management are so important. Unfortunately, because these corporate brand-building marketing and management activities may be seen as less directly related to individual products, they may be more easily overlooked or ignored. The contention of this chapter, however, is that a strong corporate brand—by allowing the firm to express itself and embellish the meaning and associations for individual products—can provide invaluable marketing and financial benefits.

Building and managing a strong corporate brand have additional requirements. For example, the firm has to keep a much more public profile, especially when it comes to influencing and shaping some of the more abstract types of associations. The chairman or managing director must be willing to maintain a more public profile if he or she is associated with a corporate brand, to help to communicate news and information, as well as perhaps providing a symbol of current marketing activities. At the same time, by virtue of a more visible public profile, the firm must also be willing to be subject to more scrutiny and to be more transparent in terms of its values, activities, and programs. Corporate brands thus have to be comfortable with a higher level of openness.

In summary, building a corporate brand offers a host of potential marketing advantages, but only if corporate brand equity is carefully built and nurtured—a challenging task. The evidence is mounting as to the advantages of having a strong corporate brand. Many of the marketing winners in the coming years will, therefore, be those firms that properly build and manage corporate brand equity. It will, however, take conviction, discipline, and focus on the part of senior management to make that happen.

REFERENCES

Alwitt, L. F., and Pitts, R. E. (1996), 'Predicting Purchase Intentions for an Environmentally Sensitive Product', *Journal of Consumer Psychology*, 5/1: 49–64.

Bender, D. M., Farquhar, P., and Schulert, S. C. (1996), 'Growing from the Top: Corporate Advertising Nourishes the Brand Equity from which Profits Sprout', *Marketing Management*, 4/4: 10–19.

Biehal, G. J., and Shenin, D. A. (1998), 'Managing the Brand in a Corporate Advertising Environment', *Journal of Advertising*, 28/2: 99–110.

Brown, T. J. (1998), 'Corporate Associations in Marketing: Antecedents and Consequences', *Corporate Reputation Review*, 1/3: 215–33.

—— and Dacin, P. A. (1997), 'The Company and the Product: Corporate Associations and Consumer Product Responses', *Journal of Marketing*, 61: 68–84.

Caminit, S. (1995), 'The Payoff from a Good Reputation', *Fortune*, 6 Mar., 74.

Cunningham, P. H., and Berger, I. E. (1997), 'Cause-Related Marketing: State-of-the-Art and Directions for Future Research', working paper, Queen's University.

Dagnoli, J. (1991), 'Consciously Green', *Advertising Age*, 19 Sept., 14.

Dowling, G. R. (1994), *Corporate Reputations* (Melbourne, Australia: Longman Professional).

Drumwright, M. E. (1996), 'Company Advertising with a Social Dimension', Marketing Science Institute Working Paper no. 96–110.

Farquhar, P. H. (1989), 'Managing Brand Equity', *Marketing Research*, 1: 24–33.

Gilly, M. C., and Wolfinbarger, M. (1996), 'Advertising's Second Audience: Employee Reactions to Organizational Communications', Marketing Science Institute Working Paper no. 96–116.

Goldberg, M. E., and Hartwick, J. (1990), 'The Effects of Advertiser Reputation and Extremity of Advertiser Claims on Advertising Effectiveness', *Journal of Consumer Research*, 17: 172–9.

Gregory, J. R. (1991), *Marketing Corporate Image* (Lincolnwood, Ill.: NTC Business Books).

Ind, N. (1998), 'An Integrated Approach to Corporate Branding', *Journal of Brand Management*, 5/5: 323–9.

Joseph, L. E. (1991), 'The Greening of American Business', *Vis à Vis*, May: 32.

Journal of Advertising (1995), 'Special Issue on Green Advertising', 24: 2.

Keller, K. L. (1999), 'Designing and Implementing Branding Strategies', *Journal of Brand Management*, 6/5: 315–31.

—— and Aaker, D. A. (1992), 'The Effects of Sequential Introduction of Brand Extensions', *Journal of Marketing Research*, 29: 35–50.

—— —— (1998), 'Corporate Level Marketing: The Impact of Credibility Marketing on a Company's Brand Extensions', *Corporate Reputation Review*, 1/4: 356–78.

LaForet, S., and Saunders, J. (1994), 'Managing Brand Portfolios: How the Leaders Do It', *Journal of Advertising Research*, Sept.–Oct.: 64–76.

Menon, A., and Menon, A. (1997), 'Enviropreneurial Marketing Strategy: The Emergence of Corporate Environmentalism as Market Strategy', *Journal of Marketing*, 61: 51–67.

Roberts, P. W., and Dowling, G. (1998), 'The Value of Enhancing the Firm's Corporate Reputation: How Corporate Reputation Helps Attain and Sustain Superior Profitability', working paper, Australian Graduate School of Management, University of New South Wales.

Schumann, D. W., Hathcote, J. M., and West, S. (1991), 'Corporate Advertising in America: A Review of Published Studies on Use, Measurement, and Effectiveness', *Journal of Advertising*, 20/3: 35–56.

Swasy, A. (1991), 'P&G to Tout Name Behind the Brands', *Wall Street Journal*, 12 Dec., B1–B3.

van Riel, C. B. M., Stroker, N. E., and Maathuis, O. J. M. (1998), 'Measuring Corporate Images', *Corporate Reputation Review*, 1/4: 313–26.

Varadarajan, P. R., and Menon, A. (1988), 'Cause-Related Marketing: A Coalignment of Marketing Strategy and Corporate Philanthropy', *Journal of Marketing*, 52: 58–74.

Winters, L. C. (1988), 'Does it Pay to Advertise to Hostile Audiences with Corporate Advertising?', *Journal of Advertising Research*, 28 (June–July): 11–18.

9

··

Building the Unique Organization Value Proposition

Simon Knox, Stan Maklan, and Keith E. Thompson

The key issue facing companies today is how to add more customer value in the face of product commoditization, increased service levels, faster innovation, and diminishing brand loyalty. We argue in this chapter that the marketing community is not responding sufficiently to the challenge: many of our brand and marketing tools are dated, worse still, they focus on creating brand values not customer value. Before marketing management can return to their place at the heart of value-adding activities, they will need to work much more closely with business process owners and acknowledge the need for creating value across the organization, rather than just through products and brands. We offer a methodology that enables marketing to reinvent itself as the architect for branding the customer value proposition at an organizational level.

BRAND MARKETING IN TRANSITION

The business community was alerted to the increasing obsolescence of brand values in April 1993 when Philip Morris accepted that its flagship brand Marlboro no longer offered sufficient customer value to support the premium prices it had once enjoyed. There followed an article in *The Economist* questioning the future of brand management and marketing departments themselves. At the heart of the matter is the fundamental shift in what customers perceive as value that is challenging the way that business activities create customer value (*The Economist* 1994). For most of this century, strong brands have been the key vehicle for the delivery of customer value. In a world of rapid innovation and ever increasing choice, reliance on a familiar and trusted brand name was the antidote to the perceived risk generated by all this change and unfamiliarity. It worked for Kellogg's in low-cost, simple consumer markets, and it worked for IBM in high-cost, complex business markets. However, new ways of coping with risk have changed all that. Business buyers have developed partnerships with suppliers involving much closer relationships, as well as more sophisticated purchasing processes (Thompson *et al.* 1998). Thirty years of consumerism, higher disposable incomes, and improvements in product performance and reliability have led to more confident, less risk-averse consumers. Brands designed to slay the dragon of perceived risk are now becoming redundant. Unfettered by the need to manage the downside risk, customers look increasingly for positive added value to discriminate between products and services. But these value-adding activities, such as total solutions, supply chain leadership, managed lifetime costs, and expert advice are in the hands of the process-owners in logistics, manufacturing, and information systems and not brand managers (Doyle 1995).

Brand value was a promise of sameness and predictability. That is no longer enough, as Heinz conceded when it announced its intention to supply supermarkets with own-label baked beans. Even when the product is less easily imitated than baked beans—and is also acknowledged to be of excellent quality—if the value offered to customers gets out of line with their expectations the choices are stark: change or fail. Mercedes Benz built one of the world's most powerful brands in terms of engineering quality, luxury, and exclusivity. Yet, in the USA during the early 1990s, the marque no longer met customers' perceptions of good value and they were not willing to pay Mercedes Benz prices. Mercedes had not let its quality slip, nor were its cars relatively more expensive to buy or own than before. Neither did the brand have the disassociative connotations that makers such as Rolls Royce and Porsche experienced. Mercedes lost their following in the USA to a competitor whose brand appeared to lack credibility in the relevant market segments when Toyota's Lexus was recognized as offering better perceived value against the costs of ownership. This superior value was primarily a result of Toyota's breakthrough developments in manufacturing processes and the resultant cost management capabilities, in conjunction with excellent design and customer care.

Concentrating on image, quality, technical competence, or what is understood by 'marketing' is no longer sufficient. Neither is offering the world an even better mousetrap: Xerox, inventors of many of the most important personal computer innovations such as the mouse, local area networks, and graphical user interfaces, have simply failed to benefit commercially from the millions of dollars invested in researching these innovations at their renowned Palo Alto laboratories.

Customer value is increasingly being generated by business processes outside the remit of marketing. Consequently, in the face of lower-priced competition, brand managers are being forced to reduce the price premiums of their brands (Richards 1997) and rationalize their brand portfolios. Concentrating largely on product-related benefits like quality, innovation, prestige or risk reduction, can leave an opening for competitors to create better customer value on a wider, organizational basis.

It follows that an organization can no longer compete effectively unless all its efforts through *external* alliances, networks, and partnerships and its *internal* business systems are directed towards delivering better customer value.

BUILDING BRANDS THAT CAN DELIVER CUSTOMER VALUE

Despite the textbook definitions of marketing as a business philosophy centered on serving the customer (e.g. Kotler 1997), the content of most marketing textbooks reflects a 4Ps approach (O'Driscoll and Murrey 1996). The *practice* of marketing has largely been subsumed into a business function in which the marketing department is tasked with delivering a Unique Selling Proposition (USP) by manipulating the 4Ps of product, price, promotion, and place through marketing programs. Over time, this has resulted in an escalation in the use of expensive stimulus-response applications, such as TV advertising, in an attempt to persuade customers to buy.

Despite the diminution in the efficacy of brand marketing, most firms need to face a serious crisis before even contemplating a radical reappraisal of the way they do business and how they create customer value. Even then, most marketing textbooks seem to offer a blend of exhortations to be customer centered whilst propagating the conventional tools of brand engineering and customer manipulation (Jain 1993; Lancaster and Reynolds 1995; Kotler 1997).

In the face of this, we propose a new modeling tool, the Unique Organization Value Proposition® (UOVP), which facilitates the integration of core business processes and positions the organization in the supply chain to create the superior customer value proposed by Hooley and Saunders (1993). The methodology we outline is to encourage brand and marketing management to make the transition from traditional 'make-and-sell' product branding to organizational branding in which the whole organization can be aligned to compete more effectively.

THE UNIQUE ORGANIZATION VALUE PROPOSITION

In essence, the UOVP brand is the organization's visible set of credentials throughout the supply chain. We use the metaphor of a cable and wires to describe the UOVP (Fig. 9.1). The wires are the core business processes that *deliver* value through the supply chain to the customer, while the cable houses and directs these processes end to end. The cable is the organization brand that *defines* the value proposition. It is the means by which customers and other stakeholders assess the credentials of the organization. The UOVP is, therefore, a tool both of differentiation and of process integration for the com-

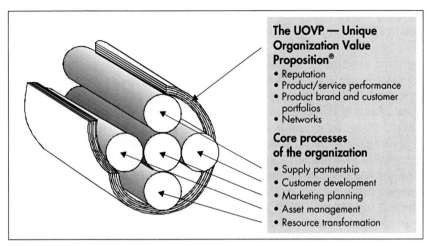

The UOVP — Unique
Organization Value
Proposition®
• Reputation
• Product/service performance
• Product brand and customer
  portfolios
• Networks

Core processes
of the organization
• Supply partnership
• Customer development
• Marketing planning
• Asset management
• Resource transformation

Fig. 9.1. Defining and delivering customer value across the organization
©Knox and Maklan (1997).

pany; it becomes the organization brand. It is how the organization is positioned in the value chain through the management of its reputation, product/service performance, product brand and customer portfolio, and networks. These components are discussed in the following sections.

Reputation

Product brand companies build corporate reputation only as a by-product of the marketing efforts behind individual brands. In the UOVP methodology, reputations are built through customers' understanding of the organization's values and its commitments, as well as their experiences of its products and services. These are conveyed through the relationships that each organization builds, as articulated by the Corporate Marketing Director of Heinz Europe, 'We as brand owners, need to build relationships with our consumers, to create a dialogue, expose them to our corporate values; establish a bond based on something more deep-seated than mere product quality, brand image or even simply meeting consumer needs' (Bailey 1997: 10). UOVP reputation differs from traditional corporate positioning because it is based upon the total capabilities of the company—as opposed to its desired market position. Neither the company's individual product managers, nor its Marketing Director, currently have the authority or scope to manage the full range of stakeholder relationships or to commit the entire organization in building its reputation. Marketers must now earn the right to develop the UOVP and to lead this new branding process in areas of reputation management since it can no longer be automatically conferred by dint of job title.

Product/Service Performance

Customers experience the brand values delivered by an organization through the performance of its products and services during their purchasing cycle. In the second half of the 1990s, for example, Tesco gained market share and moved ahead of its closest rival, Sainsbury, in the UK grocery market simply by performing better; being the first to introduce new services, such as loyalty cards, financial services, and guaranteed short queues at the checkout. At the same time, Tesco did not lose sight of its customers' costs, retaining its reputation for competitive product prices and by doing more than Sainsbury to manage customers' time, convenience, and purchase risk throughout the shopping experience. Tesco is using its reputation as the more progressive grocer to develop strong relationships with the most profitable consumer segments (Mitchell and Peck 1997). Establishing measures of performance through which customers evaluate the firm (Carlzon 1987) is one of the strategic roles within the UOVP design. Marketing, with its skills in understanding customer motivation and purchasing processes, is well positioned to develop and manage these new metrics across the business processes.

Product Brand and Customer Portfolio

In traditional brand management, the portfolios of products and services are managed as business units that must justify their continued existence on the basis of Net Present Value. Sometimes, as in Procter & Gamble, brand managers are encouraged to compete with one another. Dividing a large company into discrete product brand groups in this way is a useful way of dealing with organizational complexity. However, it does not contribute to the alignment of the whole organization with the customer, and can even result in tension between individual product brands and the overarching corporate identity.

Brand portfolios create value by endowing the product with instant recognition, enabling customers to know exactly what they will get, and allowing the company to transplant the brand values into different situations, locations, and products. Yet, they are just one *component* of customer value creation, and not the *object* of it. Value is also created by more effective customer portfolio management. Some, but not all, customers are very valuable to the organization and justify a relationship management approach that goes beyond selling them an often unintegrated portfolio of products. As Hallberg (1995) points out, research shows that, for many consumer companies, less than 20 per cent of households contribute the majority of the profits. His work also shows that many brands can actually be losing money when sold to as many as one-third of their light-spending customers.

The tools of customer portfolio management are database management, loyalty management, and effective discrimination of offers between customers. A customer-based equivalent to net present value is customer lifetime value (Reichheld and Sasser 1990). Customer portfolio management offers the potential to deliver more value to individual customers who satisfy appropriate criteria of customer lifetime value. However, the necessary marketing systems and applications cannot readily be integrated within an organization divided into product brand groups, each with a different, and possibly competing, relationship with the customer. Management of the UOVP ensures that the balance between managing product portfolios and customer relationships is struck at a sufficiently senior level to ensure that customer relationships are not merely the by-product of a product management structure, but are central to business developments that deliver most value to the most profitable customers.

Networks

The UOVP methodology enables the value added through a firm's network of suppliers and alliances to be an explicit part of the customer proposition. Managing brands that depend upon the contribution of others does represent a difficult challenge, but leading-edge companies are finding that co-branding is one of the best ways of differentiating themselves from their competitors. These companies are forming highly visible alliances aimed at enhancing customer service and providing customized solutions rather than targeting cost or capacity reduction as in more traditional alliances. For example, AirMiles was created by British Airways as an anchor for a vast network of well-known brands associated with travel. Customer value is created by enabling customers to collect points towards free air travel through this network. In the investment banking sector, JP Morgan outsourced information and communication services worth $300 million a year to a consortium led by Computer Sciences Corporation, winning the contract against EDS, the worlds largest IT services supplier, which bid as a single company.

The extent to which business partners add value to your final offer, and the level at which this contribution is made visible to the customer, determine the extent to which an organization brands its network of relationships. Arguably, marketing, in conjunction with process-owners, should be determining this and managing these relationships accordingly.

The UOVP Marketing Mix

The mix between the components of the UOVP creates the organization brand and the means by which the organization brand is differentiated from its competitors. An example of competitive positioning is provided by the airline industry, where companies can be found that have well-conceived brand mixes at the corporate level (Box 9.1).

Box 9.1. UOVP marketing mix for airlines

UOVP components	BA	Virgin	easyJet
Reputation	Reliable, predictable	Challenging, exciting, unconventional	Cheap
Product/service performance	Extensive routes, range of service, excellent recovery from problems	Limited routes, innovative services	Fit for purpose, few routers
Product brand and customer portfolios	Strong business class sub-brand, focus on longstanding distance business traveler	Trades on corporate name, mostly targets 'Virgin' devotees	Corporate brand focused on budget traveler paying for own trips
Networks	Emerging global alliances deliver worldwide capability, AirMiles scheme a major part of loyalty strategy	Focused on 'Virgin' to appeal to 'Virgin' devotees	Not part of the brand

BA's market strategy is rooted in its history as the UK's flag carrier. Now privatized, it has retained a high-priced high-service-level mix aimed at the profitable, long-distance business traveler. In pursuit of this segment, BA has used its market pre-eminence, size, and power to develop a worldwide capability through global alliances. In contrast, easyJet is positioned to offer a limited, but highly credible brand proposition as a cheap no-nonsense alternative for non-business travelers, paying for their own flights. EasyJet has neither the bargaining power nor (so far) the time to develop networks, and they do not figure in the OUVP marketing mix. Virgin has become a major player in the scheduled international airline business by carving out a position between these two extremes. Although it appeals to both business and independent travelers, Virgin has avoided becoming just a 'mini-BA', on the one hand, or a low-margin 'no-frills' operator, on the other, by building on the emotional appeal of the Virgin brand. Sir Richard Branson, the founder of Virgin, has imbued that brand with an enviable reputation for corporate integrity and transparency, as well as a higher-than-average level of service delivered through a highly motivated workforce. These Virgin brand values have been applied to businesses as diverse as recording, retailing, computers, drinks, beauty products, financial services, and travel with varying degrees of success. In the airline business, the Virgin service offering works particularly well. However, such a unique brand proposition is hard to extend to a network of explicit business partners. So Virgin Airline's ability to add customer value through networks is limited—a shortcoming that has had serious implications for Virgin's ill-fated foray into the computer market.

Finally, BA has launched GO as a low-priced brand extension to compete with price-cutters like easyJet. Clearly, BA's networking muscle offers a competitive advantage over its smaller rivals, but it is difficult to see how GO can be integrated into BA's UOVP marketing mix without compromising it.

PROCESS MANAGEMENT AND THE UOVP BRAND

When the company's core processes are driven by the UOVP brand, the UOVP moves deep into the organization and creates a proposition that is relevant to customers. These core processes, which deliver customer value, will vary by industry and by company within industries. The UOVP does not presume to prescribe what these processes are nor how many should be considered of strategic importance, but the methodology does acknowledge their importance in delivering the organization brand to customers on a consistent basis and is instrumental in determining process priorities. For illustrative purposes, this section is based upon the following five core processes:

1. marketing planning;
2. supply partnership;
3. asset management;
4. resource transformation;
5. customer development.

In our experience, these five processes are reasonably universal. They constitute the wires in the 'cable and wires' metaphor used to describe the organization (see Fig. 9.1), where marketing planning has the central position, since it links the other core processes together. Each is now discussed in turn below.

Marketing Planning

Marketing planning is discussed first, as it is the internal 'glue' that links the 'process' wires to each other and to the brand positioning (the outer cable) in order to deliver the customer value proposition. The three stages to the UOVP planning process are, then, (1) customer value proposition, (2) brand positioning, and (3) value delivery. These are mapped against the equivalent traditional marketing planning procedures in Fig. 9.2, and each is briefly discussed below.

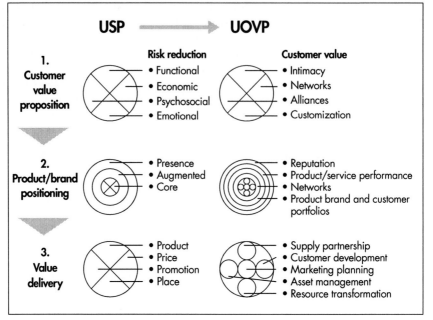

Fig. 9.2. Marketing planning and strategy focus

The Customer Value Proposition

The traditional marketing planning model used to build the USP is product centered and tends to limit the planner's thinking to what already exists in terms of market definition, product position, sales potential, and so on. Furthermore, it is an incremental process that takes an annual view of the market and aims to make step changes in market share mainly through 'good housekeeping' activities. Breakthrough thinking is not encouraged by this sort of planning; rather the marketing imagination is constrained to think within boundaries that were created in the past.

The UOVP toolset helps break these habits by encouraging a constant reappraisal of what customers perceive to be of value, with the emphasis on seeking 'order-winning' criteria through dialogue with customers. Identifying these and positioning the company against the competition with a unique value proposition is the first step in the marketing planning process.

Brand Positioning

The next step is to define the UOVP brand in support of the value proposition, through the components of the cable sheath. UOVP planning starts by revisiting the whole notion of customer value, and the ways in which it could be delivered. Compared with traditional techniques, the UOVP brand actively encourages holistic thinking, challenging the planner to look for solutions from the entire value chain, and from outside the organization where internal capabilities do not meet the competition's standards or where competitive advantage can be gained by delivering differently from the rest. UOVP brand positioning results from the creation of an appropriate mix of reputation, performance, portfolios, and networks that distinguishes the organization's customer value offer from those of its competitors. This has already been addressed in more depth, with an example from the airline industry, above.

Value Delivery

Finally, the marketing planning process determines how the brand value will be delivered by the business processes and provides action plans for all the activities involved in the customer value proposition. For example, in 1994 Guinness recognized that its performance in mainland UK pubs was not consistent with its brand positioning, which could only be implemented through end-to-end delivery of the product to its consumers. Consequently, Project Condor was launched to deliver the customer proposition, *the Perfect Pint in Every Pub* (Christopher 1997). This involved re-engineering the delivery system and channel management. Special founts to aid the famous two-part pour were installed, and licensees trained in storage and the art of serving the perfect pint. Guinness achieved its promised customer value by utilizing the entire delivery chain. Marketing planning in this example is a very different planning approach from that advocated in the past and is a call to action across Guinness's core business processes.

The nature and extent of marketing planning needed for each business process is dependent upon its prominence in building the organization brand. Examples of how the business processes can be managed to deliver brand values are discussed in the context of the remaining 'universal' processes discussed earlier.

Supply Partnership

Traditionally, the management of suppliers was hidden from customers and divorced from the process by which marketers sought to create brand value through the USP. However, arm's-length relationships with suppliers are no longer typical of progressive organizations. Modern competition is based on rapid exploitation of opportunities, quick response to customers' increasing expectations, and experimentation with new technologies and techniques. Such rapid change in core products and services is hard enough in itself to manage. Few can succeed while also dragging along a lengthy supply chain.

This switch in the way companies work with suppliers is epitomized by the car industry, where uncompetitive Western manufacturers were exposed by the newly arrived Japanese, forcing the established firms to rethink how they worked with suppliers. After some failed attempts to eliminate time and cost from the entire supply chain simply by forcing suppliers to accept lower prices, the car-makers changed their approach to one of forming open relationships with partner suppliers. This new way of working led to significant cost reductions and much faster cycle times for new product development, and provided the opportunity for suppliers to begin to contribute to customer value. The intimacy of these relationships continues to develop as suppliers take more responsibility for complete systems such as braking, drive train, steering, and engines, allowing the car-assemblers (which is increasingly a better description of the traditional manufacturers) to derive maximum benefit from suppliers' greater knowledge in their areas of specialization. This synergy will continue to develop as cars become even more sophisticated and components become more complex (e.g. microchips), making in-house specification and supply almost impossible. Consequently, the UOVP will evolve as car-assemblers shift their focus to developing their offer through service provisions, developing relationships with customers, and becoming excellent at choosing and managing their supplier network (Lamming 1993).

The automotive industry example is part of a trend in which suppliers contribute an increasing proportion of the final customer value. We propose a partnership continuum that can be divided into four discrete levels (Fig. 9.3).

- *Level 1*: Traditional supplier that has a transactional relationship with the brand-owner. The supplier sells specified goods and services to the brand-owner on the basis of prices, service, and quality.

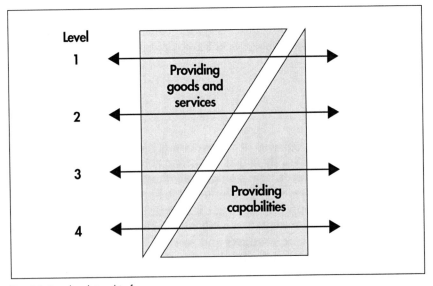

Fig. 9.3. Supply relationship focus

- *Level 2*: Supply chain optimizer that works cooperatively with the brand-owner to reduce total cost (increase total benefit) of the brand's customer value proposition.
- *Level 3*: Supply chain partner that takes responsibility for a significant proportion of the brand's value delivery. Partners not only optimize the supply chain; they take some responsibility for innovation in their area of expertise.
- *Level 4*: Value chain partner that enables the brand to extend past its traditional competencies.

One consequence of these higher-level supply partnerships is the development of increasingly effective third-party suppliers, contributing a growing proportion of customer value. This raises two problems. First, their skills are also available to competitors, so the values they contribute will become less and less effective as brand discriminators, and brand-owners will eventually need to develop new areas of value creation. Second, management of supply partnerships will need to evolve to take account of the increasing power of suppliers, as delivery of the UOVP brand proposition becomes ever more dependent upon their contribution (Knox and Maklan 1998).

Asset Management

'Our people are our greatest assets', has been one of the most commonly used and most hypocritical statements made by business executives (Wickens 1996). This observation can also be extended to other corporate assets, which have often been managed for cost efficiency rather than excellence or value creation. However, it is becoming generally accepted that assets, especially those that are less tangible, such as know-how (Teece 1998), or brands and culture (Tyrrell and Westall 1998), can be significant sources of competitive advantage. The definition of assets used here includes both the intangibles and the tangible items of plant, people, equipment, and location.

Whilst there are many examples of companies using their assets in imaginative ways, there does not appear to be a widely accepted systematic means by which companies can release more of their assets to the creation of customer value. The UOVP can provide such a framework by asking managers to:

1. Think not about individual product markets, but about the entire industry value chain and how it could be reconfigured to deliver differential value. At First Direct, for example, information technology does not automate the inefficient practices of traditional financial services companies. New technology and business processes fundamentally change how customer value is created and delivered.
2. Free asset management from the constraints of product planning. Consider the case of the $110m. invested in the 'Intel Inside' advertising. Was this justified through incremental volume? Or did the senior management

understand that, as IT became a consumer good, an investment in a brand asset was necessary? The development of organizational assets should not be held hostage to the needs of the profit and loss account if they are to build superior and lasting differential value.

3. Create structure and purpose to empowerment. The UOVP provides a blueprint whereby managers can visualize the extent and nature of their potential contribution to delivering customer value. It provides a common language and understanding of what is important to the customer and how the company is going to differentiate itself from competitors. Against that understanding, empowering all managers to add more value to customers will prove to be more productive than the 'initiativitis' that grips many companies today.

Resource Transformation

The organization's capabilities in turning inputs (supplies and assets) into outputs (goods and services) have long been recognized as a vital part of creating value and have been the subject of much of the management literature, most notably that on business process re-engineering (Hammer and Champy 1993). Re-engineering does create value, largely by lowering costs through productivity improvements, and is an important part of remaining competitive. However, improvements in productivity devoid of any understanding of customer motivations or the competitive environment must fail to optimize customer value. By contrast, within the UOVP, the cable transmits a consistent customer proposition with every component of the internal and network supply chain, ensuring that all business processes contribute to the desired customer value proposition.

Dell Computer Corporation has created a position for itself in one of the toughest markets by implementing this approach. Dell now sells directly to its customers and assembles to order from industry standard components. There is no inventory of finished goods, or middlemen between Dell and the customer. Dell's resource transformation model removes non-value-adding inventory and distribution costs from the system, and enables the customer to develop a direct relationship with the manufacturer. It is critical to Dell's UOVP brand positioning.

Customer Development

Not all customers are created equal (Hallberg 1995). In fact, American Express found that the best customers outspend the others by ratios ranging from 5 to 1 in hotels/motels to 16 to 1 in retailing (Peppers and Rogers 1993). Although it has been demonstrated that the most profitable customers are almost invariably existing, loyal customers (Reichheld 1996), it is still common for firms to weight their sales, advertising, and pricing strategies towards the acquisition of new, less-profitable customers at the expense of their loyal customers. Of course, winning new customers is not a bad thing in itself; it is really a question of striking a balance between customer acquisition and nurturing the most profitable customers through customer development and loyalty management.

Loyalty management prescribes that the existing customer base becomes a priority and that resources are assigned on a differential basis. High-worth customers are supported in their behaviors and beliefs with a package of benefits that befits their estimated economic worth to the organization and low-worth customers receive the reverse treatment (Knox 1998). American Express responded to the challenge by turning itself into a customer management organization. Each card member is now assigned to a loyalty group, such as frequent business travelers or high-value card members, so that they can be differentially rewarded according to their patterns of transactions with the company. However, traditional multiple product brand management organizations are poorly suited to company-wide customer development (Mitchell 1998). If the product manager of Nestlé's KitKat is even aware of the customers who also purchased other Nestlé products, such as Branston Pickle, the organizational structure tends to hinder, rather than help, individual managers, who are isolated in their product/brand management 'silo'. By comparison, the integrative nature of the UOVP makes it a much more effective tool for determining customer development priorities, once 'customer portfolios' are being managed more effectively.

THE REHABILITATION OF MARKETING

In this chapter we have chosen five core processes to illustrate how customer value is delivered through the UOVP brand. Some organizations may decide that they have different core processes from these or, indeed, choose to manage a greater number. Regardless, the UOVP architect plays a major role in building a team from the individual process-owners, ensuring that trade-offs between individual processes are made in consideration of the overall customer value proposition. The architect also works with process-owners to facilitate closer relationships with customers, suppliers, and potential alliance partners. Whilst process-owners will build many of these relationships through their own initiatives, ultimately, someone must facilitate their integration. If not, companies may only succeed in replacing functional silos with process ones.

We argue that money invested in building product brands, using traditional marketing tools such as the USP and 4Ps, is likely to be wasteful of effort and resources and, possibly, even part of the business problem. Many other business functions have revitalized themselves, re-engineering their structure and processes to generate superior customer value. Yet marketing, the function tasked with representing the customer within the organization, lags behind, relying instead on an outdated toolkit and a narrow philosophy customer value creation. Through the UOVP, we offer a means by which marketing can be rehabilitated. Alignment of the organization with its external environment has always been the mandate of marketing in its broadest sense. As the architects of UOVP brand design, marketing can be revitalized to align the company behind a clear and manageable customer proposition, while avoiding the trap of creating process silos. We urge marketing managers to embrace new methods of achieving that alignment and take their place in the modern, process-centered organization.

REFERENCES

Bailey, R. (1997), 'Heinz is Coming Home', transcript of a speech given at the Relationship Marketing Conference, Cranfield University.

Carlzon, J. (1987), *Moments of Truth* (Cambridge, Mass.: Ballinger).

Christopher, M. (1997), *Marketing Logistics* (Oxford: Butterworth-Heinemann).

Doyle, P. (1995), 'Marketing in the New Millennium', *European Journal of Marketing*, 29/3: 23–40.

The Economist (1994), 'Death of the Brand Manager', 9 Apr., 79.

Hallberg, G. (1995), *All Consumers are not Created Equal* (New York: John Wiley).

Hammer, M., and Champy, J. (1993), *Reengineering the Corporation* (London: Nicholas Brealey).

Hooley, G. J., and Saunders, J. (1993), *Competitive Positioning* (Hemel Hempstead: Prentice Hall).

Jain, S. C. (1993), *Marketing Planning and Strategy*, 4th edn. (Cincinnati, Oh.: South-Western Publishing).

Knox, S. D. (1998), 'Loyal to the Core', *Campaign*, July, 30–1.

—— and Maklan, S. (1998), *Competing on Value* (London: F. T. Pitman).

Kotler, P. (1997), *Marketing Management: Analysis Planning, Implementation and Control* (International edn.; Englewood Cliffs, NJ: Prentice Hall).

Lamming, R. (1993), *Beyond Partnership: Strategies for Innovation and Lean Supply* (Hemel Hempstead: Prentice Hall).

Lancaster, G., and Reynolds, P. (1995), *Marketing* (Oxford: Butterworth-Heinemann).

Mitchell, A. (1998), 'Customer Demands May Spell a New World Order', *Marketing Week*, 11 Apr., 32–3.

Mitchell, H. G., and Peck, H. (1997), 'Does Tesco Hold all the Cards?', case study, The European Case Clearing House, Cranfield University: 598–032–1.

O'Driscoll, A., and Murray, J. A. (1996), *Strategy and Process of Marketing* (Hemel Hempstead: Prentice Hall).

Peppers, D., and Rogers, M. (1993), *The One-to-One Future* (London: Judy Piakus).

Reichheld, F. F. (1996), *The Loyalty Effect* (Boston: Harvard Business School Press).

—— and Sasser Jr., W. E. (1990), 'Zero Defections: Quality Comes to Services', *Harvard Business Review*, Sept.–Oct.: 105–11.

Richards, G. R. (1997), 'Burger Flip-Flop', *Wall St. Journal*, 26 Feb.

Teece, D. J. (1998), 'Capturing Value from Knowledge Assets', *California Management Review*, 40/3: 55–79.

Thompson, K. E., Knox, S. D., and Mitchell, H. G. (1998), 'Business-to-Business Brand Attributes in a Changing Purchasing Environment', *Irish Marketing Review*, 10/2: 25–32.

Tyrrell, B., and Westall, T. (1998), 'The New Service Ethos, a Post-Brand Future—and How to Avoid It', *Journal of the Marketing Society*, Autumn: 14–19.

Wickens, P. (1996), 'The New Enterprise Culture', *Demos Quarterly* (White Paper Series, No. 8; London).

V

THE VALUE OF STORYTELLING

10

Corporate Communication Orchestrated by a Sustainable Corporate Story

Cees B. M. van Riel

Communication enables an organization to begin a dialogue to create awareness, understanding, and appreciation for the firm's strategic goals, ideally resulting in the satisfaction of the interests of both the firm and its environment. Stakeholders will, in my view, be more receptive to corporate messages if the contents of organizational messages are coherent and appealing (contributing to the personal advantage of stakeholders, and above all not irritating them). I shall claim that communication will be more effective if organizations rely on a so-called sustainable corporate story as a source of inspiration for all internal and external communication programs. Stories are hard to imitate, and they promote consistency in all corporate messages.

An ideal (normative) sustainable corporate story is a realistic and relevant description of an organization, created in an open dialogue with stakeholders the organization depends upon. Below are four criteria that, if met, can make a corporate story more effective. First of all the story has to be realistic. Stakeholders must know that the story indeed pertains to the 'distinctive' and 'enduring' characteristics of the organization as a whole. Second, the story must be relevant. Stakeholders should be aware that the key message has added value for them. These first two serve to typify the contents of the story. The third one describes the style of communication in a definitive manner, more specifically the necessity to apply a 'two-way symmetrical communication style' (Grunig 1992). Such communication is achieved by developing a responsive attitude. A corporate story is a dynamic entity invented and reinvented by the permanent interaction between external and internal stakeholders. It is a continuous dialogue testing the relevance and reality of the corporate story. Being prepared to apply changes resulting from this dialogue will improve the appealing nature of the story. Recent developments in technology (web sites) make it much easier for organizations to develop a responsive attitude. However, it is not the technology that is relevant here, but the mentality behind it. Establishing a web site does not make much sense if the company is not really interested in reacting to messages received. Finally, the fourth characteristic that will improve the effectiveness of corporate stories is the degree to which the story is sustainable. A corporate story will only be sustainable if it succeeds in finding and maintaining the right balance between the competing demands of all relevant stakeholders and the desires of the organization itself.

The contents of the story should in my opinion be based on the aggregation of a set of words evoked by qualitative and quantitative research among internal and external audiences. My chapter focuses mainly on the methods to be used to create and implement such a sustainable corporate story. This will be explained below. First, however, I will explain why organizations at the beginning of the twenty-first century are more inclined to disclose their visions and driving forces to stakeholders, compared with the situation in the early 1980s. Theoretical notions explaining the two key concepts in 'a sustainable corporate story' will be discussed in the next two sections—sustainability and storytelling. I will then explain the methods that can be applied, and how a combination of qualitative and quantitative methods can help create and implement a sustainable corporate story. Using hypothetical examples of a company active in logistics, the application of these methods will be illustrated in order to increase understanding about the nature of the results.

CAUSES OF INCREASED DISCLOSURE OF CORPORATE STORIES

Commercially driven organizations seem to have adopted the now broadly accepted corporate conviction that it is necessary to publicly announce the nature of their activities and missions, at least addressing the financial world, the labor market, and most of all to their own employees and clients. The iron curtain shutting off private companies from public life seems to be a token from the past. The necessity to disclose corporate stories can be seen as a logical consequence of a global trend in which the transparency of companies has become a basic requirement. Growth in corporate disclosure (Higgens and Diffenbach 1989) can be explained by three practical aspects (legal constraints, increased media attention on developments in the business world, and pressure on headquarters to disclose strategy by business unit management) and several theoretical notions (for example, resource dependency).

A practical driving force explaining the growth in communication is legal constraints forcing businesses to disclose actions, including formal obligations like publishing an annual report (financial, social) and other aspects of increased governmental control (such as forcing companies to explain specific plans before allowing implementation). This enforcement is without doubt a logical consequence of the social trend in which a variety of stakeholders demand accountability for corporate choices. The mass media appears to be a follower of fashion (Klapper 1960) for this trend. The frequency of business news in newspapers, radio, and television broadcasting grew significantly during the 1990s (Chajet 1997). Business creates news itself (mergers, success, and failures in the market) and interest in business news has expanded due to the growth of private investors who want to have background information about the companies in which they own shares.

Campbell, Goold, and Alexander (1995) have pointed to another interesting antecedent of the intensification of corporate disclosure stemming from greater communication. They state that corporate management is now faced with increasing pressure from managers working in lower-level business units to legitimize the added value for these units of corporate headquarters decisions. As a consequence, informing its own employees, especially middle management, has become a standard requirement for top management.

A more theoretical explanation for the intensification of corporate disclosure can, for example, be found in the resource dependency model of Pfeffer and Salancik (1978). The authors state that organizations will become more effective if they succeed in getting permanent access to five types of resources (human, natural, capital goods, legitimization, and reputation) companies depend upon. Access to these resources can be achieved through the mechanism of negotiation and the creation of a new set of rules impacting on the behavior of actors within the relevant business domain. Pfeffer and Salancik do not stress the importance of communication to reduce dependency on relevant resources. However, it will in my opinion be impossible to successfully implement negotiation mechanisms or the creation and acceptance of new rules of the game if a company does not apply professional communication, using specialists in advertising, public relations, and above all general managers.

Increased communication by firms is not equal to appealing communication. Mission statements, corporate brochures, and other corporate communication outlets pretend to express the central characteristics of the organization, often claiming nearly the same characteristics that their competitors claim. This applies not only to the official statements of identity and mission, but also to informal stories, which are supposed to express what the organization is actually like. Berg and Gagliardi (1985) observed a striking similarity between the different corporate value systems, as expressed by 'this we believe' brochures, corporate bibles, mission statements, and the like. Martin, Feldman, Hatch, and Sitkin (1983) observed how the same stories that made a claim to uniqueness occurred in virtually identical form in a variety of organizations.

SUSTAINABILITY: NECESSARY ELEMENT OF A CORPORATE STORY

Uniqueness might be a characteristic that will be very hard to find in a world that has a lot in common. Nevertheless, companies will often want to demonstrate what makes them different from their competitors. Distinctiveness is an important element to having a competitive advantage (Porter 1985). The distinctive characteristics of a firm should be appealing to every stakeholder a company depends upon. Stakeholders are 'groups and individuals who can affect, or are affected by, the achievement of an organization's mission' (Freeman 1984: 52). Organizations with high stakeholder management capability actually involve multiple stakeholders to help design and implement communication processes (Freeman 1984: 78). These organizations explicitly negotiate with stakeholders on critical issues and seek voluntary agreements. High stakeholder management capability also implies the integration of boundaries into the strategy formulation process, combined with a proactive approach and an allocation of resources in a manner consistent with stakeholder concerns (Freeman 1984: 79–80). Multiple stakeholder management implies the construction of stakeholder maps summarizing and above all selecting the main groups an organization depends upon. Stakeholder maps can be created using several methods, such as the linkage model of Grunig and Hunt (1984). Grunig and Hunt (1984) distinguish five categories of stakeholders that act as gatekeepers enabling access to resources a company depends upon to deliver products or services. These five categories are:

1. enabling linkages (e.g. stockholders as facilitators of capital goods);
2. functional input linkages (e.g. employees as human capital);
3. functional output linkages (e.g. customers buying the output of the company);
4. normative linkages (e.g. branch organizations; setting the norms and values);
5. diffused linkages (e.g. pressure groups, impacting public opinion).

Prioritization of these five stakeholder groups can be established by identifying the main stakeholders based on the perceived 'power, legitimacy and urgency' (Mitchell *et al.* 1997) that a company attributes to specific groups. 'Power' refers to the perceived ability to impact business actions. 'Legitimacy' refers to the degree to which management perceives the demands of stakeholders as justifiable, and 'urgency' is seen as the perceived time span that management foresees to solve the potential conflict. High priority will be given to those groups that 'score' high on one or more of these dimensions.

Determination of priorities is the responsibility of top management. Their point of view is strongly colored by what is called the insider's view: the perspective of the members of the target organization (Dunbar and Ahlstrom 1995: 172). The insider's view is pragmatic, but also bound to organizational or professional associations. Commitment to the insider's view at the exclusion of the outsider's view is associated with: (*a*) assertions of unique insider knowledge of practice that outsiders do not appreciate, and (*b*) denials that such knowledge and contributions can be assessed adequately in terms of universal effectiveness, efficiency, and fairness measures (Dunbar and Ahlstrom 1995: 175).

This notion is related to what Bettis and Prahalad (1995) label as the dominant logic, the gradually developed vision of the dominant coalition within an organization about how to react to external developments that may have the greatest impact on the company. Organizational attention, according to this theory, focuses mainly on data deemed of relevance to the dominant logic. Other data are largely ignored (Bettis and Prahalad 1995: 7). The nature of the filter mechanisms determines the size of the gap between insider and outsider points of view. Selective perception mechanisms based on the principles of the dominant logic explain the tendency of organizations to apply a bridging-dominated strategy towards stakeholders with a high priority (chosen by the dominant coalition) and apply buffering-dominated strategies towards stakeholders with a perceived low priority (Mitchell *et al.* 1997). Insiders and outsiders will be able to understand each other only if they begin a true dialogue, which, in the terminology of Grunig (1992), is a two-way symmetrical process. This implies the willingness of both parties to create a mutual understanding of each other's points of view. They both have to learn how to cooperate with one another, 'to share problems and vulnerabilities, and to become empowered through the process of working with one another so that the blindness of institutional competitiveness can be avoided' (Dunbar and Ahlstrom 1995: 188). Royal Dutch Shell applied this approach after the experiences of Brent Spar, Per+, and other touchy subjects. The company labels this approach the Triple D model: begin with a dialogue, followed by decision making, and then implementation. It positions this model as an alternative to the so-called DAD model (decide, announce, and defend) (van de Veer 1997).

Ecocentric Management

High stakeholder management capabilities have become more of a necessity in the post-industrial society than they were in the industrial. In the previous era, companies were primarily focused on the creation of wealth through technological expansion, while post-industrial societies are centered on the risks that accompany the creation and distribution of wealth (Shrivastava 1995: 118). A substantial group of authors (e.g. Freeman 1984; Etzioni 1988; Post 1991) linked the responsiveness of corporations primarily to societal needs. Shrivastava points out the necessity of enlarging the scope of company responsibility towards less financial and more nature-oriented issues. He labels this 'ecocentric management', in contrast to traditional (financially dominated) management. This focus implies taking into account the 'welfare of stakeholders instead of shareholder value, post-patriarchal feminist values versus patriarchal values, environmental efficiency versus technological efficiency, creating a meaningful workplace instead of increasing labor productivity as the main HRM-goal' (Shrivastava 1995: 131). The author provides evidence showing that ecocentric management as described above not only improves the quality of life, but also contributes to the financial performance of businesses. Following the publication of this article in the *Academy of Management Review*, several management gurus undertook a similar approach, including Arie de Geus in his book *The Living Company* (1997) and Chris Macrae in *The Brand Chartering Handbook* (1996). Both authors enrich the statements of Shrivastava by observations like: 'capital is no longer a scarce resource; people and knowledge are the key resources that will be fought about in the near future.' In addition to this they provide an extensive set of examples in which they underpin Shrivastava's normative claims with empirical, although mostly anecdotal, evidence about the necessity to shift from traditional management paradigms towards ecocentric management. One example given was the 3M program 'Planet, People and Profit', which led to the reduction of waste by 500,000 tons, saving the company $482 million. Other examples were Interface Inc., a carpet factory that began leasing carpets, stimulating 100 per cent recycling, and Fanny Mae (Federal National Mortgage Association), providing opportunities to minorities to take out mortgages.

Briefly summarizing this section, I have stated that high 'stakeholder management capability' increases the competitive advantage of a firm. Companies have to choose the most relevant stakeholders they are willing to work with, though in some cases they may be forced to work with certain stakeholders. The process of prioritization can be simplified by a combination of the notions formulated in the linkage model of Grunig and Hunt (1984), and the PUL-elements (power, urgency, and legitimacy) of Mitchell, Agle, and Wood (1997). This selection will be colored by the dominant decision-making logic of top management. One of the characteristics of the dominant logic of nearly all top managers of listed companies is the strong focus on shareholder value. However, stakeholder demands are much broader than merely return on investment. That is why I have introduced the notions of Shrivastava, who stresses the necessity to make a shift towards ecocentric management, placing nature-oriented issues at the forefront of management decision-making in the near future.

STORYTELLING: LESSONS TO BE LEARNED FROM THE NARRATIVE APPROACH

The work of Shrivastava (1995), de Geus (1997), and Macrae (1996), emphasizes the necessity for companies to apply a holistic long-term policy in the way they communicate with all stakeholders. Avoiding contradictory messages can be achieved through integrated communication (Nowak and Phelps 1994; Schultz *et al.* 1994). The output of the wide range of communication specialists within organizations (marketing communication, press relations, investor relations, employee communication, corporate advertising, and last but not least management communication) does not automatically result in coherent communication messages. These various specialists are naturally inclined to consider their own departmental interests rather than the strategic interest of the total organization. This often results in fragmented, even contradictory pictures being communicated by the company when viewed as a whole. Companies are aware of the dangers of fragmented communication and strive to increase mutual coherence in all forms of internal and external communication. Orchestration of the contents of communication can be achieved in various ways. Visual coherence can be guaranteed by house-style guidelines, or in marketing communications by applying the same pay-off, packaging, or visual aspects as commercial communication (Olins 1989). The communication of the organization as a whole can be orchestrated using common operational systems, cooperative structures for communication decision-making, and common starting points (van Riel 1997). Common starting points (CSPs) are central values that function as the basis for undertaking any kind of communication envisioned by an organization. Examples of CSPs are 'innovativeness', 'quality', 'rooted in the local community', 'non-profit orientation', 'strong in-product design', 'warm', 'shareholder value', and 'global player'.

CSPs are mostly written down in individual words, summarizing the key attributes a company wants to express to illustrate what the organization is and what it stands for. There is a danger involved in this approach:

1. Companies apply 'only' separate words that can be imitated quite easily by competitors.
2. A collection of words does not guarantee a similar, coherent, interpretation of the strategic intent of the company by all communication specialists. The focus of each individual in a company is different, and at least colored by the nature of the task and environment he or she is responsible for. As a consequence, this will result in differences in interpretations of the relevance and applicability of the CSP.

A *solution* to this problem, in my view, is *to connect the words in a story in such a way that the content is perceived by internal and external audiences as a reflection of their own input.* In other words, it has to be a story to which all stakeholders can relate or in which they can invest.

Boje (1991: 106) concurs that storytelling is 'the preferred sense making currency of human relationships'. The narrative approach recognizes the meaningfulness of individual experiences by noting how they function as parts of the whole. Its particular subject matter is human actions and events that affect human beings, which it configures into wholes according to the roles these actions and events play in bringing about a conclusion (Polkinghorn 1988: 36).

Stories are vital to sense-making within organizations. However, referring to the previously discussed notions about dominant logic, caution must be exercised regarding the author(s) who develops the script (Hatch 1996). It is important to take into consideration who dominates the process of creating the storyline. Is this mainly or even solely to be the responsibility of the dominant coalition in an organization, or are other decision-making units (at a lower level) to be involved also? As I will explain below, it is my view that it is necessary to involve a representative group of decision-makers in the process of creating the sustainable corporate story in order to increase its effectiveness.

Effective corporate stories are based on two outcomes: credibility and novelty (Barry and Elmes 1997: 434). Credibility will improve if the corporate story is perceived by external and internal stakeholders as illustrations of the centrality and continuity of the organization, while novelty has to express the distinctiveness compared with players in the same or a comparable league. Both aspects are important, but are dialectic in character: credibility impacts on novelty negatively, and the other way around. Thus, authors must apply both perspectives adequately in order to create an effective narrative (Barry and Elmes 1997: 434). Barry and Elmes (1997: 435) believe that credibility will increase if the story is first of all printed, 'assuming an undeniable corporeality'. Further, they concur that it is even better if it is possible to show it on screens (television, slides, and so on). One subtle credibility technique consists of developing strategic narratives according to familiar plot lines: Folk tales, fairy tales, epic hero journeys, or some other romanticist form. The first two categories do not appear useful for the creation of corporate stories. The other two seem more relevant. With the epic form, the hero/company finds itself confronting a number of enemies and/or obstacles. If everyone in the company were to pull together, the company should emerge victorious with growing market shares, profits, and job security. Romanticist plots are enacted when the company is portrayed as recovering from a fall from grace, stemming perhaps from excessive growth or divergence from the founder's vision. This type of plot results in a return to a purer self, which for a time had perhaps been obscured, but was there all along (Barry and Elmes 1997: 437–8). With respect to narrative content, novelty may be created through periodic shifts in orienting strategic problems. Thus, competitors may be assigned the antagonist role for a year or two, only to be replaced by issues of quality, mergers, or governmental compliance (Barry and Elmes 1997: 438). My personal view is that the success of corporate stories is in telling them, not so much in showing them in written or audio-visual material. Writing down a corporate story will increase the codification, but reduce especially the novelty.

CREATING AND IMPLEMENTING A SUSTAINABLE CORPORATE STORY

Creating corporate stories should not be seen as a goal in itself, but as an aid to help stimulate reflective conversations in order to create shared understanding (Roth and Kleiner 1998: 44). It should enable an organization to find an inspiring frame of reference for orchestrating the future communication of the company as a whole. An ideal way to do this is by gathering information based on the combination of internal data (from meetings with top management and surveys among a sample of all layers in the organization) and external data (the multiple stakeholders approach). The process of creating stories, especially involving the integration of internal and external resources, has received limited attention in the literature, with certain exceptions like Van Maanen (1988), Collins and Porras (1994), Senge (1994), and Roth and Kleiner (1998). The common denominator in all these publications seems to be the emphasis on involving organizational members with internal decision-making about strategic intentions in order to ensure a successful implementation. The majority of these publications seem to focus primarily on internal processes. In my view, however, it is impossible to neglect the external perspective entirely. In the next section, I will try to provide an overview of methods that can be used to create a sustainable corporate story based on the input of organizational members and conversations with key external stakeholders.

How to Create a Sustainable Corporate Story?

A sustainable corporate story should be based on the aggregation of a set of words evoked by qualitative and quantitative research among internal and external audiences. Here I will explain how to combine these words to create a story that can be perceived as relevant (having added value for society in the broadest sense of the word), realistic (typical for the organization), and indicating a responsive attitude (stimulating supporters and opponents to have an open dialogue with the firm about its ambitions and operating choices).

I suggest a combination of six steps resulting in the creation, implementation, and, if necessary, adaptation of the sustainable corporate story for a specific company (see Fig. 10.1). This approach will be in the narrative style of an epic hero journey, strongly focusing on a rational explanation of why the company was, is, and will be successful, with what kind of activities, and which results have been achieved or can expected to be achieved in the near future.

Step 1. Positioning

Positioning is the making of strategic choices for the purpose of a competitive advantage in the market (Porter 1985). It is a process in which management

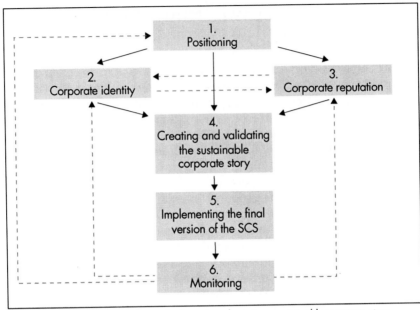

Fig. 10.1. Steps to be taken to create, implement, and monitor a sustainable corporate story

tries to find the right match between internal desires and external possibilities, allowing a company to achieve its dreams. A sophisticated strategy formulation focuses on both aspects, as well as on the nature of the choices to be
made by the organization. Decision-making about strategic positioning often
starts with the study of reports from trend-watchers in the relevant line of
business (or interviewing them personally), followed by an inventory of the
performance and communication styles of competitors. Important internal
information can be gathered by studying the long-term plans of the business
groups, the divisions and the holding, acquiring data about developments in
turnover, research and developments investments, and return on capital
employed during the previous five years. Realization of plans linked to
planned investments will be affected by 'market attractiveness' (e.g. maturity
of the market, impact of regulation, entry barriers, substitutes) and 'ability to
compete' (e.g. product life cycle, marketing power, market share, cost leadership, innovation). The position of a business unit on the market attractiveness
'scale' and the ability to compete 'scale' (see Fig. 10.2) should be based on
manager perceptions of these aspects, in combination with judgements on
the same items based on external evidence.
    Finding the right positioning requires consideration of all stakeholders a
company depends upon. The above-mentioned map in Fig. 10.2 tends to concentrate strongly on an analysis of the 'commercial' environment (potential
customers). In order to involve other stakeholders in the positioning analyses,
the previously discussed notions about the linkage model of Grunig and Hunt

can be applied, combined with the criteria of Mitchell, Agle, and Wood (1997), enabling an organization to select the most relevant stakeholders. First, managers are asked to describe the most important stakeholders (based on the five categories of Grunig and Hunt). In the next phase they are requested to evaluate every type of stakeholder in terms of urgency to interact with them, the power they can have over the organization, and the degree to which the managers perceive the claims of the stakeholder to be legitimate. An example of the application of these methods is depicted in Table 10.1.

Step 2. Actual and Desired Corporate Identity

Corporate identity deals with how you present yourself to external and internal stakeholders, to be distinguished in cues showing the logo and corporate name(s), and cues describing what the company does, why it does it, and what makes it a preferred partner in business. The first mentioned element refers to what I call 'parent visibility': the degree to which the constituent parts of an organization want to profile themselves under the name of the holding. The

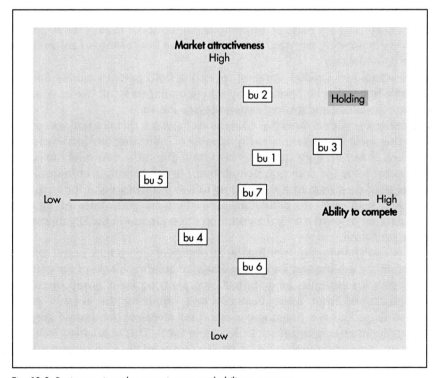

Fig. 10.2. Business unit market attractiveness and ability to compete

Table 10.1. Evaluation of stakeholder power, legitimacy, and urgency

Stakeholders	Power	Legitimacy	Urgency
Financial market		•	
Labor market	•	•	•
Branch organizations	•		
Regulatory agencies	•••	•••	•••
Politics	•••	•••	•••
Government	••	••	••
Unions	•	•	
Consumer organizations			
Clients	•	••	
Employees	•	••	
Airlines			
Environmental groups			
Transportation market			

second element is reflected in what I call 'content agreement': the degree to which all constituent parts of the company agree about the key message of the company expressing the why, the what, and the how of the organization as a whole (van Riel 1997).

The actual and desired situation regarding both parent visibility and content agreement can be described by asking managers in all business units to indicate the actual and desired situations (see Fig. 10.3).

Experiences with a variety of companies in which this method was applied show that most managers are easily capable of indicating the degree of parent visibility. However, they are rather uncertain about the nature of the content that seems to be the common denominator in the corporate communication messages of their own company. Using this as a starting point for further discussions, managers are nearly always willing to participate in follow-up research that helps to clarify the common denominator in the key messages of the organization.

More clarity about interpreting the attributes of a corporate brand (and as a consequence, adding and improving essential building blocks of the corporate story) can, for example, be acquired by organizing focus group discussions with managers from every business unit, applying the *cobweb method methodology*. This is a pragmatic method for revealing the desired corporate identity (content) characteristics (Bernstein 1984). This qualitative technique, based on a group discussion involving key representatives of the organization, stimulates managers to tell their interpretation of the corporate story, such as how they would describe the story at birthday parties, conferences, and so on.

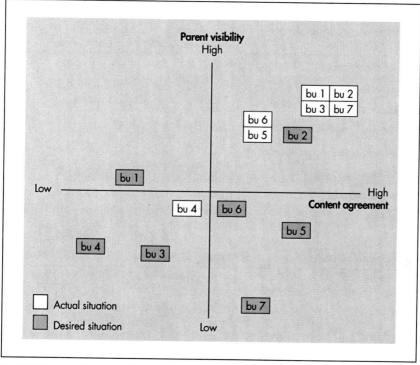

Fig. 10.3. Degree of parent visibility and content agreement

Managers are stimulated to present a description of their company as extensively as possible. After these 'open' discussions, people are invited to select the most important words to be used as the best indicators of what the company really is and/or should be. These selected words, which are perceived by a consensus of the focus group participants as being most relevant, have to be evaluated on a scale from 1 (not relevant at all) to 10 (highly relevant) for both the actual and the desired situation, resulting in a table such as Table 10.2.

This is only a hypothetical example, as was said before. Nevertheless, it does represent results that could have been gathered quite easily within a real organization. This material is a good starting point for the creation of a sustainable corporate story. One has to realize that the words acquired here are terms that indicate the internal idiom. Therefore, certain words will be seen as being relevant mainly to internal stakeholders. This implies that one has to consider these words as a starting point. Such words have to be checked against external points of view. These first internal results should not be primarily evaluated by the nature of the selected words itself, nor can the weight of these issues in positive and negative characteristics be seen as vital in the creation of the corporate story. The most important lesson to be learned from data acquired during such focus group discussions is that the richest information

Table 10.2. Results of cobweb analyses

Results of cobweb analyses	Actual			Desired			Gap
	min.	max.	mean	min.	max.	mean	
Global company	5	8	7.2	8	9	8.6	−1.4
Partner in business	6	8	6.9	8	10	8.8	−1.9
Quick delivery	8	9	8.6	8	10	8.9	−0.3
Customer oriented	4	7	6.2	8	9	8.5	−2.3
Ability to handle large volumes	7	8	7.5	8	9	8.4	−0.9
Excellent employer	6	7	6.9	8	10	8.6	−1.7
Service provider	4	7	6.0	7	10	8.7	−2.7
Reliable	8	8	8.0	8	10	8.7	−0.7
High tech	5	8	6.9	8	9	8.6	−1.7
Informal/open culture	6	7	6.8	8	9	8.1	−1.3

to be found will be what lies 'behind' the words provided by the participants. Remember that participants merely express their own interpretations about key elements of a story they prefer to tell about the company.

Step 3. Reputation Analyses and Trends in Public Opinion

The reputation of a company can be studied in a variety of ways. Most large companies can use publicly available reputation rankings, like Fortune, Price Waterhouse, Coopers–Financial Times, Asian Business, and so on (see Fombrun 1998). These popular rankings are based on the input of decision-makers, people with responsible positions in leading companies and public-sector organizations in specific countries. They are asked to participate in reputation surveys because it is believed that they have better-than-average knowledge about companies they have to evaluate in terms of familiarity and appreciation. Academic researchers heavily criticize reputation rankings. Fryxell and Wang (1994), for example, state that such rankings primarily indicate the financial appreciation of a company. Other authors view rankings as biased, because they are based on the opinions of a selected group of respondents. Even so, whether or not this might be true, it does not seem to harm the popularity of these rankings in practice. I think that rankings offer, among many other things, an interesting point of reference for creating a sustainable corporate story. The unique aspect of rankings is the potential to analyze over a long period of time trends in reputation scores for a given company compared to its direct competitors.

In crucial developments in the life cycle of a company, like when a sustainable corporate story is being created, it is necessary to execute a more tailor-made measurement of company-specific reputation scores. These data can be acquired by a wide variety of methods (for example, attitude scales, Q-sort, Photosort, laddering, Kelly Repertory Grid, Natural Grouping). In an article in *Corporate Reputation Review*, my colleagues and I analyzed the pros and cons of these six different methods (see van Riel *et al.* 1998). We concluded, theoretically speaking, that the most ideal approach would be a combination of at least one open method (preferably two) and one closed method. Open methods appear to provide relevant (as perceived by external audiences) qualitative descriptions of the organization that can be used as input for closed methods. An often used and relatively cheap closed method is the survey. Such a survey, based on combined input from internal and external attributes, could produce the results shown in Fig. 10.4.

Step 4. Creating and Validating the Sustainable Corporate Story

The gathered internal and external data will enable a consultant to make a first draft of the sustainable corporate story. This can be done by simply

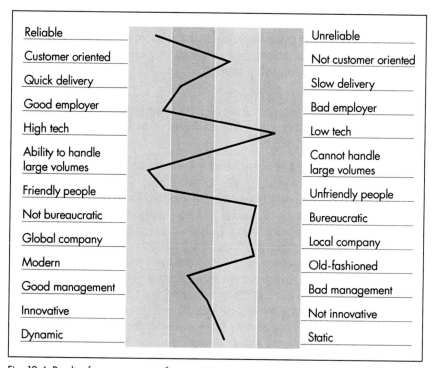

Fig. 10.4. Results of a company-specific reputation survey

writing down the *key promise* of the company, based on the interpretation of data gathered in Steps 1 (positioning), 2 (identity), and 3 (long-term shifts in public opinion regarding the company, as well as organization-specific reputation scores). A promise statement should be a full text with normal sentences and an understandable structure. This is a crucial moment in the creation of the sustainable corporate story. Now, for the first time in the process of decision-making, words are transformed into sentences, forcing managers to be clear about what the preferred words really mean within the context of their own firm. A full sentence stating, for example, what a 'partner in business' really means clarifies a lot about what the company is and/or wants to be.

The creation of this promise statement text can (and in my opinion should) be done with a small group of no more than four to six people. It seems rather risky to outsource this completely to an external consultant. The small group constructing the draft text of a positioning statement, to be considered as the beginning of a sustainable corporate story, should then have their output reviewed and critiqued by as many people as possible, both inside and outside the company. This will achieve two things. First, it will collect adaptations improving the relevant and realistic character of the story. Second, the involvement of numerous people in the decision-making processes will increase consensus about the relevance of the text.

There are various ways to acquire information that can be used, increasing involvement in the creation of a realistic and relevant text. *Internal data* can be acquired by a written questionnaire distributed to, for example, all marketing and communication managers in a company, asking them to evaluate a draft text describing the following aspects:

1. the key *promise* of the company;
2. the kind of *proofs* they can come up with to support these claims; and
3. the *tone of voice* they would like to apply to make it an appealing message.

Table 10.3 shows the kind of output that will be created when one applies this technique.

An often-applied method to test *external support* for the draft version of the corporate story is a survey of crucial external audiences based on the IDU-method of Rossiter and Percy (1997). The selection of stakeholders should ideally be based on the preferences formulated by internal managers (see Table 10.1). The IDU method focuses on the evaluation of external audiences regarding the degree to which they perceive specific attributes of the organization to be 'important' and 'unique'. It also evaluates the degree to which external audiences think the company will be able to deliver on these characteristics. Keep in mind that the word choice used in the survey of external audiences will need to be reformulated, since these respondents cannot be expected to understand internal terminology. The results of the IDU-method are shown in Table 10.4.

Table 10.3. Results of internal survey evaluating the promise statement

Characteristics mentioned in promise statement	Cobweb results	Internal support for these elements	Proofs given by internal managers
Global company	8.6	Moderate	Delivery in 200 countries all over the world
Partner in business	8.8	Good	Customer testimonials
Quick delivery	8.9	Excellent	95% is delivered the next day
Customer oriented	8.5	Excellent	Grades for customer satisfaction
Ability to handle large volumes	8.4	Moderate	Figures of volumes handled
Excellent employer	8.6	Moderate	Salary and conditions of employment
Service provider	8.7	Good	From information to delivery
Reliable	8.7	Excellent	99% is delivered at the right address
High tech	8.6	Good	State-of-the-art machinery
Informal/ open culture	8.1	Good	Personnel testimonials

A more sophisticated analysis of data acquired with the IDU method is achieved by statistically calculating the impact of importance and uniqueness on delivery, which will highlight specific clusters of words (summarized with specific labels) that appear to be most vital in the eyes of external audiences. Following this, the best way to further adapt the story is to use the same method in reverse, using several stakeholders that are considered to be crucial in the eyes of management. An example of the results from one stakeholder group (in this case, a customer) can be seen in Fig. 10.5.

The previously gathered information makes it possible to take the next step in the creation of the sustainable corporate story. Based on the internal evaluations of the promise statement (including the proofs, and tone of voice suggestions), as well as the external evaluations, I recommend setting up another *focus group session with top management*, inviting them to construct a so-called CAR model. This is a practical aid for translating the format of the story, according to the epic hero journey narrative style, into an antecedents–consequences story line. CAR is the abbreviation for critical success factors, activities, and results. The *critical success factors* focus, for example, on elements such as:

Table 10.4. Results of external survey testing the perceived relevance and reality of the promise statement

Characteristic	Importance	Delivery	Uniqueness
1. Delivery to the right address	10.0	7.2	6.6
2. Keep your promise	9.9	7.0	4.4
3. Delivery throughout the whole world	9.8	6.9	7.2
4. Express services	9.1	7.2	5.3
5. Good in logistics	9.5	7.0	5.3
6. Easy access	9.0	7.1	3.8
7. Delivering added value	9.1	6.8	4.8
8. Client is king	8.9	6.7	3.6
9. Professional	8.8	7.1	4.0
10. High tech	9.3	7.1	6.5
11. High quality	9.4	6.9	4.8
12. Integrity	9.8	7.5	4.7
13. Personal contact	7.9	6.8	3.5
14. Feeling of confidence	7.8	6.6	3.8

1. how the organization operates;
2. in which respect it is different from its competitors;
3. what makes the organization's identity enduring.

The second element of the CAR model (*activities*) addresses the repeatedly asked (but difficult to answer) question regarding which business we are in:

1. what are the main product market combinations of the organization?
2. in which countries?

The last cluster of the CAR model represents the *results* of everything an organization is aiming to achieve, such as:

1. customer satisfaction;
2. increased market shares;
3. high return on investment;
4. appreciation by external and internal stakeholders;
5. 'prestige'.

Participants in the focus group should first of all be informed about all information gathered on the visions and preferences regarding the strategic choices of the organization (the positioning), the identity, and the reputation, combined with the internal and external evaluations of the promise statement. After discussing the results achieved at this point, all participants would then be invited to jointly construct a visualization, as detailed as possible, of the 'critical success factors', 'activities', and 'results' of the company they work for. An aid to stimulate elaboration for creating such a model is to start by simply showing boxes (for 'C', 'A', and 'R'), connected with arrows suggesting causal relationships between the three elements of the CAR model. A next step might be to provide an example of a company in a completely different branch. Important instructions to be given to the participants of the focus group are as follows:

1. Start with what seems to be the most simple, which is a description of the core activities of the company.
2. Continue with the type of results you think the company already achieves or should and can achieve.
3. The next step is to start thinking about the causal relationships between the different concepts visualized *within* the boxes in the antecedents part of the CAR model (critical success factors).
4. Allow yourself to move quickly from one element of the CAR model to the other, since decisions made in one part significantly impact decisions in other parts.

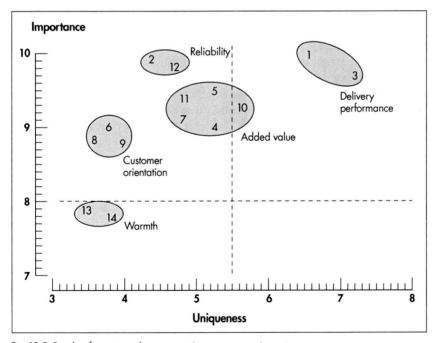

Fig. 10.5. Results of an external survey—uniqueness versus importance

5. Allow yourself (or force the group) to make at least two updated (that is, discussed with all members of the focus group) versions of the CAR model.

6. Analyze the final CAR model, separating elements to be marked RED (referring to elements of the CAR model that need to be improved first before being promoted as a key element in the identity of the organization to the outside world), or GREEN (meaning that these elements can already be justified based on past performance).

In order to clarify what the application of this method might result in, a hypothetical model is shown in Fig. 10.6.

Step 5. Implementating the Final Version of the Sustainable Corporate Story

Visualizing an idea (in this case a corporate story) seems to stimulate enthusiasm, especially for managers that are directly involved. In contrast to the construction of the promise statement text, the visualization of the CAR model allows something that is crucial in storytelling: it enables people to some extent to use their own 'interpretation' of the company story. On the other hand, it forces organizational members to stay within the context from which the model has been visualized, stimulating at least a minimum level of coherence in the way the story is told.

The corporate story can be used as a source of inspiration for various platforms. However, if it is used as a briefing tool for the production of practical media-related messages, it must be pragmatic. A solution could be to orchestrate the transformation of the story into definitive messages with the help of so-called common starting points (CSPs). As was mentioned before, CSPs can be described as central values that function as a basis for undertaking any kind of communication envisioned by an organization. These values will or should remain fairly stable, though they will eventually change over time due to internal and external influences. Every two to three years, the director of corporate communication should select a set of no more than five CSPs. Naturally these CSPs have to be rooted in the CAR model (and its underlying corporate story). In order to stimulate the application of these issues, they must receive regular attention by all crucial (corporate) communication channels. This can be structured as shown in Table 10.5.

However, working with CSPs is only an aid to stimulating coherent formal communications in a company. It should (in my opinion) never be seen as a corporate rule, which would kill creativity and not contribute to acceptance. As I see it, the power of a sustainable corporate story is in creating it and telling it. The greater the number of representatives from the dominant coalition who act as storytellers, the higher the impact will be.

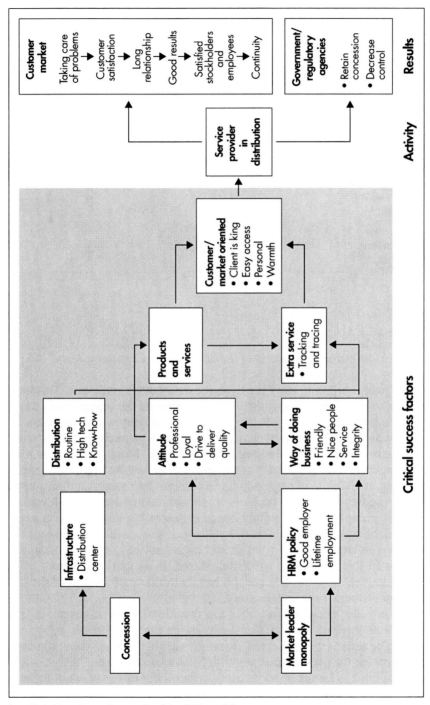

Fig. 10.6. Hypothetical example of the CAR model

Table 10.5. Transformation of the sustainable corporate story into common starting points as a frame of reference for orchestration of all communication

CSP/ channels	Speeches of top manage- ment	Internal media	Web site	Annual report	Corporate advertising	Exhibitions
Capabilities: high tech						
Reliability: loyal						
Added value: tracking and tracing						
Customer orientation: integrity						

Step 6. Monitoring the Success of the Sustainable Corporate Story

A sustainable corporate story is a dynamic entity, not a static one. This means that the story will never be finished. It is as alive as the organization itself. If the organization or its environment changes, the story will change too. Like was said before, an important characteristic of a sustainable corporate story is the style in which it is created and communicated. Most preferable is a style that stimulates both supporters and opponents to have an open dialogue with the company. Web sites are a popular technique for creating a dialogue with external audiences nowadays. More traditional means are also still valuable. Consider companies that simply organize 'captain's dinners' on a regular basis, enabling key stakeholders to readily hear about and respond to what is perceived as attractive and what should be improved in the organization. In addition to this, the whole spectrum of traditional market research can be applied to track and trace important trends in the appreciation of the company, consequently altering the story.

Not only the creation, but also the continuation, of a successful story depends on internal support. Continuity in internal support can in my opinion only be achieved by repeated inventories, gathering data about the degree of support for the present interpretation. There can be no doubt that external opinions have to be taken very seriously, but there does not seem to be any good reason to assume that external views should be more important than internal beliefs.

DISCUSSION AND CONCLUSIONS

A sustainable corporate story is not a guarantee for success, but a tool to increase mutual understanding between an organization and its stakeholders. The creation and implementation of a successful corporate story is not only a matter of using the 'right' methods and the 'right' approach, but above all the sincere desire to develop a story that will really improve the quality of the corporate communication of an organization.

A sustainable corporate story can be written down in a formal document (a corporate brochure, a web-site page, internal publications, and so on).The story has to be used in a variety of media and should have a long-term focus. Above all, a story should be told; the act of storytelling is more important than the written proof of its existence. Verbal communication is more convincing (personal communication is more effective than the indirect approach by mass media), allowing the storyteller to focus on those aspects that will be appealing to a specific audience. Such stories can stimulate the realization of internal purpose (setting implicitly the rules regarding desired behavior of organizational members) and it can provide guidelines for external aspirations (enabling a company to obtain all the resources a company depends upon). The extensiveness of the story, format, and creative style can differ, depending on the goals of the initiating organization and the context in which it is operating. The core idea should, however, remain visible, especially in company messages aimed at improving the reputation of the organization with crucial stakeholders.

In this chapter I have discussed a combination of several methods that can be applied to create and implement a sustainable corporate story. Three conclusions can be drawn:

1. A corporate story will only be sustainable if it respects all stakes. This implies a multi-stakeholder perspective that consequently requires an open dialogue with all stakeholders. However, voluntary usage of input from stakeholder opponents and supporters does not exclude the organization from having the right and the duty to accept responsibility for the way it represents itself to internal and external audiences.
2. Experience with a variety of organizations in creating sustainable corporate stories has taught me the necessity not only of acquiring data from both internal and external audiences, but of doing so in both a qualitative and a quantitative way. A story that lacks input from any vital stakeholder, or that utilizes input based 'only' on either 'facts and figures' or 'subjective impressions', will never be a success.
3. It requires at least as much effort from organizational members to create a story as it does for external stakeholders to develop an appreciation for it. Learning to be patient (internal actors), both in the creation and in the implementation of a sustainable corporate story, is therefore a necessity.

It can be concluded that sustainable corporate stories are effective instruments for achieving higher degrees of prestige and trust among internal and external stakeholders, provided four criteria are met. The story has to be perceived by these groups as 'relevant' (describing those activities that appear to have added value), 'realistic' (describing what the company really is and does), 'sustainable' (finding the right balance between the competing demands of all stakeholders), and 'responsive' (really stimulating people to have an open dialogue with the organization). The effectiveness of a sustainable corporate story will also improve if the story is told and retold, especially by the dominant coalition, each in its own style and with its own interpretation within the confines of the description in the CAR model.

Last but not least, no matter how appealing a story may be, appreciation for that story can only be maintained if the discrepancies between what is told and what is actually done by organizational members are as limited as possible.

REFERENCES

Barry, D., and Elmes, M. (1997), 'Strategy Retold Toward a Narrative View of Strategic Discourse', *Academy of Management Review*, 22/2: 429–52.

Berg, P. O., and Gagliardi, P. (1985), 'Corporate Images: A Symbolic Perspective of the Organization–Environment Interface', paper presented at the SCOS Conference on Corporate Images, Antibes, France, 16–29 June.

Bernstein, D. (1984), *Company Image and Reality: A Critique of Corporate Communications* (Eastborne: Holt, Rinehart & Winston).

Bettis, R. A., and Prahalad, C. K. (1995), 'The Dominant Logic: Retrospective and Extension', *Strategic Management Journal*, 16: 5–14.

Boje, D. M. (1991), 'The Storytelling Organization: A Study of Story Performance in an Office-Supply Firm', *Administration Science Quarterly*, 36/1: 106–26.

Campbell, A., Goold, M., and Alexander, M. (1995), 'Corporate Strategy: The Quest or Parenting Advantage', *Harvard Business Review*, Mar.–Apr.: 120–32.

Chajet, C. (1997), 'Corporate Reputation and the Bottom Line', *Corporate Reputation Review*, 1/1–2: 19–23.

Collins, J. C., and Porras, J. I. (1994), *Built to Last: Successful Habits of Visionary Companies* (New York: Harper Business).

de Geus, A. (1997), *The Living Company: Habits for Survival in a Turbulent Business Environment* (Bosten: Harvard Business School Press).

Dunbar, R. L., and Ahlstrom, D. (1995), 'Seeking the Institutional Balance of Power: Avoiding the Power of a Balanced View', *Academy of Management Review*, 20/1: 171–92.

Etzioni, A. (1988), *The Moral Dimension* (New York: Free Press).

Fombrun, C. J. (1998), 'Indices of Corporate Reputation: An Analysis of Media Rankings and Social Monitors' Ratings', *Corporate Reputation Review*, 1/4: 327–43.

Freeman, R. E. (1984), *Strategic Management: A Stakeholder Approach* (Boston: Pitman).

Fryxell, G. E., and Wang, J. (1994), 'The Fortune's Corporate "Reputation" Index: Reputation of What?', *Journal of Management*, 20/1: 1–14.

Grunig, J. (1992) (ed.), *Excellence in Public Relations and Communication Management* (Hillsdale, NJ: Lawrence Earlsbaum).

—— and Hunt, T. (1984), *Managing Public Relations* (Fort Worth, Tex.: Holt, Rinehart & Winston).

Hatch, M. J. (1996), 'The Role of the Researcher. An Analysis of Narrative Position in Organization Theory', *Journal of Management Inquiry*, 5/4: 359–74.

Higgens, R. B., and Diffenbach, J. (1989), 'Communicating Corporate Strategy: The Pay-Offs and the Risks', *Long Range Planning*, 12: 133–9.

Klapper, J. T. (1960), *The Effects of Mass Communication* (Glencoe, Ill.: Free Press).

Macrae, C. (1996), *The Brand Chartering Handbook: How Brand Organizations Learn 'Living Scripts'* (Harlow, England: Addison Wesley).

Martin, J., Feldman, M. S., Hatch, M. J., and Sitkin, S. B. (1983), 'The Uniqueness Paradox in Organizational Stories', *Administrative Science Quarterly*, 28/3: 438–54.

Mitchell, R. K., Agle, B. R., and Wood, D. J. (1997), 'Toward a Theory of Stakeholder Identification and Salience: Defining the Principle of Who and What Really Counts', *Academy of Management Review*, 22/4: 853–86.

Nowak, G. J., and Phelps, J. (1994), 'Conceptualizing the Integrated Marketing Communications Phenomenon: An Examination of its Impact on Advertising Practices and its Implications for Advertising Research', *Journal of Current Issues and Research in Advertising*, 16: 49–66.

Olins, W. (1989), *Corporate Identity: Making Business Strategy Visible through Design* (London: Thames & Hudson).

Pfeffer, J., and Salancik, G. R. (1978), *The External Control of Organizations: A Resource Dependency Perspective* (New York: Harper & Row).

Polkinghorn, D. (1988), *Narrative Knowing and the Human Sciences* (Albany, NY: State University of New York Press).

Porter, M. E. (1985), *Competitive Advantage: Creating and Sustaining Superior Performance* (New York: Free Press).

Post, J. E. (1991), 'Management as if the Earth Mattered', *Business Horizons*, 34/4: 32–8.

Rossiter, J. R., and Percy, L. (1997), *Advertising Communications & Promotion Management* (New York: McGraw-Hill).

Roth, G., and Kleiner, A. (1998), 'Developing Organizational Memory through Learning Histories', *Organizational Dynamics*, Autumn: 43–60.

Schultz, D. E., Tannenbaum, S. I., and Lauterborn, R. F. (1994), *Integrated Marketing Communication: Pulling It Together and Making It Work* (Chicago: NTC Business Books).

Senge, P. M. (1994), *The Fifth Discipline: The Art and Practice of the Learning Organization* (New York: Currency Doubleday).

Shrivastava, P. (1995), 'Ecocentric Management for a Risk Society', *Academy of Management Review*, 20/1: 118–37.

van de Veer, J. (1997), 'Buffering and Bridging in Reputation Management', conference lecture, Erasmus University/Royal Dutch Shell, Rotterdam.

Van Maanen, J. (1988), *Tales of the Field: On Writing Ethnography* (Chicago: Chicago University Press).

van Riel, C. B. M. (1997), 'Research in Corporate Communication: An Overview of an Emerging Field', *Management Communication Quarterly*, 11/2: 288–309.

—— Stroeker, N. E., and Maathuis, O. J. M. (1998), 'Measuring Corporate Images', *Corporate Reputation Review*, 1/4: 313–26.

11

Planning and Communicating Using Stories

Gordon G. Shaw

Every culture has used stories to pass on the past to newer members. Some cultures had no written language and used past stories to save their history and values. For example, writing did not exist for the New Zealand Maoris, or other Polynesian cultures, until the Christian missionaries set about reducing their language to written form. The narrative was their only option other than petroglyphs.

Many corporate cultures such as 3M and Hewlett-Packard have used stories to explain the importance of innovation to the corporation. Lessons are learned from these stories, such as when 3M scientists kept their new product ideas alive even when counter to their superior's orders. At Hewlett-Packard they tell stories of their most famous entrepreneurs, Bill and Dave. Personally, I collected a group of our stories at 3M and published them so that they would not be lost (Shaw 1998).

In most cases, the narrative is used to preserve the past and to learn from it, usually with an internal focus, communicating to the same organization that the stories are about.

THE CASE FOR STORIES

What I propose is to gather and build stories for the future, and then communicate them not only to the organization, but in some cases also to customers, distribution, suppliers, stockholders, and investment analysts. Then stories will include not only 'sagas' of the past but also—more importantly—stories of the future. In my experience, using the narrative format is the best way to develop and communicate the strategic plans of the business.

The strategic planning process is one of the only times that all functional areas of the company sit down together and discuss their future. Unfortunately, most business people dread the time spent in planning sessions. There is little excitement or enthusiasm, and most of the output is a list of 'good things to do', many of which are defensive in nature in order to respond to competitive pressures. The objective is to become functionally stronger in areas where the organization is weak, such as logistics, customer service, factory costs, mature product competitiveness, and so on. Over time, a list that either addresses weaknesses or exploits internal capabilities becomes hard for executive management to argue with, and opinions are such that, if it was accepted in last year's plan, 'don't change what ain't broke'. When results do not meet the plan's forecast, poor implementation is believed to be the cause. In fact, as Hamel and Prahalad (1994) have argued, it is more likely to be poor strategic architecture that is at fault. This implies the lack of a clear vision of strategic intent or a clear rationale as to how and why you will be able to build the future you envision.

One problem is the use of bullets or an outline format for the plan. Bullets or items do allow the complex to be condensed to a brief presentation, but in doing so we leave out 'how' and 'why' we should expect to achieve our goals. An outline will not create enthusiasm for the plan, since it only acts as a 'to do' list. Lists present only an illusion of clarity—and it can be an expensive illusion.

In contrast, a narrative or strategic story takes advantage of what stories do best: they are more believable, they are more memorable, and they generate more enthusiasm. Executives often state that they want to improve employee satisfaction. What good, talented employees want is excitement about their work. Developing a winning story should be a stimulating activity for competitive people. Business people tend to be of a competitive nature. Many business people play competitive sports or support their favorite teams. They enjoy competitive games and like to wager on the outcome. So why do they dislike thinking through a winning business strategy? Strategic Planning is where this should happen, but this process has become too mechanical.

Narratives are used to teach salespersons how to paint word pictures in the customer's mind of the benefits of using their product. Storyboards, which today are electronic, are used to construct advertisements. When dealing with stock analysts, we differentiate our company from others by explaining our culture using stories of the past to make the future more believable. Human resources use stories to explain the company to new employees. Why then do we resist using strategic stories for our business plans that should pull all of these other activities together?

In my experience, narrative plans that explain how the future will be accomplished are more difficult for business to develop than having each functional area provide a list of functional improvements to a designated planner, who then puts together the business plan. The latter seems to be the current practice, where the leader judges what belongs in the list of functional improvements, adds any that s/he knows will be well received by executive management, and has the planner write up any modifications to last year's plan.

Using a narrative requires an in-depth understanding of the customers, competitors, suppliers, and others in order to craft a true vision statement of significant new benefits to customers, and the sequence of events that will lead to the successful sales results that support the plan's forecast. This is more difficult to do and thus strategic stories are not written.

Excuses for not doing so include:

1. 'I am an engineer—not an English or journalism skilled person—I was not trained to write a story.'

   My response is: Lower your standards and start again. This is not about literary excellence. It is about thinking through how you can bring about the end-state for an industry you have envisioned.

2. 'Strategic stories can become fables that sound good but are not realistic.'

   My response is: Realistic stories are better than the usual lists of things to do because it is easier to recognize an unrealistic story about the future than it is to evaluate a list. This is because a list of good things to do is still worth doing and evaluators may be inclined to support a proposal on that basis alone. An unrealistic story, on the other hand, is far easier to recognize as such, and therefore the use of stories carries less risk of an unwarranted positive evaluation. With stories, the reviewing executives still have to do their job of challenging faulty logic. The narrative strategic plan must be compelling or it will be rejected.

3. 'As General Manager of this business unit, I don't have time to lead the planning process, so I delegate this to one of my staff. He or she collects what the functional heads plan to do and puts it together as our plan. I make comments and approve.'

   My response is: No one else in the business unit has the budget, the contacts and position to gather the intelligence from the marketplace leaders as to how you can make the most meaningful contributions to your customers and the industry. The leader must have foresight into the future, and should solicit contributions from her or his staff to aid in evaluating ideas. A staff planner is not in the same position to lead, and seldom has the experience that is necessary. What can the General Managers do with their time that is more important than leading their teams into the future? In my experience, not wanting to take the time to write the future story indicates a lack of foresight as to how the business can win.

DREAMING WITH YOUR EYES OPEN

'The Chinese dared to dream and outlasted the Romans, Persians, Maya and Ethiopians' (Boethius, Italy, AD 524).

We dream, not in bullet points, but in narratives. A story and a strategic plan have a lot in common. Box 11.1 shows how I construct a story from its basic components (for example, situation, purpose, conflict, plot, and climax). It also shows the outline of how I see its analog in a business plan. In constructing a story or a plan, I first set the scene. I make certain that the characters, the situation, past events of significance, relationships, trends or changes in

Box 11.1. Analogs between stories and strategic business plans

Novel or story analogy	Strategic business plan analogy
Setting the scene of the story	*Global business situation*
Identify the cast: Who are the characters?	What is the industry? What can it be—industry foresight?
Identify the situation at hand: What is the setting? What has happened before?	Who are the players? Customers, competitors, suppliers, etc.
Establish cast relationships: What are the important personal interactions that will affect the story in the future?	What trends are affecting the business (e.g. power changes, effects of government, technology, customer behavior)?
	What determines winners from losers? Key success factors?
	How global is the business? Where is the action? Where will it be?
Purpose of the story?	*What are the vision and vision objectives?*
The conflict	*The critical issues*
'There is no novel without conflict'	What are the barriers or obstacles to realizing the vision and vision objectives?
The plot	*The strategies and supporting action plans to overcome the critical issues, cross-functional and global*
Development of conflicts and actions to resolve (must be believable)	The main part of the succinct scenario The scheme to win with supporting logic and rationale
The climax	*Winning in the marketplace*
How the conflict is resolved	How sales organization will win and vision be realized

power comparisons, technology, customer processes, preferences, and competition are succinctly and clearly presented.

Next, I identify the objective or purpose of the story. In strategic storytelling, this implies creating the vision or strategic intent and confronting the conflicts involved. I argue that all stories must have conflict. Thus, in my view, business plans must accurately reveal any barriers to reaching the desired end-state. The end-state in this case is the vision of significant new contributions the company can make to its industry customers. I refer to these barriers as 'critical issues'. In most plans I have critiqued, instead of defining the real barriers, the critical issues are incorrectly defined as (1) important things that must be done, (2) failure to achieve objectives (not earning 25 percent ROI), or (3) symptoms.

Strategies must be developed that alter your strength relative to your competitors. This involves considering either your customers' current key success factors, or new success factors you can establish for them. Strategies must address critical issues or obstacles. One example would be if you were operating a narrow product line, while customers were looking for a total system solution. The narrow product line is a barrier or obstacle (in a novel it would be one of the conflicts) and could, for example, be overcome by a strategy of partnering, a joint venture, purchasing technology, or acquisitions.

Next, I include the events necessary for implementing strategies and resolving conflicts. This involves individual battles that occur as part of the campaign to win. A saga of heroic effort and sacrifice is told in this part of the story. This saga highlights the efficient use of resources, including both material and human capital.

I then complete the strategic story with the climax. I describe how the objective will be gained and how it will provide major new benefits to existing and new customers, as well as the rewards I expect for the company. By rewards I mean the financial results from accomplishing the vision and reaching the end-state through a well-thought-out scenario or story.

In strategic planning, not all stories are equally productive. The narrative format will not overcome poor content or faulty logic. In other words, the media is not the message. Stories can have a good or bad purpose. For example, two very talented storytellers were Sir Winston Churchill and Adolf Hitler. Stories can also have a positive or negative 'spin', as is often found in politics. You can feel worse after hearing the story. Weak or bad stories have poor schemes. They are not compelling. These stories are not productive because they do not result in excellence in implementation, and the scenario is flawed, resulting in end-results not being attained. Good stories keep listeners interested by being to the point rather than impressing people about what you know. The audience should be able to understand at all times just how each activity or 'chapter' fits within the plot.

STRATEGIC THINKING IMPLICATIONS

Narratives allow each of the contributors to more clearly explain the assumptions that they are making in their portion of the plan. This facilitates discussion and debate as the plan is constructed.

Cause and effect are a necessary part of a story in order to ensure a good logical outcome. Thus, strategic stories require more rigor: (1) in defining the Key Success Factors of the industry; (2) in clearly establishing the purpose of the plan or vision; (3) in correctly stating the critical issues of, or obstacles to, the vision; and (4) in reducing the situation analysis down to those facts that are necessary for setting the scene and for supporting the rationale of the strategies and action plans. Many strategic plans spend too much time showing how much we know about the industry but not enough about how we can change the future. A narrative brings to life the campaign necessary to accomplish the strategic intent and explains how the 'dream can be turned into reality' (in the words of Hamel and Prahalad 1994).

A list of core competencies and the competencies needed for the future are not compelling unless they fit into the winning story as clearly explained steps necessary for building competitive advantage and 'making the world a better place'. Thus the use of strategic stories is, in my experience, the key to the thinking required for the preparation of useful strategic plans. This use of a strategic story as an analog for a business plan within 3M is illustrated by a test case recounted in the next section.

3M Telecom Systems Division Strategic Story

Setting the Scene: Global Business Situation

This is an abbreviated version of the real plan with changes made to conceal confidential information. It is not an ideal plan model but an example of a real world strategic narrative—the first one attempted by this particular business unit.

The reality of today's global markets is intense competition, unprecedented turbulence, and, for many industry leaders, troubles with growth. This is not so for the telecommunications industry, which is growing at 15 percent each year in a market worth over US\$ 600 billion. This market is dominated by giants such as Lucent, Alcatel, Siemens, Nortel, and Cisco, with each offering a full array of communications equipment.

The World Trade Organization's 1997 Agreement on Tariffs and Trade in Telecommunications meant liberalization, and the introduction of competition in more than seventy countries. Then came a flurry of takeovers, mergers, and alliances in both service and equipment providers. To add to this, the 1990s saw the explosion of a new kind of telephony: the mobile phone. Finally, the shock wave from the increase in data traffic that overtook voice traffic in volume during 1999 was driven by the phenomenal growth of the Internet.

The Telecom Systems Division is faced with an aging portfolio of products. It needs to decide where to make new contributions to this fast-changing industry. From 1997 to 1999, through scenario planning, it identified robust customer needs.

One of these is in the premises network equipment market, which is growing by over 18 percent per year and is US$ 120 billion in size. End-users are seizing on the power of linked computer work groups as the key to business efficiency. File sharing and e-mail are today's applications, though there is a move towards next-generation solutions of converged voice, video, and data networks combined on single lines through Internet Protocol (IP) telephony.

Traditionally, 95 percent of global premises equipment, both active and passive, has been wires and systems built out of copper. Though copper systems have made considerable advances in signaling speeds, their limit as we move towards multi-application users in an IP environment becomes clear.

Purpose of the Story: Vision and Vision Objectives

The strategic vision of the 3M Telecom Systems Division is to provide a simple, complete, active and passive low-cost system for fiber-to-the-desk (FTTD). This will result in virtually unlimited bandwidth, 2–5 gigabits, and will provide 'future proofing' for the regular rewiring experienced in copper system. This represents success in this industry, meaning increased bandwidth at minimum cost without sacrificing reliability. It prepares the industry for IP telephony.

The Conflict: Critical Issues or Obstacles

Soon after identifying new robust customer needs through a 'Future First' planning exercise, it became obvious that this new market for the Telecom Systems Division will require different skill sets, both technical and marketing. 'Hiring as usual' was not going to meet the special global needs for new talent. New and technically superior products will require experienced and talented new employees.

We do not have the complete set of products to meet our vision. We also need to develop additional line extension systems so we can serve not only the premises market but also campus and metropolitan networks.

The competition from Lucent, AMP, Siecor, Cisco, etc., is intense and they have literally thousands of people deployed. Although our position will be unique and we offer greater benefits to the customer, we do not have a scheme for communicating our position that counters the defensive ploys that our competitors can be expected to use.

The Plot: Strategies and Action Plans

Now that we have established our vision, we must include human resources in our planning sessions, so they can strengthen our technical and marketing staffs to the degree necessary for aggressive sales growth over the next 5+ years. Human Resources will be communicating opportunities for experienced telecommunications personnel within both customer and competitor organizations.

Over 120 new employees will be hired worldwide, utilizing trade publications and industry shows, which provide the best means of reaching the appropriate candidates. We expect this to take one year. With the assistance of Alpha-Omega, a telecommunications consulting firm, we are preparing for technical service, central research, sales and marketing management as well as sales training to develop the necessary orientation. Training is to be completed by the 2nd Quarter of 2000. Each functional area has developed a narrative to show how the activity will be successfully implemented.

R&D has developed the Volition^{TM} system[1] to meet the definition specified in the division strategic intent. Industry experts have been involved in the process and will continue to contribute information about this new market as we expand the total system. Contacts have already been made, and discussions continue with alliance partners, OEMs, and suppliers who can help us supply complete solutions rather than discrete components. Our end-user solution will be less than half the cost of the competition's offerings. These complete systems will anticipate the convergence of voice, data, and optical transport, as well as provide solutions that lower bandwidth costs by reducing labor costs. Once the Volition system is ready for market, our staff manufacturing department will start working on ways to reduce manufacturing costs in order to keep the system competitive and profitable. Cost accounting and distribution management will contribute to this activity. Even with the right people, highest value product, and product availability, there is a challenge in moving towards unique solutions for bandwidth capacity.

Our marketing communication, sales, training, and technical service efforts must be aggressive and effective in a market dominated by larger competitors with larger staffs. The use of narratives in our strategic plans has driven us to become a more process-centered organization. All four process centers will be involved in the success of commercialization:

1. Global Business Strategy and Leadership;
2. Global Process for Commercialization;
3. Global Customer Relationship Management;
4. Global Supply Chain Management.

Our change from functional reporting to process-centered reporting will ensure strong cross-functional teamwork.

A strong brand (Volition) will be used for our current and future group of products. Communications will develop an aggressive plan and audit the results. A broad range of activities will support the establishment of the Volition brand within the industry as a whole. A strong brand will aid in our selling, OEM endorsement, approval by standard bodies, alliances, acquisitions, and supplier arrangements. This will benefit many of the process centers' activities. This is 3M Innovation at work. Direct mail to the multiple buying influences of this industry will be timed so as to precede the high level sales calls. Third-party examples will be used with real world economic benefits included.

In conclusion, our sales representatives have never been better prepared to succeed with a totally new product system as with Volition. The decision process is slow, due to the size of the investments, but we expect a high percentage of campaigns will result in success because we offer strong technical and financial advantages to our customers, delivered by a sound technical and sales staff.

CORPORATE STORYTELLING AND ORGANIZATIONAL STRUCTURE

As demonstrated in the business plan above, storytelling can overcome problems of organizational structure by gaining the cooperation and involvement of the various functional areas of the company. A good strategic story ensures that they are focused on achieving sales success—not just functional improvement. A clear plan explained as a narrative reduces the parochial outlook of the various functional departments, just as a clear military campaign gains cooperation from the Army, Navy, and Air Force. Either the functional heads support the scenario or the organizational reporting relationships are changed so that the necessary cross-functional teamwork is achieved.

At 3M, some of the business units have found that using narratives about how you will win has encouraged them to move from a functional reporting structure to a more process-centered approach. A process-centered organization, as mentioned in the strategic story of the 3M Telecom Systems Division, also supports 3M's new organizational change from sectors and business groups to market centers.

This not only results in better teaming within the business unit, such as among R & D, Marketing, Technical Service, and Sales, in testing and introducing new products, but also results in contributions from staff departments, regardless of to whom they report, including corporate departments such as Human Resources, Environmental Engineering, Staff Manufacturing, Purchasing, Corporate R & D, Cost Accounting, and so on. When you are writing a story about the future where you are working to change the strength of your company relative to competitors, the staff departments must feel they are a genuinely responsible part of the team that will help win customers. They must write their part of the story where they have expertise and be included in the meetings or campfires where the future is discussed. Storytelling helps keep organizational structure from interfering either with the acceptance of the plan or with the exceptional performance and sacrifice that will be necessary to achieve the goals of the plan.

WHO TELLS THE STORY TO WHOM?

In strategic planning, the 'cast' of the story writes the 'how and why' of the story along with the General Manager, who leads the process and provides the 'what' and the 'when'. Then they tell the story to each other. The 'key characters' of the strategic story then tell the story to Executive Management, or perhaps the leader tells the story alone. Telling the story to Executive Management helps the executives test the logic of the plan and how likely it will be to accomplish. Executives are able to judge how believable the plan for winning is, and to offer suggestions to make it more acceptable, or else to reject it as not convincing. The presenters demonstrate the 'buy in' and commitment of the leader and management team. The significance of the contributions to the industry is easier to assess, and the forecasts of sales and profits—the rewards—are easier to justify. The executives can thus more easily become supporters of the investments required for the plan.

Parts of the story are shared with outside partners, such as suppliers, co-developers, distribution, regulatory agencies, and potential customers. Also, parts of the story can be shared with stock analysts to make the financial forecasts of the company more believable and memorable. Also, a strategic story can make future financial returns, three to five years from now, more acceptable, since the need for the present investment is more easily understood and the pay-off seems less risky or vague. Any changes in the story as the plan progresses are more logical and acceptable, rather than unexpected surprises from a plan they never really understood in the first place.

I have been told by some General Managers that they should perhaps write one plan to present to Executive Management and a different one to be given to their employees, since the employees did not seem to grasp the plan that had just been presented to and approved by the Executive Review Team. I assured them that one plan should be appropriate for both audiences, and that the Executive Review Team did not understand the plan either—they just did not want to admit it.

Finally, past stories are useful in writing new stories for the future since the lessons of the past are clearer and more insightful than an outline plan of improvement activities.

INTERNAL/EXTERNAL IMPLICATIONS OF STRATEGIC STORYTELLING

Given that strategic storytelling is accepted as a means to communicate for the corporation, what is its significance in corporate internal and external communications?

Within the organization, stories bring about more enthusiasm from the members. They can see their role more clearly in the future and understand the reasons for sacrifice and the importance of their contributions. Cross-functional teaming flows more naturally from the story, as the necessary sequence of events is identified and the importance emphasized for reaching the end-states of the plan or activity. Also, it is easier to gain internal buy-in from a larger group of contributors, since they contribute to writing 'the script'.

Stories are the most effective way of orienting new employees to the company culture. The new employees can be new hires or employees from a recent acquisition who need to be integrated into the parent core.

Agreement from Executive Management increases as they become more certain that the outcome is possible, and the means plausible and worthy of support. The risk to any individual of supporting the plan is reduced because good stories are more believable. The executive group becomes more like mentors rather than only critics—the parenting concept of Campbell and Goold (1998).

External implications of stories include the increased confidence in the success of the business unit by suppliers, distributors, customers, and other companies that may be partners in the story. A more believable and clear vision of the future can be a very persuasive means of gaining this support from others, since everyone likes to take part in a significant success. This leads us to the investment community. Financial analysts respond to strategic stories that are more completely explained using solid rationale and logic. It provides the material for them to use to convince others.

Stories are utilized to prepare sales reps in their presentations to potential new customers. This fits very well with role-playing sales training designed to prepare sales personnel for typical customer questions and objections. Word pictures are painted of how the product can be utilized and what its benefits are.

HOW DO YOU FIND YOUR STORY?

No one can tell you how to find your story—certainly not as part of a chapter in a book. You can read the stories of successful entrepreneurs as to how they established their companies, but all stories are unique. Bill Gates cannot tell you how to write a story that will lead you to be as successful as he has been. There are, however, some preconditions that are important for beginning the process.

1. It is necessary to know your customers and industry very well. New general managers to a business area find it harder to write a story about the future. They do not know the story of the past and have not had the time to talk with forward-thinking industry members. Spending enough time in external discussions is most important for new-to-industry leaders, but the temptation is to try to fix all the internal problems of the company. The dilemma that results is that the new leader rejects the old story she or he inherited, but is not prepared to adequately provide a better replacement.

2. Not 'casting a large enough net' to gather participants into the writing of the story content can limit both the quality of the story and the support of those who must help implement it. I like to have everyone sitting in a big circle with a hidden video camera to record the ideas. Use lots of flip charts, even sketches, to keep everyone together.

3. It is very important to have identified your strategic intent or vision before you discuss action plans. Include your core competencies, new technology ideas, and your 'sacred bundle' (past success stories), as well as external insights into customer needs that have significant value. Look for your purpose from both internal and external perspectives. You need to establish your purpose first, as you would for a novel.

4. Keep the leader leading. She or he cannot be drawn away because of other important matters. She or he must be the ultimate author of the story.

5. Set the ambiance in the meeting so that everyone is comfortable and eager to contribute. Do not let a few people dominate the discussion. There must be collective excitement that keeps focusing on a sequence of events leading to a meaningful result.

6. If the story does not seem to be developing and results only in discussions of what is wrong with the business unit, someone, preferably the leader, should start telling a story of the future so that others can add to or correct it. Everyone should be encouraged to envision the future and how the organization will reach it.

BUSINESS RELEVANCE OF STORIES

Within 3M, some stories of how new innovations came about and what lessons were learned in the process were published internally for 3M in 1998 as *Innovation Chronicles* (Shaw 1998). One of the lessons passed on from the past is how R & D inventors kept their new product ideas alive, even when told to discontinue the programs. The Life Sciences part of 3M began that way. Lew

Lehr, past CEO and Chairman of 3M, kept his surgical drapes product alive, even after being told to drop the product.

During 1999 all 3M business units prepared their strategic business plans as strategic narratives. It allowed them to get to the issues quickly, to really think out what must happen over the next 5+ years, and to determine what resources will be needed. In the past, the plans had included numerous tables and charts that resulted in very lengthy documents of facts not utilized to support the winning scenario. Now the plans were much more succinct and to the point, describing how the business unit will win by providing superior value to the marketplace.

When Robert Brullo of 3M proposed a joint venture between 3M and Hoechst, he used a story or narrative to sell his vision of the future. After the successful joint venture (JV) was put in place, he used the stories to communicate the business plans to the JV team, which included members from both companies. Subsequently, an additional JV was approved using the narrative format. Since 1998 Dyneon, the successful JV company, has continued to use strategic stories in planning its future. Robert was able to persuade both 3M and Hoechst executives that his plans for the future were realistic in the sophisticated business of high-performance chemical products. Both 3M internal management and external Hoechst partners were comfortable with the strategic story of the future. Robert Brullo, the President of Dyneon, believes it would have been much more difficult to gain acceptance of his plan without the use of the narrative.

IN CONCLUSION

In a knowledge-led world, the winners of tomorrow will be those organizations that invest most effectively in their intellectual capital. As companies become more global, that intellectual capital content must become globally aligned—all must understand and support with their hearts as well as their minds.

Using the narrative is a formidable discipline for communicating clearly and logically. In a speech given during 1995, Roger Rosenblat stated, 'stories are effective in communication at all levels—not everyone is patient enough for stories. Too bad.' Storytelling is the single most powerful form of human communication. Stories allow a person to feel and see information, as well as factually to understand it. The events come alive for the listeners so that they 'see' with you and become physically and mentally involved in the story.

Storytelling allows you to create a shared vision of the future. As Howard Gardner (1995: 43) has stated so well in his book *Leading Minds*, 'it is stories of identity-narratives, that help individuals think about and feel who they are, where they come from and where they are headed—that constitute the single most powerful weapon in the leader's literary arsenal'.

The truly expressive organization will make use of this most powerful, ancient weapon. The potential leverage in conceptualizing, communicating, and motivating through the use of strategic stories (both inside and outside of the enterprise) will define superior management in the future.

NOTE

1 Volition™ is a registered trademark of the 3M Company.

REFERENCES

Campbell, A., and Goold, M. (1998), *Synergy* (Oxford: Capstone Publishing Ltd.).

Gardner, H. (1995), *Leading Minds* (New York: Basic Books, Harper Collins).

Hamel, G., and Prahalad, C. K. (1994), *Competing for the Future* (Boston: Harvard Business School Press).

Rosenblat, R. (1995), 'The Power of Stories', speech given at the Masters Forum, University of Minnesota, Minneapolis.

Shaw, G. (1998), *Innovation Chronicles* (Minneapolis: 3M).

12

Managing the Corporate Story

Mogens Holten Larsen

Managers are increasingly broadening their perspective from the strictly ratio-nal, to include more emotional and imaginative aspects of doing business. In my opinion, one of the most important implications of this shift is the poten-tial for ownership of words and images in the minds of stakeholders. Ownership of words and images relates to those (often emotional) associa-tions that occur in one's mind when a company name is mentioned. Associations that are meaningful and relate to long-term corporate strategy create differentiation of the organization from its competitors in the eyes of its customers and a sense of belonging for employees and other constituencies.

THE OWNERSHIP OF WORDS AND IMAGES

'Owning' words or images in the minds of stakeholders represents a new type of capital that differs from the traditional physical capital or market value of the organization. The economic value of this new type of capital is indicated by developments such as Standard and Poors's inclusion of corporate image in their rating evaluation formula, in which they give image a factor of 15 per-cent. It is my thesis that this type of capital is created in part by individuals responding to their emotions, interpretations, and images of organizations. These responses, interpretations, and images are constructed when corporate stories are encountered. In effect, the corporate story is boiled down to a few words that create meaningful images. These words or associations become the 'property' of the organization and can then be capitalized upon.

THE CORE CORPORATE STORY

A corporate story is a comprehensive narrative about the whole organization, its origins, its vision, its mission. However, the emotionally formulated core story is much more than just a vision or a mission statement. By incorporating elements such as competencies, fundamental beliefs, and values, it mirrors something deep within the organization and provides a simple yet effective framework guiding the organization in all its actions. An effective corporate story combines creative as well as strategic thinking and provides a common thread that can then run through all the employees' everyday activities no matter how fragmented they are (Holten Larsen and Schultz 1998). This corporate story should be only a few pages long but needs to be broad and deep enough to guide everyone's behavior in relation to the organization. Well formulated, such a story makes it easier for stakeholders to align everything that an organization is, does, or says—and the way they do it.

The origin of the organization, its vision and mission, the competencies, fundamental beliefs, and values, are all, together with those words and images owned by the organization, important parts of the post-industrial or post-information-age company's strategic platform (Kanter 1989; Hamel and Prahalad 1994; Collins and Porras 1998; Jensen 1999). These emerging organizations express themselves in all actions, internal as well as external, factual as well as imaginative. To guide these expressions and to link them to the strategic position of the organization, as illustrated in Fig. 12.1, the organization can benefit from the use of the core corporate story concept.

A story can be a powerful tool for differentiating an organization, its products, and its services. In a few years, this may even become the primary vehicle for differentiation. An organization that utilizes a legitimate reputation to explain in simple yet meaningful terms where it is going, what contributions it will make to society, and how it will continue to create value for all its stakeholders will hold a strong strategic position. Such a position will indeed affect market share, provided a uniform core story is expressed through all organizational actions.

In this chapter I use as an example the case of Astra Denmark. Founded in 1948, Astra Denmark became a subsidiary of Astra, the international pharmaceutical company (now AstraZeneca) in 1970. Astra Denmark operates both in the business-to-business as well as the business-to-consumer markets, selling to end-users as well as to general practitioners, specialists, and pharmacies. When Bergsøe 4, my communications consulting company, began working in the 1990s with organizational vision, mission, identity, and reputation as means for creating product differentiation, Astra was our first client. The management accepted a 'full-scale' redefinition of Astra, using a very early version of our corporate story method (Holten Larsen 1996). I have chosen to refer to this case here because it represents one of the few companies I have known that has measured its progress in qualitative terms over a long period of time.

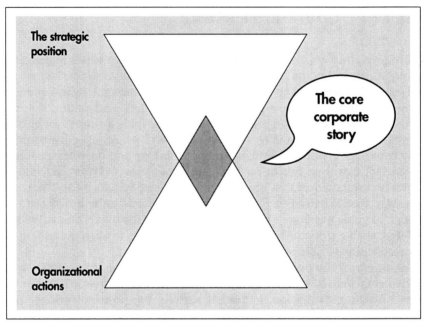

Fig. 12.1. Strategic use of the core corporate story concept

Other clients, with whom we have developed corporate stories over the past few years, have not yet collected sufficient data to allow for the analysis of any significant statistical trend.

In the case of Astra, the process involved the top management team. The core corporate story underwent a process whereby it was eventually directed towards both internal and external stakeholders. However, while core elements were presented to all audiences, specific qualitative goals, internal politics, and certain values remained internal and confidential. As the contour of the story then developed, the need to communicate it externally rose. Translating the story into communication channels, such as corporate story brochures, corporate advertising, and product advertising, led to a condensation of the story. In the case of Astra, the corporate story was boiled down to the phrase 'knowledge heals', implying that knowledge is a better medicine than pills as a means to improve the health of society. Before this, Astra had mainly measured its success in terms of product sales.

Astra now began using its corporate story to communicate that it no longer simply sold pharmaceutical products. Word was being spread that it was incorporating health-education services alongside sales of its traditional product line. Thus, since the advantages of selling on a strict product advantage basis were diminishing anyway, Astra began educating the professional market on a general therapy basis. Utilizing the Astra story made it easier for the organization to identify and focus on activities that were most important to implementing its vision of being seen as the number 1 educator in the phar-maceutical market. This new emphasis soon created very positive attitudes among important stakeholders, which Astra in turn was able to measure. The 'knowledge-heals' story appeared to be directly related to a significant increase in overall positive perceptions of the company. Within four years Astra was ranked among the top pharmaceutical companies in the Danish market.

MANAGERIAL PROCESSES INVOLVED IN DEVELOPING THE CORPORATE STORY

The process involved in creating a corporate story can potentially lead to radi-cal changes in many traditional procedures and routines, resulting in the transgression of entrenched organizational territories, and creating new frameworks for managing and organizing. An organization's ability to express itself through storytelling and reach its internal and external stakeholders in a cost-efficient manner depends on the clarity and coherence of the company vision, identity, and mission, and on an accurate reflection of its reputation. Thus, part of the challenge for management will be to clarify what the specific story content should be, and to understand how this should enhance the orga-nization's ability to communicate and create value. The distances between the four elements visualized in Fig. 12.2 may indicate the level of diversity in the organization, and point out areas requiring improvement. If the fit between the four circles is too loose, this means that the distance is too great or does not match, meaning it would be very difficult to create a strong and coherent story that will differentiate from the rest of the market. The more accurate the fit, and the better and clearer the story, the easier it will be to attract employ-ees, customers, and capital.

Translating strategic position through the corporate story into practice requires a number of managerial processes: organizing as communication, setting the stage, valuing human resources, and symbolic management. The arrows in Fig. 12.2 represent these important managerial processes for devel-oping and communicating the corporate story.

Organizing as Communication

As the number of people communicating the story of an organization increases, as the variety of communication issues expand, and as the number and diversity of stakeholders increase, aligning internal and external commu-nication becomes a senior management challenge. With storytelling, organi-zational communication is no longer equivalent to mediating a message professionally—it becomes the framework for combining strategy, organizing,

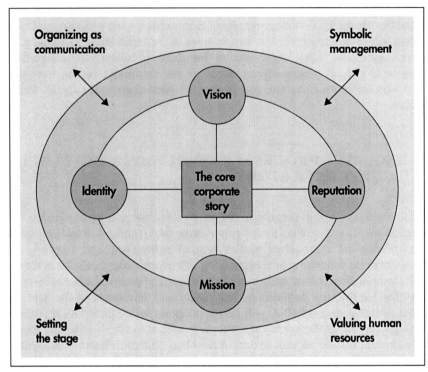

Fig. 12.2. Managerial processes for developing and communicating the corporate story

and marketing. The various forms of expression an organization incorporates to tell who it is and what it represents include everything from planned communication activities, such as name, logo, design, home page, advertising campaigns, and public relations activities (Bernstein 1984), to spontaneous and situational actions performed by management or other members of the organization. If these different types of messages lack alignment, it may be profoundly damaging to the perceived legitimacy and credibility of the organization's reputation.

Management combines the internal and external perspective of the organization's purpose, communicating to the market in order to create external images for internal purposes, thus accelerating strategic processes. This methodology is called auto communication and indicates that communication is too important an issue to be left to a product manager alone.

The aligning activities performed by Astra (Holten Larsen 1996) resulted in a rise in perceived quality of information from 48 percent in 1991 to 86 percent in 1995, and a perception of educational activities that complemented the knowledge of doctors, from 44 percent in 1990 to 82 percent in 1995. Astra increased the number of congresses and in-house session for doctors, shifting perceptions of the quality of their congresses from 47 percent in 1990 to 94 percent in 1995.

The corporate story-influenced perception of organizational core processes has shifted the emphasis from 'organizing around production' to 'organizing along the lines of communication'. The perception that the corporate story must revolve around organizational core processes is changing in favor of organizing along the lines of communication. This challenges organizational competencies. How do you learn to be a fabulous storyteller? How do you actually present an organization's reality? How do you optimize efforts in relation to communication rather than production?

Storytelling organizations are based, I argue, on the development of these new competencies among individual employees, who will learn to cross established professional boundaries, disciplines, and functions, and who are capable of interpreting and applying organizational stories to their own situations, making decentralized decisions, while still expressing a unified message.

This implies far more than simply establishing a unit that incorporates all communicating activities. For most companies, I argue, one of the first steps in organizing for communication will be to develop coherence in the application of the corporate story across differing functions and types of work. In functionally divided organizations, 'ownership' of external messages typically belongs to sales, marketing, and possibly public relations, while internal messages are typically the responsibility of human resources, training, and information functions. But, in many cases, nobody is responsible for cross couplings between, for example, human resources and marketing. Any inconsistency between various messages communicated by the organization will be enhanced by the fact that employees in human resources and marketing typically have different educational backgrounds, as well as different styles and professional frames of reference. This reinforces the creation and maintenance of various organizational subcultures, and adds to further potential differentiation in the interpretation and application of organizational storytelling. The result is confusing, not only to external stakeholders, but also to employees in particular.

It may, therefore, become necessary to break away from a functional organization structure or stiff matrix organization, making it possible to express the same core message, yet independent from influences by department boundaries, business areas, permanent teams, or well-established professional cultures. The risk of becoming a hyper-flexible spaghetti organization without identity as a consequence is obvious; therefore it is imperative to create rock-solid consistency in some of the other professional areas of an organization. Whereas products are adaptable for optimization within a global frame of reference, messages and expressions, in my opinion, need to be consistent across organizational boundaries. Communication processes should become centralized, while other tasks become simultaneously decentralized.

Setting the Stage

Stage setting involves how the organization itself becomes a platform from which the story can unfold. This refers to the 'look and feel' of the organization, with symbols and artefacts becoming more important communication tools, particularly relating to sense and emotion. Symbols and artifacts include everything from the buildings, offices, reception areas, and retail outlets to colors, logo, other symbols, and visual identity programs (Olins 1989). In setting the stage for the organization to unfold, managers should be aware of the reputational interpretations of rituals, and seek therefore to nurture those that are coherent with the core story. The look and feel of the organization determines which part of the culture to emphasize. This part of the identity complex has to be described in a way that enables it to be transplanted into all corporate activities, so that even advertising and personnel policies have the same specific look and feel.

One of the major activities involved in implementing the Astra 'knowledge-heals' story was the building of a mini-university at the company location, creating a meeting place for professionals in the industry.

Valuing Human Resources

Psychologically, people invest energy and commitment in tasks for which they are assessed. By the end of the 1990s most reward criteria were based on volume, using production and sales logic, such as market share, products sold, and number of customer contracts, the aggregated volume of which adds to the bottom line. The training traditionally offered employees supports this focus by strengthening their formal and professional competencies.

In expressive organizations, management and employees will still be assessed based on energy and commitment invested in financial tasks. However, personal reward and career opportunities are achieved based on a broader set of criteria, first among which is the ability to contribute to the development and clarification of the corporate story. The wide use of share options and the like stresses the shareholder perspective, which can result in the loss of profile and reputation, since the organization will then tend to ignore long-term, more imaginative aspects of company success. But in more and more cases the price label on a company is being connected to the perception of the corporate story which in turns reflects identity, vision, mission, and reputation. Reward systems, as a consequence, should focus on these areas as well. Thus, remuneration criteria will include abilities to:

1. communicate the corporate story to employees, colleagues, customers, and partners;
2. guide the organization in how to make unifying contributions to the corporate story;

3. contribute to the perceived internal and external trustworthiness of an organization through consistent manifestations of organizational values and attitudes.

If management only introduces change in some of the areas described in the model above, but keeps the old remuneration system, the organization will become frustrated, resulting in ineffectiveness.

Even though Astra introduced a totally different core story, its internal evaluation and reward system remained focused on financial and traditional sales performance. As a result, the focus on improving reputation eventually declined, right at the very moment that the perceived positive reputation of Astra had achieved a very high level. From this point, its reputation began to suffer, narrowing any differentiation from competitors, as traditional sales thinking continued to be rewarded.

Symbolic Management

The best leaders are the best communicators. They present employees with a consistent, forcefully told story that everyone can understand, accept, and act upon (Champy 1995). Using communication strategically across traditional functional and perceived boundaries, individual managers act as both symbols and organizational storytellers. For many managers, their careers have involved developing traditional competencies, mirroring the logic of the late-industrial 'truth' about how to create value. Post-industrial organizations create emotional bonds and messages attracting and maintaining managers, employees, and network partners, while at the same time introducing higher quality, and improving processes and technologies that save costs and time, benefiting short-term shareholder value. From being aloof problem-solvers with calculated general knowledge, managers will need the ability to enter into dialogue, developing empathy and other relevant talents needed for clarifying and linking values and objectives. Thus, storytelling and individual commitment become at least as important to the managerial role as general financial and strategic knowledge. This will challenge manager ability to create attractive images and emotional messages or stories for the numerous internal and external stakeholders, and to develop the effectiveness and communicative abilities of individual employees. In combination, this will help intensify emotional commitment to the organization.

However, it is often the case when management itself undertakes long periods of challenging strategic development, and this includes Astra, that the managers convince themselves that the organization will somehow simply accept and understand the depth of implications after a brief exposure to the new ideas. They ignore the fact that everybody in the organization will have to re-explore parts of the strategic process involving the core story in order to implement it on a local basis. The importance of the role of management in helping the entire organization understand and be able to implement the story cannot be exaggerated.

Organizations are becoming more open, frequently out of necessity. They are becoming more decentralized, with responsibilities being pushed downwards. Employees are in a position to be selective about their place of work, and do so based on company values as well as traditional financial rewards. Because of this, new managerial roles are in demand. By personally symbolizing, expressing, and demonstrating the corporate story, management can create meaning as it strives to manifest the desired specific nature of the organization. By thus guiding communication efforts involving organizational values and stakeholders, management can help create value.

COMMUNICATING THE CORPORATE STORY: MANAGERIAL DILEMMAS

The managing processes and management qualifications related to the areas of 'organizing as communication', 'valuing human resources', 'setting the stage' and 'symbolic management', focus on a number of very different and as yet unaccustomed management issues. The biggest obstacle to introducing a successful core corporate story strategy is the frequent unwillingness to throw away the old, generally accepted, 'tried-and-true' logic and methods in favor of new ways (Peters 1997). A wholehearted expressive turnaround demands the alignment of all organizational activities, and this includes the attitudes and behaviors of managers.

Some of the managerial tasks described above may conflict with established norms or traditional career training. These include:

1. finding and defining the core story, and then focusing organization activities into those areas that correlate with the core purpose of the firm;
2. creating clarity and coherence in company storytelling;
3. unifying internal and external activities by creating a common voice;
4. telling and visualizing the story and helping the organization do the same;
5. creating value by owning words and images;
6. guiding internally using external communication;
7. making the organization flexible in relation to products but more rigid in relation to the corporate story;
8. optimizing organizational processes in relation to communication rather than production;
9. setting the scene, but then allowing the organization to become the scene;
10. creating touch, look, and feel;
11. prioritizing communication efficiency by combining strategy, organizing, and marketing.

All of these topics are interrelated, painting the contours of required new management capabilities. Many personal characteristics that bred success using the old logic will not necessarily work in expressive organizations. Rational qualifications will probably still be in high demand and will continue to be taught, but how do you learn to be a fabulous storyteller and a symbol of the corporate story? And how do you balance the three?

The ideas of the storytelling organization and its implications for managers in regard to organizing, leadership, and communication thus present a series of managerial dilemmas including the dilemmas of choice, authenticity, belief, self-disclosure, simplicity, and value.

The Dilemma of Choice: To Exclude in Order to Strengthen the Core

What is the core story of the organization? What is the *raison d'être* today, and what will it be in the future? Which values and images characterize vision and mission? Answering questions like these requires experience with maintaining a dialogue and using the imagination. It also requires the ability to understand and synthesize different personal and professional views, along with a willingness to exclude ideas, activities, and attitudes that do not correspond. It also requires self-reflection and a willingness to make selections and priorities for the purpose of pursuing and sustaining the core story.

In organizations, making choices has been tied to professional competence, as well as to technical and financial rationality. In the past, planning procedures, budgets, business objectives, and closed boardrooms have set the criteria for choice. At the turn of the century, decision-making also requires taking into account attitudes, emotions, intuition, and the ability to interpret the changing feelings and attitudes of multiple stakeholders.

The Dilemma of Authenticity: Simultaneously be Yourself and be a Symbol of the Company

Stakeholders utilize the attitudes and actions of management as a kind of litmus test of an organization's trustworthiness, determining what the organization actually represents, as opposed to believing the rosy pictures painted by seductive market schemes. This raises the question of how a manager can be a symbol of the organization and of him or herself at the same time. This dilemma is amplified by the fact that managers are also expected to express the values of their organization through emotions and attitudes. This requires not only insight into the particular organization's culture, but also the ability to master expressions that are associated with the organization. A specific example might be to ask what kind of stereo or television a manager from Bang & Olufsen should own. Should a manager from Disney be a devoted 'family man'? Are Nike managers expected to 'just do it' in sports—or at least look as if they are? Is it possible to have a German as a manager representing British icons like Jaguar and Rolls-Royce?

The Dilemma of Simplicity: To Create Clarity without Losing the Ability to Acknowledge Complexity

One overall concern for stakeholders in an emerging expressive organization will be the dramatic increase in the multiplicity of interpretations of who the expressive organization is and what it is communicating. At the same time, the need for the organization to find a voice of its own will become more important in the search for distinction and visibility in the marketplace. Thus, managers seeking to communicate a set of clear messages will be confronted with a high level of complexity involving stakeholder perceptions and reactions.

The Dilemma of Value: To Create Return on Both Physical and Reputational Capital

If an organization's *raison d'être* is its ability to express itself in simple and distinct terms, while simultaneously being assessed on the basis of its short-term financial return, management will have to successfully survive such an assessment. This will expand future demands on management to create return not only on physical, but on reputational capital as well (Fombrun 1996; 1999). The managerial challenge and emphasis will be to create net corporate story value, and to ensure that existing reputational capital yields a satisfactory return.

CONCLUSION

An expressive organization will push its reputation to the extreme. Becoming expressive will have profound affects on those processes that are to be considered most important to the organization. By focusing on the core corporate story, management will help create a greater awareness of organizational learning and communication processes, as well as embedded capabilities.

The logic of a core corporate story does not merely apply to Astra and the medical sector, but to all sorts of organizations. I have seen results in public as well as private organizations, in big as well as small (Danish scale) operations, and within both business-to-business and business-to-consumer markets. These organizations have yet to invest the patience, time, and personnel resources required to tell their stories fully, using all the managerial processes mentioned above. However, the useful results of working a core corporate story into the organizational reality are, as shown in the Astra case, profound. Using an early version of this story concept has helped the value of the Astra name to increase substantially—including in relation to competitors. Within the pharmaceutical market, Astra now owns the phrase 'knowledge heals', and is associated with the very positive image of a company that offers knowledge along with its products to help implement better treatment. The profound support for Astra among its stakeholders has shown a direct relation to the manner in which the quality of its (non-differentiated) products are perceived.

In conclusion, there are indeed many factors that must be taken into consideration as organizations move towards becoming expressive. Many experienced managers, after a lifetime of experience and training in remaining aloof, will naturally find it difficult to change who and what they are in order to become open, expressive individuals capable of truly demonstrating an organization's emotions and values. Additionally, expressive managers will have to walk a tightrope between maintaining a measure of consistency with regard to the corporate story, while still allowing for any necessary flexibility. This will require a high degree of discernment, where managers themselves must remain flexible in terms of how they maintain a 'stable' story. This will not be an easy task.

REFERENCES

Bernstein, D. (1984), *Company Image and Reality: A Critique of Corporate Communications* (Eastbourne: Holt, Rinehart & Winston).

Champy, J. (1995), *Reengineering Management* (London: Harper Collins).

Collins, J. C., and Porras, J. I. (1998), *Built to Last: Successful Habits of Visionary Companies* (New York: Harper Business).

Fombrun, C. J. (1996), *Reputation: Realizing Value from the Corporate Image* (Boston: Harvard Business School Press).

—— (1999), presentation at the 3rd International Conference on Corporate Identity, Reputation and Competitiveness, San Juan, 7–9 Jan.

Hamel, G., and Prahalad, C. K. (1994), *Competing for the Future* (Boston: Harvard Business School Press).

Holten Larsen, M. (1996), *The Value of a Mission Statement* (Copenhagen, Denmark: Bergsøe 4).

—— and Schultz, M. (1998), *Den Udtryksfulde Virksomhed* (trans. *The Expressive Company*), (Copenhagen, Denmark: Bergsøe 4).

Jensen, R. (1999), *The Dream Society* (New York: McGraw Hill).

Kanter, R. M. (1989), *When Giants Learn to Dance: Mastering the Challenge of Strategy Management, and Careers in the 1990s* (New York: Simon & Schuster).

Olins, W. (1989), *Corporate Identity: Making Business Strategy Visible through Design* (London: Thames & Hudson).

Peters, T. (1997), *The Circle of Innovation* (London: Hodder & Stoughton).`

13

Valuing Expressive Organizations: Intellectual Capital and the Visualization of Value Creation

Jan Mouritsen

Intellectual capital statements, which report on firms' intellectual capital, combine digitization, visualization, and narration to account for organizational value creation. Such statements, which at the beginning of the twentieth century are published only by a limited set of companies, help explain the conditions for future value creation, rather than current financial results. They are difficult pieces of communication, however, because there is no generally accepted accounting formula that can generate an intellectual capital result, as is the case for the financial result in the financial accounting context. That is, there is no set logic behind the digits produced in intellectual capital statements. Regarding the financial accounting statement, this logic is found in generally accepted accounting and auditing principles, which are largely defined in practice by the auditing profession. The intellectual capital statement uses other means to craft a credible, cohesive, and 'true-and-fair' account. These means include sketches and narratives in addition to digits, which not only—to some extent—allow direct, formal analysis, but also facilitate the production of reputation as a category of organizational asset more general than either financial and intellectual capital.[1]

Expressive organizations attempt through various forms of communication to produce reputation or image (Fombrun and Shanley 1990; Fombrun 1996, 1998). Reputation is an effect of various streams of cues, each established in relationships with external 'stakeholders', who often, on the basis of very limited information, construct ideas about firms and their conduct. Reputation is

I wish to acknowledge the very helpful comments provided by my colleagues John Christensen, Per N. Bukh, and Heine Larsen. They are obviously not to blame for any mistakes or omissions. However, their advice has been highly influential in the production of this text.

formed by an ambiguous assemblage of hunches about what firms stand for. It is, therefore, a fragile resource, the management of which is far from trivial (Klein 1997). A 'company's reputation comes from everything the company, its employees and others say about the company, how the company behaves, and the strategies it tries to enact. Stakeholders learn about a company from a variety of sources, some of which are difficult for the company to manage and control' (Saxton 1998: 398). Consequently, there are many predictors of reputation building: accounting performance, market valuation, media visibility, dividend yield, size, charitable contributions, and advertising (Fombrun and Shanley 1990; Riahi-Belkauoi and Pavlik 1992; Fombrun 1996).

Reputation is, however, not easily defined. It is a 'black box' typically measured on its outside in terms of, for example, accounting cues, while its inside is measured in terms of organizational activities that are less visible. Intellectual capital offers one avenue for opening this 'black box'.[2] It is concerned with the mechanisms that mobilize relationships between employees, technologies, processes, and customers. In intellectual capital statements, a firm's immaterial 'hidden values' are presented—in digits, narratives, and sketches—as the interplay between human capital, organizational capital, and customer capital (Edvinsson and Malone 1997; T. A. Stewart 1997; Sveiby 1997). Together, the digits, narratives, and sketches form a 'language' that ties expression directly, albeit in complex ways, to valuing through 'grand stories' of the empowered individual (e.g. Bartlett and Ghoshal 1997), of the coming of the IT and knowledge society (e.g. Reich 1991), and of long-term relations to customers and partners (e.g. Heskett et al. 1997).

This chapter has been organized to investigate how intellectual capital contributes to (re-)producing and creating value for an expressive organization. First, there is a brief definition of intellectual capital, which leads to a section on what 'valuing' is about. Valuing through intellectual capital is argued here to be less concerned with describing and reporting value than it is with creating and fostering value. There is then a section where the whole intellectual capital statement is, perhaps too briefly, analyzed and illustrated to demonstrate that, in addition to the 'conventional' format of digitized financial value reporting, intellectual capital statements also incorporate sketches and stories. This main section, which builds on empirical material from five firms, leads to a discussion that identifies how intellectual capital works as an expressive medium, and how expressive organizations' 'operations' are constituted.

THE VALUE OF INTELLECTUAL CAPITAL

Robert Reich (1991: 105) has identified the contours of the new emerging economy of creativity as follows:

Members of the accounting profession, not otherwise known for their public displays of emotion, have fretted openly about how to inform potential investors of the true worth of enterprises whose value rests in the brains of employees. They have used the term 'goodwill' to signify the ambiguous zone on the corporate balance sheets between the company's tangible assets and the value of its talented people. But as intellectual capital continues to overtake physical capital as the key asset of the corporation, shareholders find themselves on shakier and shakier ground.

Although the reference to the 'brains of employees' is a bit exaggerated, Reich here suggests that value estimations now go increasingly beyond physical, tangible, material assets. To Reich, this is important, because we are on the verge of creating the information and knowledge society, where there seems to be a growing discrepancy between the market values of knowledge-intensive companies and their financial book values. Even if this discrepancy is not to be carried too far in terms of explaining the value of intellectual capital, it has been presented as one indication that the mobilization of immaterial assets via employees, customers, internal routines, and technologies may be a new domain for value creation. Leif Edvinsson (Skandia 1994: 5), Intellectual Capital Director at the Swedish Skandia Insurance Company, and one of the leading pioneers in the area of intellectual capital statements, suggests that intellectual capital be best understood as follows:

The aggregate sum of . . . intangible values can be called Intellectual Capital, which comprises both human capital and structural capital. Human capital represents the knowledge, skills and capability of the individual employee to provide solutions for the customers. Structural capital consists of everything that remains when the employees go home: Databases, customer files, software, manuals, trademarks, organizational structures, and so on—in other words, organizational capability. Customer capital, i.e. the relationships built up with the customers, is a significant part of structural capital. Structural capital can be owned, which is not the case with human capital.

Value creation is an effect of the interplay between human, structural (or organizational), and customer capital. This interplay can only be 'productive' if the linkages between the separate forms of capital are made strong. This requires 'management', because intellectual resources cannot be 'commanded'; they have to be 'motivated' to be productive. In Skandia, through Intellectual Capital Supplements, which are supplements to their annual financial accounting statements, management attempts to make such links durable, credible, and serious via sketches, stories, and digits. Skandia's Intellectual Capital Supplements do not 'measure' intellectual capital; they craft intellectual capital as they help produce and reproduce internal organizational identity (an on-going internal 'we' story) and external corporate reputation (a continuous external 'us' story) through expressive media. To understand how this process of valuing goes on, perhaps a brief discussion is appropriate on what 'valuing expressive organizations' may mean.

'VALUING'

To value—or valuing—is a verb, which shows a process of committing certain organizational traits to digits. It is a process of transforming a version of the firm into a digital format that can 'stand for' and represent it to an audience of 'stakeholders'. In other words, 'valuing' is a means for creating a digitization of certain organizational arrangements. This can be done in at least three ways. One is the financial accounting version, where audited financial accounts constitute a bottom line through the manipulation of the receipts that have been stored in the firm's financial database via double-entry book-keeping procedures. Another one is the finance theory version of value, which assigns cash flows to a firm's future, and then discounts them to the present. The expected future income stream of the firm can be captured in one digit when it is taken back to the present via discounting procedures. Both of these approaches attempt to *describe* the firm's value, although in different ways and on different bases, as will be elaborated on below.

The third approach to 'valuing' suggests that the object of 'valuing' is value creation. It does not assume—as the approaches above do—that the firm already has a value, which only has to be uncovered. 'To value' here means to *create (more) value*, to generate value via the transformation or 'improvement' of corporate routines and practices. Digits in intellectual capital statements do not show the value of intellectual capital; they co-produce value. Let us look a bit more closely at the three forms of 'valuing'.

The Financial Accounting View on Valuing

Value in a financial accounting statement is constructed via the rules of auditing (Power 1997). Here, the production of an accounting value in the balance sheet (as well as in the income statement) is predicated on three principles (Ekelöw 1999). First, the asset has to be separable, and must thus be identifiable as a unique item. Second, it has to be in the control of the firm, which means that the benefits that accrue from the asset are owned by the firm. Third, it has to have a market where its value can be determined. These three conditions make the recognition and auditability of an asset particular. Typically, auditability presupposes that a receipt can be produced for the asset. This makes the recognition of internally generated intellectual capital very difficult. The receipt identifies the asset, shows the controllability of the asset, and indicates a value to be bestowed on the asset. This (purchasing, replacement, or market) value is typically different from its value in use because an asset is only required if it can generate an income that exceeds its investment. Here, the idea of 'valuing' is to accumulate the receipts accruing to a firm according to generally accepted accounting principles. 'Valuing' means assigning digits based primarily on historical costs of acquisition, which will typically reflect the financial benefits that an asset will actually generate for the firm only with difficulty—if at all.

Intellectual capital has little place in such a framework. Intangibles do, however, since they represent an attempt by the accounting community to construct some accounting means for measuring immaterial assets. International Accounting Standard no. 38 (IAS 38) defines an intangible asset as an 'identifiable non-monetary asset without physical substance held for use in the production or supply of goods or services, for rental to others, or for administrative purposes' (for an extended discussion, see Ekelöw 1999). Such identification requires the asset to be separable, and to possess future economic benefits. Otherwise, there must be 'reasonable and supportable assumptions that represent management's best estimate of the set of economic conditions that will exist over the useful life of the asset'. Indeed, certain kinds of training and development may satisfy this criterion. More doubtfully, certain marketing costs, and in some situations, R & D expenses may comply with these rules. However, intangible assets are few and difficult to verify, and thus to audit. Compared to intellectual capital, this is—as will become clearer below—a very restrictive definition of immaterial assets.

The Finance View on Valuing

In finance theory, valuing is a matter of predicting the future cash flows of the firm. These are the elements of shareholder value (Rappaport 1986), or even the quest for value itself (B. G. Stewart 1991). Here, 'valuing' means defining and assigning weights to expected cash flows so that each element of cash is discounted by a risk-adjusted required rate of return to create one bottom-line indicator for value. Therefore, value is a trait of the firm, which has to be mobilized by forecasts of its future performance. The production of this value is an analysis of the financial flows of the firm as financial ratios, flows of investments, movements in productivity levels, and the more general in- and outflows of capital. The model being investigated is constructed around both the income statement and the balance sheet, which are approached using certain financial ratio analysis techniques. These are, in turn, coupled to a more general analysis of risk and return on the business of the firm in question, from which certain statistically based assumptions about risk and return can be made.

Here, 'valuing' also means assigning a digit to the firm. The digit is not based on the verifiability found in receipts, but relies on the trustworthiness of the procedures that financial analysts make use of. Estimates of the future, which can be derived via statistical analyses, remain grounded in a firm's history. The future has to parallel the present and the past for this procedure to be intelligible. This requires, in a certain sense, that the world be stable, if not at a standstill. The past must somehow be a guide to the future. 'Valuing' through financial analysis reflects a future constructed to be in continuity with the past, albeit under complex and uncertainty-ridden circumstances.

Immaterial assets, such as investments in R & D or training and education, play a role as a parameter in the forecast of cash flows. Therefore, analysts deconstruct the traditional accounting statement, attempting to qualify it and find the expenses that have effects beyond the year, but that have still not been capitalized in the balance sheet. Bennet G. Stewart (1994), for example, argues that generally accepted accounting principles in the USA will require roughly 160 changes and modifications in order to create a more proper match between expenses and their associated income stream. According to this finance perspective, proper economic value can only be constructed if the financial analysts themselves are able to judge the cash-flow implications of expenses on immaterial assets. Consequently, when financial analysts deconstruct the balance sheet, they in turn reconstruct it to fit expected values rather than conservative values. Therefore, according to Bennet G. Stewart (1991), for economic value to become transparent, R & D, training, goodwill, and other intangibles have to be put back into the balance sheet in order to account for all assets, thus facilitating a more intelligent forecast of cash flows.

The Intellectual Capital View on Valuing

Intellectual capital is highly different from the two views on valuing presented above. To begin with, it does not suggest that there is a stable object termed 'the firm' which is to be represented by a digit. On the contrary, 'valuing' here refers to transforming value. It is concerned with using digits to move value and increase it. Its digits are not constructed merely to describe the world in a set valuation of the firm. Rather than forming a bottom-line, intellectual capital digits form a loosely coupled assemblage of configurations of financial as well as non-financial indicators. As Box 13.1 illustrates, these digits are very 'mundane'.

Box 13.1 illustrates digits in empirical intellectual capital statements[3] (see Mouritsen 1998). These digits are broad, but in a particular intellectual capital statement they are assembled uniquely. This is an open-ended list, which has no logical closure. The particular assemblage of digits does not contain just one conclusion about valuing: 'Is this a definitive list? Hardly . . .' (Edvinsson and Malone 1997: 185). 'The measurement system that I propose does not present a full and comprehensive picture of a company's intangible assets; such a system is not possible' (Sveiby 1997: 150).

The digits do not measure a set value on intellectual capital. They monitor management's knowledge-management activities. In Box 13.1, the indicators of 'what is' (statistics) are concerned with the portfolio-management practices conducted to create a configuration of resources. It could be a distribution of formal employee qualifications, a distribution of customer profiles, a configuration of technologies, and a distribution of resources along corporate processes and value chains. This knowledge-management activity differs from the one supported by the 'what is done' key indicators. These refer to the

Box 13.1. A template for intellectual capital

Dimensions of intellectual capital	What is Resource statistics	What is done Internal key indicators	What happens Effect ratios
Staff	• Number of employees • Distribution of sexes • Length of employment • Formal education and training	• Share employee with personal development plan • Expenses for training and education • Number of training days per employee • Expenses for training and education per employee	• Employee satisfaction • Employee turnaround ratio • Human resource accounting • Value added per employee
Customers and partners	• Sector and market turnover • Number of customers per employee • Distribution of revenues in markets and products	• Marketing expenses • Marketing expenses per $ revenue • Administration expenses per $ marketing expense	• Customer satisfaction • Customer loyalty • Share of customers with long relations • Company image and reputation
Technology	• PCs per employee • Portable PCs per employee • Share of internal to external IT customers	• IT investments • Computer expenses per employee	• IT qualifications • IT license
Processes	• Expenses per process • Distribution of staff on processes	• Investments in R&D and infrastructure • Expertise development cost	• Errors • Waiting time • Quality • Throughput time • Product development time • Telephone availability

activities set in motion to qualify resources in the form of employee development, customer retention, technology development, and process refinement. The last category of indicators—'what happens'—are key ratios that monitor the 'productivity' of knowledge-management activities and looks at their broad effects in this area, such as motivation through employee satisfaction and turnover, customer satisfaction and retention rates, technological skills and process efficiency.[4]

Is this a conservative calculation of intangibles—referring to separable immaterial assets—in the financial balance sheet? No. Is it a capitalization of the value of intangibles and tangibles? No. It is not about the financial balance sheet at all. There is no bottom line. It is not a value of a firm, even though this has sometimes been proposed, since intellectual capital is sometimes defined as the market value of a company less its book value. This definition, however, treads on very thin ice. When writers such as Edvinsson and Malone (1997) and Thomas Stewart (1997) introduce the idea of market-to-book values, they only do so very rudimentarily. When they go on to talk about how intellectual capital works, they never return to that idea again. It is simply not a coherent description of how intellectual capital can work, at least for the individual firm. There may be other uses in the aggregate capital market.

This is not very surprising, because the rigor of the market-to-book value is questionable. In this formula, intellectual capital is a residual value, which is market value less book value. Obviously, this formula is attempting to identify intellectual capital merely by stating what it is not. However, the residual between market value and book value could be anything. It has been proposed that it is reputation, brand value, or competitive position. Therefore the market-to-book ratio does not have a 'referent' *per se*. Additionally, this formula says that a change in accounting rules would also change the value of intellectual capital. If change were made regarding which items could be capitalized in the balance sheet, or if depreciation of fixed assets were accelerated, thus constructing a different accounting result, a different value of intellectual capital would come about. Or, in other words, in such a situation, intellectual capital would be a function of the accounting rules used to construct book value. This is obviously absurd, since intellectual capital is argued to be outside the financial capital. Finally, the formula is also problematic, because it assumes that intellectual capital 'fills out' the gap between market value and book value. This is a problem, because intellectual capital information would then have no value, because more appropriate information would typically influence the financial markets' choices, and thereby the market value of the firm. In all, market-to-book value is a problem.

Intellectual capital does not posses a single bottom line. It is a loosely coupled set of digits. It does not provide the answer to 'how much' intellectual capital is. It is, when put in motion, more an inscription that helps the monitoring and guidance of a firm towards a competence-based mode of functioning.[5] Here, as Prahalad and Hamel (1990: 81) put it: 'In the long run, competitiveness derives from an ability to build . . . the core competencies that spawn unanticipated products. The real sources of advantage are to be found in management's ability to consolidate corporate-wide technologies and production skills into competencies that empower individual businesses to adapt quickly to changing opportunities.'

Intellectual capital, to paraphrase Prahalad and Hamel, is concerned with the 'real sources of advantage', which are to be found in the attention, not to outcomes but to 'technologies and skills' and thus to capabilities and competencies (Hamel and Prahalad 1994; Roos and Roos 1997; Mouritsen 1998). If this is the objective, can the intellectual capital digits illustrated in Box 13.1 really help accomplish this? Not directly. They have to be related to a supplementary set of media in order to do this: a narrative and a set of sketches.

INTELLECTUAL CAPITAL STATEMENTS

An intellectual capital statement connects narratives, sketches, and digits. It is both a vision statement that talks about or narrates the firm's preferred internal mode of functioning, explaining the importance of capabilities and competencies, and a mechanism to make it serious via the digits reported. And even though the digits are ambiguous, the narratives, sketches and digits together create not only a vision, but also the means by which to keep management accountable to it. Therefore, an intellectual capital statement combines vision with a mechanism that points out how it should be evaluated, and thus makes a critique of the implementation of a vision possible.

In the following sections, this is illustrated by five figures, each of which provides a quotation concerning the justification of the intellectual capital statement, and a visualization that makes the intellectual capital statement 'coherent'. All of the examples are obviously more complex and 'full' than can be shown here. However, the figures help illuminate how visualizations, or sketches, construct 'wholes' by virtue of an illustration, and how narratives construct a perspective from which digits are to be interpreted and made part of a meaningful account of the firm's intellectual capital.

Visualization

Intellectual capital is a form of reporting that has certain expressive characteristics, such as sketches, metaphors, and stories. Fig. 13.1 shows Skandia's system of accounting for intellectual capital (Edvinsson 1997; Edvinsson and Malone 1997): It is a set of boxes linked by lines. This is the main mechanism for understanding how various digits (of the kind represented in Box 13.1) are organized and related to each other. They 'cohere' because they can be organized according to the sketch that makes up the system of capitals defined here. The model persuades because of the indication that what is below can be said to 'explain' the top. It partly resembles a tree where output at the top—the fruit and flowers—is the result of tending the bottom—the trunk and the roots. The tree is central to the Skandia story. As the quote at the top of the figure says, the tree is made up of fruit and roots. Intellectual capital is concerned with the roots (Grafström and Edvinsson, n.d.: 29–30):

if we compare the intellectual capital to a tree, the ripe fruit of the season's efforts can be seen in the crown—i.e. in the annual report's income statement and balance sheet. The human core in the trunk is protected by the bark of customer relations and work routines. Research and planning, which the tree needs in order to survive future droughts and cold spells, is carried out in the root system. At a time marked by quick and capricious changes in the business environment, it is in the roots where the most crucial activity may take place, for future fruition.

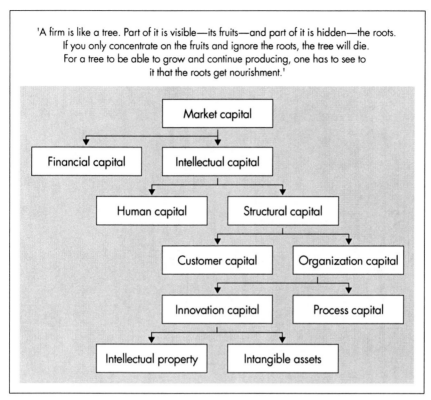

'A firm is like a tree. Part of it is visible—its fruits—and part of it is hidden—the roots. If you only concentrate on the fruits and ignore the roots, the tree will die. For a tree to be able to grow and continue producing, one has to see to it that the roots get nourishment.'

Fig. 13.1. Skandia's 'System of Capital'

The story is one of the benevolent gardener who minds the long-term future of his tree.

Likewise, Rambøll's (a Danish engineering company) 'Holistic Accounting Statement' (see Fig. 13.2) shows a sketch that takes the firm from management's vision, through human resources, and into the employee and customer satisfaction that lead to commercial success. It is a model of a large-scale integration of the managerial, technical, organizational, and human aspects of corporate life. It interrelates management potency, employee involvement, and customer satisfaction.

The case of SparNord (a Danish regional bank presented in Fig. 13.3) illustrates three themes, profitability, employee satisfaction, and customer satisfaction, inscribed via a triangle, where each corner is located between one and five units from the point of origin.[6] Here, there is a balance between the three sets of concerns visualized as purely aesthetic issues. The golden triangle is appropriate because it is beautiful, having legs of equal length. It is the balance and symmetry that provide a sense of force and coherence. In contrast, the sorry triangle is to be scorned because it is handicapped. It does not have

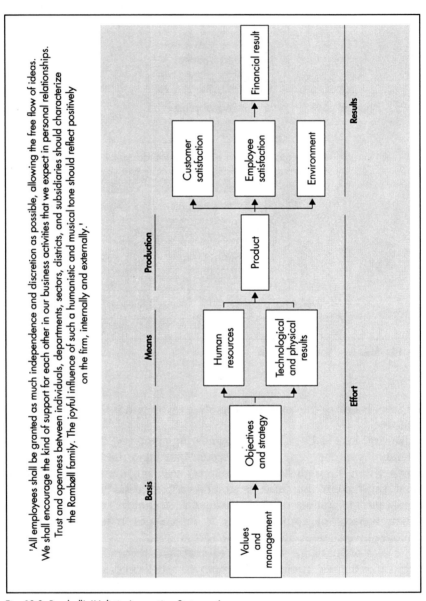

'All employees shall be granted as much independence and discretion as possible, allowing the free flow of ideas. We shall encourage the kind of support for each other in our business activities that we expect in personal relationships. Trust and openness between individuals, departments, sectors, districts, and subsidiaries should characterize the Rambøll family. The joyful influence of such a humanistic and musical tone should reflect positively on the firm, internally and externally.'

Fig. 13.2. Rambøll's 'Holistic Accounting Statement'

the beauty of the golden triangle, nor does it speak with the voice of aesthetics, and therefore the firm's position is not in balance. Visual representation renders complex relations between profitability, employees, and customers across time and space simple and communicable. Visualization grants normative implications, and here demonstrates the role of intellectual capital.

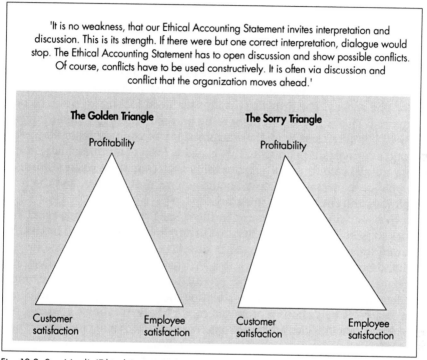

'It is no weakness, that our Ethical Accounting Statement invites interpretation and discussion. This is its strength. If there were but one correct interpretation, dialogue would stop. The Ethical Accounting Statement has to open discussion and show possible conflicts. Of course, conflicts have to be used constructively. It is often via discussion and conflict that the organization moves ahead.'

Fig. 13.3. SparNord's 'Ethical Accounting'

All three examples illustrate that the intellectual accounting statement is interesting, not for its analytical rigor but because of its visualizations. The visual—the aesthetic of representation—offers in its own way a persuasive argument to support the validity of typical accountant obsessions—namely, 'completeness', 'relevance', and 'truth and fairness'—because it produces a notion of wholeness. It enables integration of the various indicators that are utilized to tell a complex story. Not that they could only tell one story; rather, they support a very general and socially acceptable story, the one about the role of individuals in producing tomorrow's firm/society, as will be illustrated below.

The Storytelling Firm

It is no coincidence that Rambøll's intellectual accounting is termed a 'Holistic Accounting Statement' (see Fig. 13.2). It tells an extended story about the firm's work. There is, the quotation indicates, 'trust and openness', and it operates as a 'family' that pays attention not merely to financial results, but indeed to a 'humanistic and musical tone'. Rambøll in this way constructs a narrative around the sketch and makes a dynamic relationship between management, employees, customers, society, and financial results. It is an optimistic story, telling customers and employees that all take part in a project that is larger than the firm, but where the firm plays a crucial role. It is the firm that mobilizes the present and future, the internal and external, and the individual and society. The firm also inspires the need for employees to be entrepreneurial. This is the requirement to be part of a tomorrow, and terms such as 'trust', 'family', and 'joyful' are expressions of commitments that go well beyond a formal labor contract. This is a new form of accountability, emphasizing the delicate forms of responsibility that cannot be written down, but can only be expressed in a story about the firm in the future, and the role of employees and customers in this story.

Such a storyline is also present in the other firms in the examples. These stories suggest that firms grow because of employees, customers, and technology, and they are concerned to see intellectual capital as a leverage for other capitals. Developing people, for example, makes them use technology more intelligently, thus increasing the productivity of technology investments. Intellectual capital is, therefore, a storyline that makes employees' role in the firm clearer. It tells about a proposed mode of organizational routines more than about specific roles and functions. The stabilization of intellectual capital is an effect of all the network of sketches, indicators, and stories. Neither element is strong *per se*, but in combination the resulting network may be.

Individuals are important, but not—ever—alone. They are important because their motivation to engage actively in defining and solving a firm's problems is crucial, but their power is leveraged only in relation to customers, technologies, and organizational procedures and processes. Top management is left with the job of primarily seeking the development of the enduring vision, while local managers and employees are empowered to find and handle product and customer opportunities as they materialize in real time. This is the flexible firm competing in an uncertain world. A new contract simply exists now between labor and capital. Labor has to help craft itself because managers cannot do this in a world where general rather than special competencies will be required to attend to rapidly changing conditions in a hyperactive form of competition. Here, rather than merely competing on the basis of products and markets, capabilities and competencies have become central strategic levers.

This is also the case for Sparbanken (a Swedish regional bank shown in Fig. 13.4), where emphasis is placed on 'how responsible managers and employees

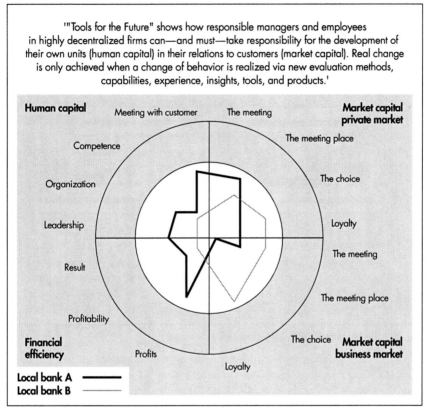

'"Tools for the Future" shows how responsible managers and employees in highly decentralized firms can—and must—take responsibility for the development of their own units (human capital) in their relations to customers (market capital). Real change is only achieved when a change of behavior is realized via new evaluation methods, capabilities, experience, insights, tools, and products.'

Fig. 13.4. Sparbanken's 'Tools for the Future'

in highly decentralized firms can—and must—take responsibility for the development of their own units in their relations to customers'. As Sparbanken's visualization shows, each organizational unit can be 'measured' on a variety of dimensions that allow a relatively detailed comparison of organizational units. This visualization illustrates where and how the individual unit differs from the rest, thus allowing analysis of relationships between employees and customers. Thus emphasis is placed on the importance of individuals, but only in relation to customers.

This is also the case for ABB (Fig. 13.5), which emphasizes 'development of competence, decentralization . . .'. The story is clear: firms have to mobilize employees and their competence to meet future customer needs. This is also why ABB has initiated a sharp reduction of levels in the organizational hierarchy, to allow more empowerment at the low end of the firm. This was followed by a policy of making work cells 'office-like', and establishing an environment of 'clean work', which was considered necessary to dramatize top management's aspiration to make workers more 'responsible' for solving the firm's

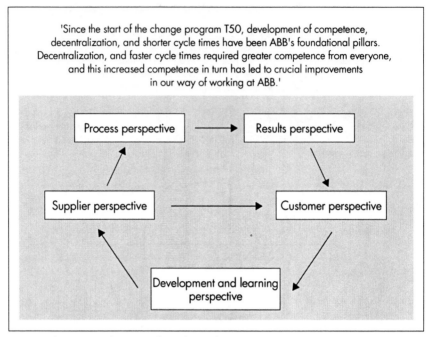

Fig. 13.5. The structure of ABB's intellectual capital statement

problems. Blue-collar work was transformed into white-collar work, and thus a certain care for 'organization', 'planning', 'foresight', and 'motivation' was installed. Work was not merely for the 'hand', it was also for the 'brain'.

Capital as Process

Intellectual capital is not a stock that will depreciate. It is a process where value is augmented when capital is put to use. In a sense, intellectual capital only exists when it is in use. In contrast to material assets, intellectual capital cannot be put on hold. It is a continual process of becoming something new. It cannot be put outside an organizational process, because if it were, it would be forgotten, which is also why stories and visualization are so important.

Consequently, intellectual capital is an integral part of ongoing organizational processes, and it leverages other capitals, including the material ones. For example, training in computer knowledge will increase the productivity of IT investments. Intellectual capital is part of a network of assets and produces effects only in combination with other assets.[7] Assets come in bundles and are complementary to each other, and intellectual capital is a 'relationship asset' that exists only in associations between people, materials, and procedures.

There is, in a sense, no direct access to competence or creativity, because it is an effect produced by a whole network of 'assets'.

All digits are therefore tangential, if anything, to competence—or perhaps more precisely to competence development. The digits are always elements in a story, which—in turn—is the only mechanism that justifies their presence in the first place. Digits are 'good' if they transform future intellectual capital. Therefore, measurements of intellectual capital are mere expressions of hope. They do not stand for competence, but they may in being put to use function as a node in a network that brings out competence development, because firms do change in the name of intellectual capital. *Managers do make arguments using intellectual capital statements*; they do point out, for example, that training is important, that customer satisfaction is more important than the product, that processes have to be enabled by technology, that new relationships have to be crafted, and that empowerment is warranted. Thus, firms change, and not because of a bottom-line-oriented computation of value. Such change is more often the result of 'hope' that this set of loosely coupled digits could eventually direct attention to a possible future, even if this future cannot be specified beforehand, apart from in metaphors and stories of how the firm is supposed to work to arrive at its future.

Intellectual capital is a process during which different types of assets cooperate. This cooperation is a dynamic process where 'investing' in one type of asset increases the value of other assets. Such complementarity exists when, for example, employee training in the usage of certain software increases the value of the personal computers they utilize. A positive chain of events can be set in motion, such as when investment in new products and marketing results in enhanced reputation, which in turn improves recruitment prospects.

Individual Capital—Organizational Capital

Since intellectual capital is a process whereby some assets support the productivity of other assets, management has been attempting to tie individual capital to various forms of organizational capital that are controlled by the firm. This desire to manage, or control, individual capital, which 'belongs' to people, has led to an endeavor to transform individual into structural capital, thus 'belonging' to firms. Management hopes to achieve this by aligning individual capital with technologies or procedures.

The paradox is that firms are interested in both setting the individual 'free', while at the same time doing so in a structured manner. Individuals are empowered to look into the firm's problems and solve them individually, since top management is too far removed from the marketplace to manage effectively at that level. In a sense, intellectual capital is used to persuade employees via metaphors, stories, and expressions, stating that firms thrive by flexibility, empowerment, demanding customers, and a continual adaptation to markets and technology. The strategy is for individuals to keep strategy in mind, and for firm's problems to be 'privatized', allowing individuals to find and solve management problems (Bartlet and Ghoshal 1997). Managers try to suggest 'strategies', but these cannot be put clearly into words simply because the new world cannot be known. Individuals are now encouraged to consider their own contributions as part of the corporate (as yet unutterable and unknowable) strategy. As was often expressed in one firm, employees must learn to 'craft' themselves as *employ-able* by demonstrating commitment to the experiment for finding the firm's strategy. Employability here refers to commitment to change, to undertake extra training, and to mind the firm's business, not just one's own. The assumption is that people, who count, will co-produce strategies for markets, customers, and products. In turn, top management will develop a competence strategy for creating a mode of organizational functioning where empowerment, sharing of knowledge, and alignment between individuals and organizational procedures and routines are central imperatives.

In implementing such imperatives, an important part of the management of intellectual capital is the packaging of individuals and technology in such a way as to tie free-floating individual capital to organizational capital, making the individual more accessible to management intervention. By *packaging* people and technology together, certain individual capabilities are rendered reusable when information systems and/or organizational procedures accompany them. This is attempted by creating new stable relations between people, technology, and customers in such a manner that no particular person or group will be critical. By putting knowledge into information technology, personal knowledge is rendered structural and can be reused in many places simultaneously. This is, for example, the case when firms develop packages of knowledge that can be inserted administratively into the corporate budgeting and accounting procedures within a very short period of time. People, manuals, technology, and procedures can then be packaged and exported to new subsidiaries. In the case of Skandia, this has reduced up-take time by 60–70 percent.

INTELLECTUAL CAPITAL AND THE EXPRESSIVE ORGANIZATION

Intellectual capital is thus a particular form of capital. It is odd and a bit incomprehensible, because it is hardly in continuity with common, ordinary conceptions about what capital is. First of all, it is grounded in a form of *aesthetic reflexivity* (Lash 1994), where the conventionally coherent grand scheme of organizational development is supplanted by the localized, step-by-step 'unmediated mediation' of the problems of the day. In other words, the grand cognitive scheme of planned strategy is replaced by localized small schemes of empowerment. Aesthetic reflexivity involves mediators—or digits, narratives, and sketches—that do not claim to represent or forecast properties of the future, as does the 'promise' of the finance view of valuation. Finance valuation makes the assumption that the net present value stands for the future, and it claims to predict the future with some degree of certainty. Alternatively, the mediators of aesthetic reflexivity do not have one grand bottom line. They are based on local relations between different kinds of heterogeneous media. They are indeed expressive, because they cannot create a cognitively satisfactory explanation of the delicate connections between them. The potential 'meaning' or 'importance' of the whole array of 'messages' conveyed by the network of mediators is not a mere analytical endeavor. It is also—and perhaps primarily—a 'debate', because it allows people to construct a practice that is only partly supported by the 'design' of the mediators, images, stories, sketches, and digits. In contrast to the financial view of valuing, this method does not profess to 'guarantee' any particular path into the future.

Second, intellectual capital is significant because it crafts stories at different levels simultaneously. It carries *extended signification* (Giddens 1987: 100 ff.) because the local is always part of a bigger game. People cannot simply invent just any kind of local interpretation. There are broader considerations, such as shareholder value, that function as barriers, limiting how far the celebration of local practices can go. Local games must remain in line with larger concerns, demonstrating that local creativity actually produces results relevant to outside actors. This has an influence on the games that can be played, the interventions that can be found relevant, and the propositions that are acceptable. The games that can be played are structurated, thereby limiting playfulness in the practice of intellectual capital development.

Third, the notion of intellectual capital brings with it a new mode of *accountability*, where a responsible person is one who commits 'psychic energy' or 'motivation' to identifying and solving a firm's problems. Here, people commit themselves and demonstrate ability and willingness to be part of a team. This kind of accountability goes beyond merely adhering to rules laid down in a formal labor contract, to not only encouraging greater recognition based on 'results', but also inspiring greater commitment to the rules of the game, to the rules of the community, and to the rules of corporate identity. The employable person is one who can be trusted to co-develop the rules of the game and make them count in new ways and new contexts.

Fourth, the *narrative* mobilized via intellectual capital is one that creates linkages and makes sequences in organizational storytelling. The plot is mobilized through expressive media, making it (re)interpretable again and again. The plot, including the whole intellectual capital account, is fabricated on three pillars. One is the sketch, which creates the boundaries for the objects to which intellectual capital refers. It thus identifies 'the whole' that it is about. The second is the storyline, which creates the legitimacy of the intellectual account, and in particular mobilizes the norms and possible sanctions inscribed in intellectual capital. The third pillar is the digits, which create a sense of seriousness on the part of management because they—even in their incomplete form—allow the critique of blatant transgressions against the rules or norms of the games suggested by the stories and sketches. These digits capture the seriousness of the whole idea of intellectual capital. This is where management is tested: will they allow the fruition of the story they themselves have espoused? The digits act as reference points for answering this question.

These four points suggest how the expressive organization produces value. Expressions such as the ones found in intellectual capital statements are communicated internally as well as externally to the firm. The internal motive explains how the firm is to work towards one or the other realization of capabilities and competencies. The external motive not only demonstrates the capabilities of the firm to customers, investors, and partners, but also shows internally that the propositions made in the stories are taken seriously. The external communication is thus not only there for the external audience; it is also—and perhaps more importantly—one of the mechanisms used to transform the firm from within. Being externally available may have a more pronounced effect internally, because the implications are not easy to neglect. Management can more easily be held accountable to it, because it may now be considered more than 'mere words'.

CONCLUSION

Intellectual capital is concerned with the value creation of long-term developing capabilities and competencies, which are said to be needed in a society of demanding customers and empowered employees. The digits in intellectual capital statements are not a coherent whole. Instead, they are a justification found in sketches, metaphors, and stories that connect intellectual capital to a future.

Intellectual digits do not purport the ability to form any kind of grand bottom-line determination of, for example, net present value, as is the case with the finance view of value. Intellectual capital digits do not claim any ability to uncover hidden truths about the value of a firm, or even the value of intellectual capital itself. These digits are, however, pertinent and interesting in their ability to instigate certain practices involving interplay between human, organizational, and customer capital.

Intellectual capital statements are media for expressive organizations. Through storytelling and sketches, intellectual capital incorporates an aesthetic dimension to account for the direction of corporate activities. By suggesting that capital is a process rather than a stock, it claims that assets come in bundles or in networks of relationships, and that they cannot be separated without loss of value. Management is often interested in stabilizing both this process and these relationships, the result of which is that individual capital is often 'transformed' into structural or organizational capital. This interest derives from management's desire to gain access to intellectual capital and to control organizational arrangements.

The interplay between stories, sketches, and digits is important, because stories provide the promise of mechanisms that will allow intellectual capital to work. Sketches provide the wholeness that legitimates a certain set of digits. Digits, in turn, provide authority, because they allow the promises made to be followed up and acted upon if they are not abided by.

NOTES

1 Here, I leave aside the philosophical accounting issue of how capital (a credit) is related to assets (a debit). This issue here is concerned with the transformations that capital moves through to become debits. This may thus be an issue of what the referent for intellectual capital is. Other approaches to 'capital' may be found in anthropology and sociology (social capital and its transformation into economic capital), and in economics (capital as generic investment).

2 The presentation of intellectual capital offered here is typically 'Scandinavian', since it focuses on the detailed exploration of the strategies and motives managers mobilize when they direct attention to intellectual capital (e.g. Roos and Roos 1997). This stands somewhat in contrast to the typical 'American' approach, which is focused on the outside of intellectual capital through statistical analyses of its correlation with profitability (e.g. Bontis 1998).

3 These propositions are based on results from interviews with ten Scandinavian firms that all produced and published intellectual capital statements (see Mouritsen 1998), of which only five are presented here. Interviews were conducted with people responsible for intellectual capital statements. The issues covered were the content, role, and implementation of these firms' intellectual capital statements.

4 Notably, some firms measure indicators of image and reputation. Via questionnaires, these firms ask internal as well as external stakeholders—sometimes very targeted groups—about image and reputation. The specific role of image and reputation in thesis statements is narrower than in the typical reputation research. For these firms, reputation is not an overall, broad outcome indicator, as it is in most literature on reputation (e.g. Fombrun 1996).

5 The intellectual capital movement (in Scandinavia, but also to a certain extent in Europe and the USA) is a product of the work carried out in the Swedish Association of Service companies, which in the beginning of the 1980s started to experiment with new measurement systems for service firms. These discussions (Konrad Group 1989; Tjänestforbundet 1993) appear to have direct linkages with the present models of intellectual capital reporting, such as Sveiby (1997), and Edvinsson and Malone (1997), which were all part of the original Konrad Group. An intellectual capital approach is oriented towards the expansion of corporate value (Mouritsen 1998), and it is thus different from the stakeholder approach, which is concerned with the distribution of results. It is also different from social responsibility accounting, which is concerned with how firms help solve broader social problems.

6 Based on questionnaires sent to customers and employees, an index covering multiple topics is created and laid onto a scale from 1 to 5. This is a piece of mathematical

work, but it is fragile, because Likert scales do not lend themselves easily to averaging, which is what has been done. In addition, the underlying questions are themselves compiled by inspiration more than by models and taxonomies.

7 This is also likely to be the case for material assets, since they work in concert with other material assets. There is complementarity between assets. However, pointing out intellectual assets as a special case is nevertheless interesting, because they are simply not interesting at all, except in their use and deployment. They are only present when in combination with other assets, some of which most likely have to be material assets, such as tools, buildings, IT systems, or trucks.

REFERENCES

Bartlett, C. A., and Ghoshal, S. (1997), *The Individualized Firm* (New York: Harper Business).

Bontis, N. (1998), 'Intellectual Capital: An Exploratory Study that Develops Measures and Models', *Management Decision*, 36: 2.

Edvinsson, L. (1997), 'Developing Intellectual Capital at Skandia', *Long Range Planning*, 30/3: 266–373.

—— and Malone, M. S. (1997), *Intellectual Capital* (London: Piatkus).

Ekelöw, G. (1999), 'The Logic of Auditability as a Classification Base for Intangible Assets', working paper, Stockholm University, School of Business.

Fombrun, C. J. (1996), *Reputation: Realizing Value from the Corporate Image* (Boston: Harvard Business School Press).

—— (1998), 'Indices of Corporate Reputation: An Analysis of Media Rankings and Social Monitors' Ratings' *Corporate Reputation Review*, 1/4: 327–40.

—— and Shanley, M. (1990), 'What's in a Name? Reputation Building and Corporate Strategy', *Academy of Management Journal*, 33/2: 233–58.

Giddens, A. G. (1987), *Social Theory and Modern Sociology* (Cambridge: Polity Press).

Grafström, G., and Edvinsson, L. (n.d.), *Accounting for Minds: An Inspirational Guide to Intellectual Capital* (Stockholm: Skandia).

Hamel, G., and Prahalad, C. K. (1994), *Competing for the Future* (Boston: Harvard Business School Press).

Heskett, J. L., Sasser, W. E., and Schlesinger, L. A. (1997), *The Service Profit Chain: How Leading Companies Link Profit and Growth to Loyalty, Satisfaction and Value* (New York: Free Press).

Klein, D. B. (1997) (ed.), *Reputation: Studies in the Voluntary Elicitation of Good Conduct* (Ann Arbor: University of Michigan Press).

Konrad Group (1989), *Den Ösynliga Balansräkningen* (Stockholm: Konrad Group).

Lash, S. (1994), 'Reflexivity and its Doubles: Structure, Aesthetics, Community', in U. Beck, A. G. Giddens, and S. Lash (eds.), *Reflexive Modernization* (Cambridge: Polity Press), 110–73.

Mouritsen, J. (1998), 'Driving Growth: Economic Value Added versus Intellectual Capital', *Management Accounting Research*, 9/4: 461–82.

Power, M. (1997), *The Audit Society, Rituals of Verification* (Oxford: Oxford University Press).

Prahalad, C. K, and Hamel, G. (1990), 'The Core Competence of the Corporation', *Harvard Business Review*, 68/3: 79–91.

Rappaport, A. (1986), *Creating Shareholder Value: The New Standard for Business Performance* (New York: Free Press).

Reich, R. B. (1991), *The Work of Nations* (New York: Alfred A. Knopf).

Riahi-Belkaoui, A., and Pavlik, E. L. (1992), *Accounting for Corporate Reputation* (Westport, Conn.: Quorum Books).

Roos, G., and Roos, J. (1997), 'Measuring Your Company's Intellectual Performance', *Long Range Planning*, 30/3: 413–26.

Saxton, M. K. (1998), 'Where Does Reputation Come From?', *Corporate Reputation Review*, 1/4: 393–9.

Skandia (1994), *Visualizing Intellectual Capital* (Stockholm: Skandia).

Stewart III, B. G. (1991), *The Quest for Value* (New York: Harper Business).

—— (1994), 'EVA™: Fact and Fantasy', *Journal of Applied Corporate Finance*, 7/2: 71–87.

Stewart, T. A. (1997), *Intellectual Capital: The New Wealth of Organizations* (New York: Doubleday).

Sveiby, K. E. (1997), *The New Organizational Wealth: Managing and Measuring Knowledge-Based Assets* (San Francisco: Berrett-Koehler).

Tjänsteförbundet (1993), *Tjänsteföretagens värden, rekommendationer om styrtal i tjänsteföretag* (Stockholm: Tjänsteförbundet).

VI

COMMUNICATING
ORGANIZATIONS

14

The Communication Advantage: A Constituency-Focused Approach to Formulating and Implementing Strategy

Paul A. Argenti and Janis Forman[*]

Since the 1970s, numerous studies have identified how organizations develop their strategies and, in some instances, how they succeed or fail as they attempt to move from a formulated strategy to its implementation. These studies include Collins and Porras's book *Built to Last* (1994) on the long-term corporate success of eighteen visionary companies; Prahalad and Hamel's (1990) work on core competence, as well as the Hamel and Prahalad (1989) article on strategic intent; and D'Aveni's (1994) work on hypercompetition. Some of these studies also discuss the importance of communication to the process of implementing strategy, but none of them considers communication to be a central focus. Moreover, with few exceptions (Fimbel 1994; Seiter 1995; Tucker *et al.* 1996; Botan 1997), little attention has been given to the links between strategy and communication in published research appearing in the flagship journal for business communication, the *Journal of Business Communication*. This is also the case for publications in management communication, public relations, marketing, and strategy. (The exceptions are: Ice 1991; Eccles and Nohria 1992; Lippitt 1997; Tyler 1997; Argenti and Forman 1998; Bobrow 1998; Gray 1998.)

Even studies of strategic implementation (e.g. Galbraith and Nathanson 1978; Lorange 1982) make communication a peripheral concern, focusing, instead, on issues such as organizational structure and processes, reward systems, and resource allocation. Despite the importance of these issues, the lack of focus on communication leaves a significant gap in managers' understanding of how to move from formulating to implementing strategy.

[*] We are equal contributors to this chapter.

This chapter bridges this gap by answering the question, how can senior management use communication effectively to formulate a strategy and to ensure that the strategy is implemented? Our goal is to give executives a systematic approach to thinking about how they can communicate their plans and vision to significant constituencies.

We turn first to Aristotle's *On Rhetoric* (1991 edn.) as the theoretical basis for bridging the gap between strategy and communication, and use his constituency-focused approach to persuasion as a departure point for building a communication framework that can be used by 'expressive organizations'— that is, organizations that risk expressing their values in the marketplace to attract and form relationships with varied constituencies on which their survival and success ultimately depend. We then offer an extended illustration of the communication framework in action. We conclude by suggesting how the consistent use of the communication framework can enable expressive organizations to enhance their reputations with key constituencies.

USING ARISTOTLE'S *ON RHETORIC* TO FORGE LINKS BETWEEN STRATEGY AND COMMUNICATION

In Aristotle's day, the fundamental unit of organizational life was the city state. In his case, it was Athens. As an instructor of rhetoric in fourth-century BC, Aristotle offered his students, among whom were future leaders of the city state, training in the major challenge of civic discourse in his era, persuasion.

In *On Rhetoric* (Aristotle 1991: 36), a compilation of his lectures on the theory and practice of persuasion, he defines rhetoric as 'an ability, in each [particular] case, to see the available means of persuasion', be it in the law courts or political assemblies—the key public arenas for debate in his time. By persuasion, he does not mean manipulation or coercion; rather, he means a process of discovery and interaction with the audience by which the speaker both creates a message collaboratively with the audience and communicates that message to the audience (see Lunsford and Ede 1984: 44). Rhetoric, then, has an epistemic, or 'knowledge-making', as well as a communicative function (Lunsford and Ede 1984: 46).

Despite the historical gap between classical times and our own, Aristotle's *On Rhetoric* (1991) contains two important elements that inform our understanding of how expressive organizations can effectively design and communicate their vision statements and strategic plans. The first of these is his notion of *deliberative rhetoric*, or speeches made in political assemblies where debate occurs for or against a particular kind of future for an organization—in his case the city state, in ours the expressive organization.[1] The second element is his constituency-focused approach to communication—that is, the centrality of the audience to persuasive discourse. The latter serves as the basis for our communication framework.

According to Aristotle (1991: 53), deliberative rhetoric involves topics of grave importance to the future of the city state, such as 'finances, war and peace, national defense, imports and exports, and the framing of laws'. It is discourse by which the speaker postulates a particular kind of future for the city state as well as the probable unfolding of events that create this future. The purpose of such discourse is to identify and support the most advantageous policy or action for the city state. In today's expressive organization, deliberative rhetoric is most akin to the discourse of strategy formulation and implementation. For example, the whole idea behind Gary Hamel's (1996) notion of 'strategic revolution' is to postulate a future and move constituencies towards it. According to Hamel, a company can either surrender the future to revolutionary challengers or revolutionize the way it creates strategies.

For instance, under the leadership of CEO Arthur Martinez, Sears, Roebuck, & Co. developed a new vision statement in the mid-1990s that was a hallmark of a huge company transformation, a radical departure from the company's earlier strategic direction: 'Sears: A compelling place to work, shop, and invest.' Martinez and his senior management team devoted considerable attention to ensuring that the three constituencies implied in this vision statement—employees, customers, and investors—understood and internalized the vision statement, and took action on the basis of it.

Like the ancient *rhetor*, a leader and public speaker in the city state whose task was to persuade his constituencies to imagine a future for the state and to support his vision, the leaders in expressive organizations need to know how to motivate key internal and external constituencies to help formulate, accept, and implement the strategic change or vision for the company that the leadership advocates. Managers who use communication to formulate and implement strategy are, then, engaged in deliberative rhetoric transposed from the political assembly to the expressive organization. In informal terms, the leadership is saying to its key constituencies, 'picture this future for the organization, help shape it, find it compelling and achievable, and support its enactment'.

Despite the shift in the cultural, economic, and sociopolitical situation from Aristotle's time to our own, our notion of strategic communication resembles Aristotle's idea of deliberative rhetoric in several ways: the emphasis on the organization's future (the city state for Aristotle, the expressive organization for us); the advocacy for or against actions and policies of serious import to the organization; and, finally, the role of audience as judges rather than as mere spectators or recipients of the ideas proffered, which, in the case of deliberative rhetoric, concern the future course of action for the state.

The central role that Aristotle granted to the audience as judge of a particular argument provides the basis for our constituency-focused framework for using communication to formulate and implement strategy. The particulars of audience have changed since Aristotle's time—his audiences judged legal cases or made decisions about issues of state; the audiences for today's expressive organizations judge strategic plans, vision statements, and key corporate actions. Yet, despite these differences of historical circumstance, the central place of audience in Aristotle's *On Rhetoric* furnishes an ample platform upon which to develop a framework for using communication to formulate and implement strategy.

A COMMUNICATION FRAMEWORK FOR FORMULATING AND IMPLEMENTING STRATEGY

In *On Rhetoric*, Aristotle used a constituency-focused approach to consider the individual speaker as he tried to persuade others to think or act according to the speaker's agenda. We have adapted this approach to look at the communication challenges that expressive organizations and their chief spokespeople face as they attempt to formulate and implement strategy. See Fig. 14.1

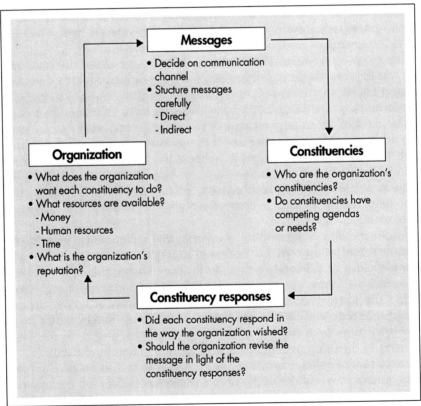

Fig. 14.1. A constituency-focused approach to communication for organizations
Source: Argenti (1998); Argenti and Forman (1998).

(this framework has been adapted from Argenti 1998, and Argenti and Forman 1998). Each element of the framework—the organization, its messages, its constituencies, and its constituency responses—focuses attention on specific communication challenges for implementing strategy.

As the framework illustrates, the *organization* must determine its objectives for a particular communication with each constituency (*what does the organization want each constituency to do?*); evaluate the resources (*in terms of money, human resources, and time*) available to accomplish the task; and determine the organization's overall *reputation*. This process sets the wheel in motion as organizations try to communicate.

For example, an entrepreneurial organization might try to establish itself as a worthy competitor to an established incumbent, as is the case today in the telecommunications industry following the 1996 Telecommunications Act in the USA. RCN, an entrepreneurial company that sells bundled communications services to residents in the densest and most profitable parts of the USA, competes with larger established firms, including AT&T, Bell Atlantic, Time-Warner, TCI, and AOL. All are far bigger than RCN, but the upstart company has convinced potential customers, investors on Wall Street, and employees that only an entrepreneurial company can successfully provide telecommunication services by building a new network.

RCN wants to become the dominant provider of telecommunication services from Boston to Washington and from San Francisco to San Diego. The company's idea of success is to get investors to bid up its stock, employees to provide the best services on the planet, customers to buy all of its available services, and communities to be proud to have RCN in the neighborhood. To achieve its objective, the company has invested millions, and both the company and its CEO have built a very powerful reputation in the process. In fact, the CEO was named entrepreneur of the year by both the Harvard Business School and Ernst & Young in 1999.

RCN has used a number of *communication channels* to reach its constituencies, including advertising to reach customers, presentations to reach investors, and face-to-face communication to reach employees. *To structure its messages*, the company uses a direct approach that seems to work with all constituencies. A direct approach from a communication strategy perspective (see Munter 1999) means to state your main ideas first and prominently in specific communications, as opposed to an indirect approach in which you state your main ideas at the end. The direct approach is more bottom-line focused and has three advantages (according to Munter 1999): it improves constituency comprehension; it is constituency focused; and it saves time. Companies and individuals tend to underutilize this approach out of habit and academic training (which stresses a more indirect approach).

RCN's CEO David McCourt has successfully used an advertising campaign on television and in his speeches to Wall Street that features a picture of Lenin with a noose around his neck and the headline, 'No empire lasts forever; especially one that keeps you waiting five hours for a repairman' (see Fig. 14.2).

Fig. 14.2. RCN corporation advertisement
Source: Printed with permission of RCN Corporation.

McCourt's 'David vs. Goliath' strategy addresses his constituencies' need to find an alternative to large companies that provide poor service.

Of course, messages such as RCN's have been delivered successfully through advertising over the course of the twentieth century. Today, however, organizations have many more channels at their disposal. They can rely exclusively on the Internet, as is the case with Amazon.com, for example. This company has created more shareholder value than large bookstores, such as Barnes & Noble, solely by using a new channel to appeal to customers. Online communication can, however, be a mixed blessing. Although it offers a company the ability to send communications instantaneously to multiple constituencies, the channel puts control of who receives company communications into the hands of anyone with access to the system. As a result, the company is left in the dark about who, other than the company's intended audiences, receives its online communications.

Determining who your constituencies are can be straightforward, as is the case for RCN with its customers and the investment community. On the other hand, this process can be very challenging, as several high-tech companies are finding when they market their products to both their direct customers and to their customers' customers. Once identified, a company's constituencies need to receive communications tailored to their specific requirements. In RCN's case, the company tailors specific messages to different analysts depending upon whether they are covering the company as a telecommunications company, an Internet company, or a cable company.

Constituencies may also have competing agendas or needs. For example, RCN's aggressive push to dominate both coasts appeals to shareholders, but creates demand among consumers that is difficult for employees to satisfy in the short term. The company's effort to dominate both coasts leaves the three constituencies—the shareholders, consumers, and employees—feeling anxious and puts pressure on management; however, this tension is the price organizations may have to pay to create a revolution in their industries.

Ultimately, an organization must determine *whether each constituency responded in the way the organization wished.* Evaluating responses to communication can be done in many ways—for example, through traditional marketing research techniques that measure attitudes or by more sophisticated reputation quotients, which are being developed by some of the authors of this book. More than ever, communication professionals have the ability to judge the success of a communication strategy in terms of dollars and cents. For instance, if RCN's CEO David McCourt goes on a roadshow to address groups of investors and the stock price climbs significantly during and after the time of the presentations, it is safe to say that the presentation caused the stock to climb. If the company has 65 million shares and the stock climbs $5 based on the presentation, it has a value of $325 million dollars in terms of constituency response.

Finally, companies must determine whether the communication was successful. This can be ascertained by asking the question: *did each constituency respond in the way the organization wished?* If so, there is obviously no need to repeat the process; however, if the organization did not meet its original objectives(s), the following question must be answered as well: *should the organization revise the message in light of constituency responses?* RCN was able to succeed with the investment community as measured by the meteoric rise in its stock price. With customers, however, the company had to change its approach to service to live up to the promises of the advertising campaign.

The section that follows presents an extended illustration of how expressive organizations may use the communication framework, with one particular organization serving as an example.

NAVISTAR'S CONSTITUENCY-FOCUSED APPROACH TO COMMUNICATION FOR FORMULATING AND IMPLEMENTING STRATEGY

A good way to see the benefits of a constituency-focused approach to formulating and communicating strategy is to examine an organization that employs such an approach. Although CEO John Horne of Navistar, a heavy truck manufacturer headquartered in Chicago, did not formally design and use such an approach, his ideas about communication evolved to clearly illustrate his focus on persuading the company's multiple constituencies to help formulate and implement the organization's strategy.[2]

Before Horne was named CEO at Navistar, the company's idea of corporate communication was 'crisis communication'. When Horne took over as CEO in 1993, he recognized that the company had significant problems with its constituencies—employees, unions, senior management, the financial community, and the media. The company was plagued with a history of union conflict, including a long strike in the 1970s. In turn, the general discontent of the workforce made investors lose confidence in the company's ability to prosper.

As he confronted these problems, Horne believed—in the words of the Vice-President of Corporate Communication, Maril McDonald (1998)—that the company 'couldn't muscle our way out [of the problems]. We had to sell our way out.' At the same time the company's view of communication was very limited. Communication consisted of newsletters and videos.

Believing that he had to bring his employees on board before raising the confidence of the financial community, Horne supported early initiatives to gather information from employees about their concerns. He used a three-pronged approach: extensive plant visits, an employee survey with follow-up, and direct involvement of union representatives in employee issues.

Horne and a group of senior managers began visiting the plants. Initially, plant managers did not want senior management to visit, fearing that they would be greeted with hostility. Despite this, Horne persisted, keeping in mind his 'rule of three'—that is, he believed that, due to the employees' lack of trust in senior management, he would be unable to communicate successfully with employees until his third visit to the plant. In fact, first meetings tended to be gripe sessions, but, by the third visit, management and employees began to engage in serious discussions about how to beat the competition.

The dialogue between senior management and plant employees became so successful in raising morale and in formulating strategy that the plant visits became a formalized communication practice by the fall of 1996. Each month every plant is visited by a member of the senior management group. Meetings include the senior manager and about thirty or forty employees, who represent a cross-section of the plant. The employees are asked to talk about a few things that are working well and a few that need attention. Before the meeting, the employees speak to people whom they work with to learn about their concerns; after the meeting, the senior manager publishes management's response to employees' concerns in the plant publication and gets back to the plant with answers to questions that he or she could not provide at the session. Senior management's responsiveness to employee concerns has gone so far as to include inviting assembly-plant workers to visit headquarters, observe its operations, and discuss work issues directly and informally with the top decision-makers there (Brooke 1997).

The plant meetings were initially conceived of as an effort to open up dialogue with the employees and to identify their concerns. But very soon the monthly meetings proved to have benefits that reached far beyond this. Senior management brings back to corporate headquarters what they learn at the plants and, in this way, the employees' voices are brought into top management's discussions of strategy. Employees are, then, involved in strategy formulation, not just in the implementation of strategy devised solely by senior management. A communication practice—monthly meetings between senior management and employees—became a technique for strategy formulation. In this regard, the communication practice of Navistar's management represents a process of discovery and interaction with one of its key constituencies, its employees. This has allowed the company to create its message collaboratively with this constituency, a role for communication that Aristotle envisioned long ago in his study of rhetoric.

Surveying employee concerns was another technique Navistar used to open up dialogue. In designing the survey, Navistar's communication group conducted extensive employee research, using one-on-one interviews with a cross-section of employees. Through this exploratory research, the communication group identified questions for the survey, which was administered in every plant. Soon thereafter, survey results, which were presented jointly by management and union leaders at every plant and published in the plant newsletter, became the basis for action plans that plant management developed to address employee concerns and to establish deadlines for completion of these plans. Plant management is held accountable for the goals they choose.

To strengthen the relationship between senior management and plant employees, the CEO also initiated and maintains dialogue with another constituency, union representatives. More specifically, union members have been invited to join education and training committees and to recommend changes in this aspect of employee life. Believing that employees can be dealt with directly, the CEO has also worked collaboratively with the United Auto Workers (UAW) on wage and other employment issues. (Aware of Navistar's interest in involving union leadership in top management decisions, the company's lawyers have fostered rather than obstructed such dialogue.)

Along with the plant employees, Navistar's CEO also targeted senior management as a key internal constituency with which he wanted to improve communications. To do so, he instituted a 'leadership conference' in 1995, a three-day conference for the top 550 managers in the firm. Horne's goal at the first conference was to 'pump life back' into the leaders, who were, in general, risk-averse survivors of years in which the company had been fighting for survival. He used skits and humor—including Rap performances by the most senior members of the management team to the accompaniment of boom box music—to illustrate new strategic initiatives and to poke fun at the old ones. On the first day of the first conference, Horne learned that only 24 percent of the top executives knew that the company had a strategy. By the end of the conference, 98 percent knew. These leadership conferences continue to be a permanent component of the company's approach to communication.

When the company turned its attention to the external world, its first concern was its customers. Customer focus is, in fact, one of the core values it espouses. Since Horne became CEO, the company has taken actions to revitalize this core value: doing research on the customers' overall experience of the brand and expectations of the brand, rethinking each target market group, holding press conferences, and giving speeches at industry events for the purpose of projecting Navistar as an industry leader in its product lines. Among other things, the company has worked to extend its brand image beyond that of 'reliability' and 'durability'—qualities that its customers identified—to include technological leadership and excellence for its extensive distribution network.

To address the skepticism of another external constituency, the financial community, about Navistar's ability to resolve its union problems, senior management at Navistar developed a powerful, consistent story about how the company was going to resolve its difficulties—that, although management would take the blame for the problems, the company needed the employees to work collaboratively with them to solve it. As for the media—another key constituency—Horne persisted in opening up dialogue with them even in the face of media stories that exacerbated the strife between unions and management and resulted in low morale within the plant communities. Despite initial lack of trust on both sides—the company's and the media's—the CEO's willingness to respond to questions and his ability to present a consistent story about the company's strategy gradually improved relations. The company also, now, tries to get to know reporters rather than dismissing them as the 'evil press'.

As a result of Horne's constituency-focused approach to communication, he has been able to change the image of the company, raise employee morale, and improve its reputation and financial status (see Box 14.1 for a summary of Navistar's key constituencies). To accomplish these goals, he has been ably assisted by his corporate communications vice president, Maril McDonald (1998), who considers that her role is to 'help John understand where all of our publics are relative to what we're trying to accomplish'.

Box 14.1. Navistar's key constituencies

- **Employees**
- **Union representatives**
- **Senior management**
- **Customers**
- **The financial community**
- **The media**

THE CONSTITUENCY-FOCUSED APPROACH TO COMMUNICATION AND THE NEEDS OF THE EXPRESSIVE ORGANIZATION

Historically, the exigencies of public life have stimulated interest in rhetoric. Aristotle's work grew alongside Athenian democracy and its needs for public debate in the contested arenas of the law courts or public assemblies where issues of great consequence to the individual or the state were decided. Today's expressive organizations face other but no less compelling challenges: the need to influence and motivate key constituencies and to engage them in formulating as well as implementing strategy.

Reputations are built on the basis of how well all of the constituencies of an organization buy into its overall meaning, as it is expressed by its leaders. It takes many years to build organizations into icons such as General Electric in the USA, Asea Brown Boveri in Europe, and Matsushita in Asia. Every one of the organizations mentioned built and transformed its reputation using a similar process to the one we describe in this chapter. What the legendary leaders who have run these organizations drew upon for their success—without recognizing their indebtedness—is a rhetorical tradition based upon the work of Aristotle.

The RCN and Navistar examples discussed in this chapter illustrate how leaders in expressive organizations engage in complex rhetorical activities that focus centrally on the analysis of their constituencies. For these organizations, communication is not a mechanical, elementary skill that is 'split off' from the organization's significant strategic initiatives. Instead, the leaders in expressive organizations, like the individual speaker in the public assemblies of Athens, advance their strategic agendas by attending to their significant constituencies as collaborators in the creation of meaning and as parties to be influenced and moved to carry out those agendas.

NOTES

1 Aristotle identified three kinds of rhetoric: *deliberative rhetoric,* or speeches that persuade citizens to endorse a course or action that the speaker believes will enhance significantly the well-being of the state; judicial *rhetoric,* or speeches in defense of an individual brought to trial for real or apparent wrongdoing; and *epideictic rhetoric,* or ceremonial speeches. Taken as a whole, the three kinds of rhetoric relate to three 'different human tasks relating to planning for the future [deliberative rhetoric], criticizing the past [judicial rhetoric], and appreciating the fuller meaning of the present [epideictic rhetoric]' (Edel 1982: 344).

2 Much of this case study is based upon extended interviews with Maril McDonald, Vice-President of Communication for Navistar.

REFERENCES

Argenti, P. (1998), *Corporate Communication,* 2nd edn. (New York: Irwin/McGraw-Hill).

—— and Forman, J. (1998), 'Should Business Schools Teach Aristotle?', *Strategy & Business,* 12/3: 4–6.

Aristotle (1991), *On Rhetoric: A Theory of Civic Discourse,* trans. G. A. Kennedy (New York: Oxford University Press).

Bobrow, W. (1998), 'Is your HR Department in Shape to Support your Business Strategies?', *Bobbin,* 39/8: 64–8.

Botan, C. (1997), 'Ethics in Strategic Communication Campaigns: The Case of a New Approach to Public Relations', *Journal of Business Communication,* 34: 188–202.

Brooke, G. (1997), 'Mr. Assembler Goes to Chicago', *Inside Navistar,* July–Aug.: 6–7.

Collins, J. C., and Porras, J. I. (1994), *Built to Last: Successful Habits of Visionary Companies* (New York: Harper Business).

D'Aveni, R. A. (1994), *Hypercompetition* (New York: Free Press).

Eccles, R. G., and Nohria, N., with Berkeley, J. D. (1992), *Beyond the Hype: Rediscovering the Essence of Management* (Boston: Harvard Business School Press).

Edel, A. (1982), *Aristotle and his Philosophy* (Chapel Hill, NC: University of North Carolina Press).

Fimbel, N. (1994), 'Communicating Realistically: Taking Account of Politics in Internal Business Communications', *Journal of Business Communication,* 31: 7–26.

Galbraith, J. R. and Nathanson, D. A. (1978), *Strategy Implementation: The Role of Structure and Process* (St Paul, Minn.: West Publishing Co.).

Gray, R. (1998), 'PR Does the Business', *Marketing*, 11 June: 24–7.

Hamel, G. (1996), 'Strategy as Revolution', *Harvard Business Review*, 74/4: 69–71.

—— and Prahalad, C. K. (1989), 'Strategic Intent', *Harvard Business Review*, 67/3: 63–76.

Ice, R. (1991), 'Corporate Public and Rhetorical Strategies: The Case of Union Carbide's Bhopal Crisis', *Management Communication Quarterly*, 4: 341–62.

Lippitt, M. (1997), 'Say What You Mean, Mean What You Say', *Journal of Business Strategy*, 18/4: 18–20.

Lorange, P. (1982) (ed.), *Implementation of Strategic Planning* (Englewood Cliffs, NJ: Prentice Hall).

Lunsford, A. A., and Ede, L. S. (1984), 'On Distinctions between Classical and Modern Rhetoric', in R. J. Connors, L. S. Ede, and A. A. Lunsford (eds.), *Essays on Classical Rhetoric and Modern Discourse* (Carbondale, Ill.: Southern Illinois University Press), 37–49.

McDonald, M. (1998), Interviews on Navistar's Communication Practices, 6 Nov.

Munter, M. (1999), *Guide to Managerial Communication*, 5th edn. (Upper Saddle River, NJ: Prentice Hall).

Prahalad, C. K., and Hamel, G. (1990), 'The Core Competence of the Corporation', *Harvard Business Review*, 68/3: 78–91.

Seiter, J. S. (1995). 'Surviving Turbulent Organizational Environments: A Case Study Examination of a Lumber Company's Internal and External Influence Attempts', *Journal of Business Communication*, 32: 363–81.

Tucker, M. L., Meyer, G. D., and Westerman, J. W. (1996), 'Organizational Communication: Development of Internal Strategic Competitive Advantage', *Journal of Business Communication*, 33: 51–69.

Tyler, L. (1997), 'Liability Means Never Being Able to Say You're Sorry: Corporate Guilt, Legal Constraints, and Defensiveness in Corporate Communication', *Management Communication Quarterly*, 11: 51–73.

15

Self-Absorption and Self-Seduction in the Corporate Identity Game

Lars Thøger Christensen and George Cheney

> . . . we are too preoccupied with saving our identity to undertake anything else . . . the need to speak, even if one has nothing to say, becomes more pressing when one has nothing to say . . .
>
> The solicitation of and voraciousness for images is increasing at an excessive rate. Images have become our true sex object, the object of our desire.
>
> (Baudrillard 1988: 29–30, 35)

Contemporary organizations are—no matter what sector they occupy or what products or services they produce—in the communication business—that is, in the business of expressing themselves deliberately in their environments. And for good reasons. The market of today seems to be demanding well-crafted identities, identities that are able to stand out and break through the clutter. At the same time, organizations are expected to be able to adapt, modify, or radically alter their identities at a moment's notice. As a consequence, organizations are investing more resources than ever in articulating, expressing, and celebrating their identities. But who is listening to them? And who *really* cares about the careful and, often, detailed considerations behind these organizational efforts? In a world saturated with corporate symbols asserting uniqueness and calling for attention and interest, such questions are important to ask not only for academic reasons but also because they invite organizations to reconsider radically the role that their formal communication campaigns play in the market of symbols and messages of today.

This chapter discusses and critiques prevailing assumptions about corporate identity[1] and the role it plays in contemporary society. More specifically, the chapter questions the assumptions that the general public is genuinely interested and deeply involved in the expressions that contemporary organizations choose to manufacture and that organizations consequently adjust their communication to the wishes and demands among such external constituencies. By contrast, this chapter sets out to demonstrate that the demand for corporate identities is primarily generated by organizations themselves in their relentless pursuit of visibility and legitimacy in the marketplace. In their desire to be heard and respected, organizations of today participate in an ongoing *identity game* in which their interest in their surroundings is often overshadowed by their interest in themselves. Although identity is fundamentally social, inasmuch as it rests on its reflection and accreditation in its surroundings (e.g. Berg and Gagliardi 1985), we see today a tendency for corporate identity campaigns to become rather self-centered undertakings.

CORPORATE IDENTITY AS COMMUNICATION

The Quest for Distinctness and Visibility

Corporate existence, it seems, can no longer be separated from the question of communication. Although bottom-line concerns still shape the logic of many business and non-business operations, at the turn of the century organizations are convinced that their continued success in the marketplace is contingent upon their ability to justify their existence through powerful corporate symbols. While British Petroleum (BP), for example, continues to 'tweak' its logo and its version of green (now patented) to try to strike the 'perfect' corporate image, the organizations behind products like Absolut Vodka and Silk Cut cigarettes have become almost one with the aesthetic images they project in their surroundings (see e.g. Schmitt and Simonson 1997).

With a growing number of similar products, relatively easy and inexpensive to copy, the market has become a battlefield of brand names, images, and logos striving to be heard. Indeed, we have witnessed such battles in the soft drink industry for decades, where struggles for existence imply that products and brand names are situated within a larger cluster of cultural icons. And, as expressions of 'service' or 'customer service' are now *de rigueur* in corporate mission statements, organizations work desperately to add distinctiveness to those expressions with adjectives such as 'constant', 'ever-improving', 'smiling', 'unquestioned', 'outrageous', 'super', and 'happy'. The practices of identity management extend beyond the corporate world to include governmental agencies, cities, social movements, and religious denominations. And now it is almost required that even cities and nations will have catchy slogans and identity 'packages' (e.g. Kotler 1987).

By placing more emphasis on the identity of products or services, organizations clearly hope to add some uniqueness or 'soul' to an otherwise anonymous and unstable world of goods. Although this hope is shared by most organizations, the desire for distinctness in the marketplace of today constantly sparks new efforts to contrive and communicate identity (Cheney and Christensen, forthcoming).

The Search for Accreditation and Legitimacy

At the same time, a growing number of organizations feel the need to explain their existence and activities in terms of current social and political values. Whereas the *raison d'être* of most private organizations is still the generation of profits, they often justify their existence in *other* terms. Until the 1980s, the justification was typically given implicitly by the satisfaction of specific consumer needs or by the numbers of jobs provided by production. Organizational legitimacy, however, seems to require more conscious and *explicit* attempts on the behalf of the organization to justify what it *is* and what it stands for. Hence we find that most large organizations, regardless of sector, are issuing mission statements, identifying core values, and promoting ethical codes. Moreover, in industries ranging from transportation to breakfast cereals, companies are stressing social responsibility and subscribing to a type of stakeholder theory that allows their constituencies to play more active roles in corporate governance.

This trend—which is not entirely new (see e.g. Marchand 1998)—is explained by reference to the increasing critique of private business corporations by various interest groups, growing media attention to scandals and hypocrisy, and new demands from so-called political consumers (Hatch and Schultz 1997). And clearly, these developments can be seen as significant challenges to corporate legitimacy. The fact, however, that a growing number of organizations outside embattled industries such as oil, chemicals, and tobacco are now subscribing to what Dahler-Larsen (1997a) calls 'moralized discourses'—discourses through which organizations account for their existence and behavior in terms of current social norms and values—calls for a deeper social-historical explanation beyond the scope of this chapter. The new moralized discourses of organizations, however, have a relatively narrow aim: to facilitate consensus or 'smooth organizational life', as Dahler-Larsen (1997a: 321) puts it, or simply to demonstrate an adherence to the organizational crowd. Thus, while contemporary organizations tend to see their new moral standards as being related to grand social principles, they typically are used simply as markers of corporate respectability and as an ingredient in their ongoing efforts to assert their identity.

Redefining Corporate Boundaries

With the advent of new organizational forms with transient or unclear physical boundaries, many organizations have begun to articulate their existence in new and more symbolic ways. Along with an urge to become more flexible and responsive to external demands, and thus to move beyond traditional boundaries, contemporary organizations feel a need to formulate more clearly their purpose through elaborate vision, mission, and values statements (Bergquist 1993; see also Hirschhorn and Gilmore 1992).

Where an organization's identity used to be given with its products or its specific technology, it now hinges on the ability of management to convey purpose and a sense of belonging relatively independent of time and space. Clearly, corporate logos and larger 'identity packages' are seen in this light as compelling and enduring points of reference, not only for employees and consumers but also for other constituencies. Moreover, companies such as Daimler-Benz, McDonald's, and General Mills rely on a strategy of 'essentializing' (or capturing) the organization, its products, its history, and its reputation through immediately recognizable symbols. As we have already suggested, such identity-management efforts go far beyond branding to include attempts to make sacred a constellation of symbols representing the organization. For example, the State Farm Insurance Companies do this with a detailed policy statement that specifies the treatment of the corporate logo and shield, even prescribing the exact placement of the plaque with the logo in corporate offices. In this case, the official packaged corporate identity is presented rigidly as the univocal expression of the organization and is exalted with a degree of reverence that borders on the absurd. Here, as in many other cases, corporate policy seeks to instill reverence and awe for master symbols of the organization. And a host of organizations do so by insisting that they represent the 'one true' purveyor of a product or service in their industry and that all competitors are merely imitators or impostors. Again, identity is the issue, and communication seems to be the answer.

A Volatile Communication Environment

Interestingly, however, communication has become a double-edged sword: Where media consultants seek to convince organizations to communicate more in order to gain a larger 'share of voice', many decision-makers have come to realize that what they gain is primarily a larger share of noise. Paradoxically, it is precisely *because* of professionally planned communication that identities of many products and organizations are not what they used to be—distinct, independent, and relatively stable.

The identity of Volvo, for example, as a very safe car with strong welds—and, as it is put in an ad from the 1980s, a built-in 'child's welfare organization'—was seriously challenged during the 1990s, not because Volvo had difficulties living up to its promises but because other car-producers began to emulate the *same* safety theme. In a similar manner, the identity of IBM is constantly being challenged by competitors paraphrasing its slogan 'Think'. While ICL for a while suggested 'Think ICL' (Olins 1989: 67), Apple began in the late 1990s to market its Macintosh computers under the theme 'Think Different', appropriating images of an array of world figures and, in this way, suggesting inspiration as well as innovation. Although the imitators may not be in a position to threaten the companies they copy, their persistent efforts to position their identities on the names, the slogans, or the goodwill of other and more well-known organizations provoke constant adjustments of established identities, even among market leaders (Christensen 1999).

Leaning on or plagiarizing the identities of other organizations in the same industry or category can also be seen in the domain of corporate ethics and social responsibility. Following the success and criticism of The Body Shop, a variety of cosmetics and toiletries manufactures have now positioned themselves against animal testing, for recycling, and against pollutants. As a different kind of example, Mobil Corporation led the way in the 1970s for a variety of other businesses and organizations to blend advertising, public relations, and policy statements with an explicit 'corporate-advocacy' campaign. In response to low public opinion of big business, crises in government, the first oil crisis, and the threat of windfall profits taxes, Mobil began to rethink its methods of public persuasion (Crable and Vibbert 1983). The company *re*acted to its own environment by becoming more proactive with respect to its various audiences. Specifically, the Corporation became more concerned with managing its general image and speaking about socio-political issues than with discussing its products and services. Mobil's op-ed columns, which still regularly appear in major newspapers and magazines, called 'Observations', are just one example of a genre of corporate communication now known as the 'advertorial'. These ads comment on topics ranging from governmental regulation to 'common sense'. Such messages, which are used by many other organizations, are expected by their corporate creators to influence public values and in turn to reshape policy in the corporations' favor.

In sum, the corporate communication environment has become extremely complex and volatile, with, on the one hand, blurred lines between traditional modes of advertising, public relations, marketing, and lobbying and, on the other hand, constant attempts by organizations to exploit the positions and identities of each other (Cheney and Christensen, forthcoming). In spite of this complexity and the difficulties associated with the expression and maintenance of distinctness in a cluttered environment, communication is seen by many decision-makers as *the* central vehicle of identity. Identity-related communication has, in other words, become an imperative in almost all sectors of society.

CORPORATE SELF-ABSORPTION

While contemporary organizations know that their identity hinges on their ability to express themselves professionally in their surroundings, they rarely question the relevance of their communication outside their own formal boundaries. As a consequence, the development of corporate communications campaigns and especially identity 'packages' are typically one-way affairs. Although the notion of market-related communication traditionally suggests some kind of interaction and relatedness with the world, today it simultaneously indicates that organizations are engrossed or absorbed in their own symbolic constructions.

Corporate self-absorption is manifested in a number of different ways: on the one hand, as a growing preoccupation with ritualistic expressions of identity; on the other hand, as a previously unseen vanity with respect to the signifiers that organizations themselves choose to manufacture. Both dimensions of corporate self-absorption will be discussed below.

When the Sender is the Receiver

Expressions of identity are not only more plentiful in the marketplace of today; they are also delivered with more force, vigor, and intensity. Like sports teams before a game, contemporary organizations feel a strong need to remind themselves on a regular basis about the symbols, values, and catchwords that unite them. However, while the recurring articulation of identity and community is essential to the organization itself, the 'environment' does not necessarily share the exuberance (see Fig. 15.1).

Fig. 15.1. Hagars vikings
©KFS/Distr. Bulls.

What is regarded as an important ritual of unity for the organizational representative may be seen by the external spectator as nothing more than an undue repetition of the obvious. This we sense most clearly when TV commercials restate the same simple slogan week after week. Other examples include continuous attempts by organizations to spell out the specifics of their identity, like we find, for example, in design manuals, identity programs, and job announcements. While such attempts typically assume a priori that the external audience is involved in what the organization has to say, we ought to be sensitive to the possibility that the environment knows what the organization 'is' and does not need to hear it once more.

For the organization, however, the function of communication goes beyond knowing. Ritual expressions of identity are not messages in the traditional sense of sending and receiving information. Rather, they are *meta*-messages— that is, messages that communicate through their very existence. In this capacity, the messages are typically more relevant to the sender than to the receiver. Corporate communication often fills such function. As Broms and Gahmberg (1983) have argued, organizations often communicate with themselves through strategic plans projected into their surroundings. Following the same line of thought, Christensen (1997) points out that market-related communication— including advertising, identity programs, annual reports, job announcements, and corporate architecture—speaks as much to the sender organization as it does to the external world. By being visible in proper external media, organizations not only communicate with their environment but demonstrate to themselves that their identities are authentic and based on something real and respected 'out there' (cf. Christensen 1995). The fact that many organizations now feel a strong need to 'be' on the Internet, even when they have nothing to say, illustrates this point with cynical clarity: communication *is* existence, even when the message is only relevant to the sender. Much market communication, thus, can be described as *auto-communication*—that is, communication through which organizations establish and affirm their own self-images or their own cultures.

According to Lotman (1990), all societies and social institutions communicate with themselves to a higher or lesser degree. Through the process of auto-communication, cultures not only maintain but also construct or develop themselves (see also Sherry 1987). In fact, social systems must do this to demarcate themselves and the 'environment' (Christensen and Cheney 1994; cf. Luhmann 1990). Although this construction is often a rather self-centered activity, the role of the 'external' world is not insignificant. By providing media (for example, television or graphic signs) with a higher degree of status in society than traditional *internal* media, the external world endows the messages that organizations convey to themselves with authority and 'supplementary value' (Lotman 1990: 21). Thus, in the process of auto-communication, the 'external' world becomes a reference point rather than a receiver, a 'mirror' rather than an audience.

Although all organizations auto-communicate, we should expect organizations with lots of front-line personnel, like service organizations, to feel a stronger need to remind their employees on an ongoing basis about their commitments to the organization and its customers. And clearly, in the service sector (for example, banking, insurance, and the airline industry) we find many examples of messages to employees via external media (Christensen

1997). Today, however, organizations in *all* sectors of society feel a growing need to project their identities in their surroundings. And, while this projection is not in itself auto-communicative, the growing competition for attention implies that organizations become more preoccupied with their own symbols than any external audience can be expected to be.

Obviously, the logic of auto-communication does not rule out the possibility that the messages in question *also* communicate to external audiences. In fact, as Lotman (1990) points out, any text may simultaneously stimulate both kinds of communication. Still, in a cluttered communication environment saturated with messages asserting importance and uniqueness, it is highly unlikely that corporate messages will be able to stimulate more than a passing interest, let alone engagement, outside the organization's formal boundaries. Of course, some corporate slogans are able to spread like wildfire. Research on the effects of advertising, however, suggests that, with time, messages typically become detached from their source, meaning that people may be able to remember the slogan but not who the sender was (Belch *et al.* 1987). Even if we acknowledge the fact that brand loyalties and the emergence of 'political consumers' indicate some deeper involvement in organizations, it would be erroneous to assume that the *specifics* of corporate identities are perceived as important by the general public. As Schudson (1993: 3–4) puts it:

If we think of popular culture as a variety of forms ranging from those that are avidly followed to those that are barely acknowledged, then popular movies like *E. T.* or *Star Wars* or celebrations like the 4th of July fireworks would be at the high-involvement pole. They are cultural forms that people go out of their way to see, they become 'events' in the foreground of people's lives, and they may provide grounds for talk and even critical reflection. At the low-involvement pole are forms of culture that surround us without our taking notice. Design, typically, touches people without their focusing on it—the design of buildings, of products, of packages. Television and radio are somewhere in the middle, with soap operas and sports near the fireworks end of the spectrum and most other programming far closer to the unattended end, existing for most people as a kind of background noise. Television commercials, though often noticed as a phenomenon—they are interruptions, after all—are less attended to than television programs. They are, as Shakespeare said of the cuckoo in June, 'heard but not regarded'.

While it is disputable whether external audiences have *ever* been *deeply* interested in what business corporations have to say, the mere accumulation of corporate signifiers in contemporary markets suggests, as Schudson (1993) points out, that one of the scarcest resources today is attention and interest. And this reality causes organizations to be ever more vigorous (and sometimes outrageous) in their advertising and marketing strategies. Benetton's famous campaigns depicting misery and disaster (aids, flooding, war, and so on) offer many good cases. Other examples include the New Zealand-based clothing company Glassons's campaign 'Wear It Your Way', which portrays dark images of urban life suggestive of despair, and a campaign by the Danish watch producer REM REM that suggested killing yourself is better than killing time.

A New Era of Corporate Vanity

The lack of involvement and interest among consumers does not make organizations less concerned about themselves. Facing a blasé environment in which cynicism is rampant and novelty commonplace, a growing number of organizations are becoming absorbed in their own symbolic expressions and their own appearance.

For many organizations, appearance has always been an important issue. Banks and large industrial corporations have a long history for investing in their visual style (Olins 1989). This, of course, is true also for many department stores and specialty shops selling, for example, fashionable clothing. Corporate vanity is not a new phenomenon. In fact, the Art Deco architectural and design movement, which was at its height in the early 1930s, was closely linked to images of industrial progress and corporate pride. However, as Berg and Kreiner (1990: 41) point out, contemporary organizations are more involved than ever in expressions of identity: 'It is an indisputable fact that organizations increasingly care about their physical appearance. Huge amounts of money are being invested in improved corporate "looks", in terms of slick, stylish corporate buildings, new office lay-outs and decorations, landscape gardening, graphic designs, corporate "uniforms" and color codes, visual identities, etc.'

With an increased focus on their 'surfaces', contemporary organizations are, according to Berg and Kreiner, adapting to the emphasis of postmodern society on appearance and mass-communicated images. The emphasis on appearance, however, is not limited to a concern about *physical* 'looks'. Organizations in the 1990s demonstrated a remarkable preoccupation with, for example, their history, their values and their reputation (see e.g. Fombrun and van Riel 1997). Still, the primary focus of many organizations when considering their identity is still on how these more abstract dimensions are *presented* or *communicated* in the general public. Many organizations now regulate external images with detailed design manuals that are supposed to govern external communications by staff. Olins (1989) presents a long checklist of visual elements to be included in a design manual and illustrates this with examples of how Q8, the international petrol brand from Kuwait Petroleum International, has implemented such principles in practice. Also universities and other public or non-profit organizations are developing elaborate manuals to guide internal and external communications in an attempt to centralize and standardize uses of their symbols.

The preoccupation with appearance and presentation is understandable given the competition between visual signifiers in the corporate landscape. Clearly, many of the principles put forth by identity consultants like Olins and his associates are both logical and sound when viewed in this light of increased competition. However, the identity efforts of *competing* corporations do not seem to figure prominently in the concerns with appearance of contemporary organizations. Following Baudrillard (1988: 40 ff.), this indicates an important shift in the emphasis on difference and identity:

Formerly we were haunted by the fear of resembling others, of losing ourselves in a crowd; afraid of conformity, and obsessed with difference . . . All that matters now is only to resemble oneself, to find oneself everywhere, multiplied but loyal to one's personal formula . . . Resemblance is no longer concerned with others, but rather with the individual in his vague resemblance to himself; a resemblance born of the individual's reduction to his simple elements.

Not only do organizations expect their 'selves' to be seen and heard everywhere; they are also careful to ensure that what is seen and heard across space is always the same. Where difference used to refer to distinctions between subjects, it now refers, in the words of Baudrillard (1988: 41), to 'an internal, infinite differentiating of the same'. And this we clearly see in the way contemporary organizations are handling their own symbols of identity. In the development of new communication campaigns, organizations typically work vainly and meticulously with their own established symbols in order to make sure that the new corresponds to the old. Moreover, in order to speak with one voice (e.g. Phelps *et al.* 1994), many organizations have become increasingly preoccupied with controlling the behavior of their employees, even outside the workplace. While the design manual is one such attempt, more recent and controversial steps include bans on certain behaviors, including driving motorcycles after work.

The attempts of contemporary organizations to align all symbolic representations within one coherent image is typically explained as necessary to avoid inconsistency between words and action—a project stimulated by globalization, the splintering of mass markets, growing media attention, and critique by consumers and interest groups (e.g. Schultz *et al.* 1994). But, although few identity managers seem willing to accept this, the detailed preoccupation of many organizations with their own symbols cannot be explained simply with reference to such *external* trends. The Danish shoe producer Eccolet, for example, is carefully designing its retail outlets all over the world using the same kind of maple wood material. As managers at Eccolet have told students of the first author, using this material is imperative for the organization in order to convey the same image to consumers in all countries and this way increase global awareness and recognition of the Ecco brand. Although the strategy of standardizing communication and design across different cultures may have a number of advantages in terms of coordinating the dissemination of corporate symbols and controlling communication costs (e.g. Onkvisit and Shaw 1987), these measures are usually not dictated by *consumer* interests or concerns. Still, Eccolet managers seem to imagine that their target consumers are highly enough involved in their shoe brands to compare store design across different countries. This is quite unlikely and demonstrates well how easily corporate vanity turns into self-absorption.

Given the stress on consistent presentation of an organization's image across diverse contexts and for diverse audiences, we might wonder how serious most organizations really are about taking account of multiple stake-holders (Leitch and Motion 1999). Moreover, the fact that even universities and religious groups are demanding *consistent* presentations of their organizations across different audiences and through various media indicates that much corporate communication has developed its own logic. While it makes perfect sense for organizations to *integrate* their communication efforts and to strive towards *consistency* across traditional organizational boundaries (e.g. Schultz *et al.* 1994), in practice the art of managing corporate identity across organizational boundaries is often reduced to a relatively simple, but rigorous, exercise of coordinating and harmonizing carefully designed corporate signifiers. Such efforts are noticeably autocratic or top down in most organizations, even in those that claim to have identity packages derived from their 'whole cultures' and from bottom-up processes. The growing emphasis on corporate identity thus breeds a new kind of corporate vanity, which corresponds to what Baudrillard calls a ' "narcissistic" faithfulness to one's own sign and to one's own formula' (1988: 41).

Who's Telling the Story?

But the organizational 'formula' or identity is not predetermined or given once and for all. As Ashforth and Mael (1996) rightly point out, identities of organizations are *narratives*—that is, idealized accounts or stories about organizations and their self-perceived role in the marketplace of today (see also Czarniawska 1997). But who is orchestrating such accounts, and who is telling the story?

Clearly, many organizations hope that their members will internalize their narratives, make them their own and perhaps even become ambassadors of the organization. And, this is one way in which organizations today are consolidating their internal and external communications functions. This strategy is not new. Kaufman's (1960) classic study of the US Forest Service, for example, shows how ostensibly external communications, like public talks by forest rangers, are used to solidify those employees' organizational identification. However, as some organizations have come to realize, identification cannot be inspired through simple reliance on traditional communication channels, like internal seminars in which employees are informed about the latest version of the corporate profile. To have employees internalize corporate narratives requires a more direct involvement of them in the articulation of the organization's identity. Some companies have regular luncheons where employees comment on the popular management books of the day and explain what their company's corporate culture means to them. In other words, to allow members to rearticulate organizational narratives in an apparently open and creative manner is to stimulate identification. Such employee communication programs thus become part of the new emphasis on participation and involvement (see e.g. Kunda 1992), although they are highly variable in their motives, processes, and effects.

Few managers, however, seem to be willing to take the chance of allowing relatively unfettered communications by employees to external stakeholders. Although they are often aware of their multiple identities (cf. Cheney 1991) and the advantages of strategic ambiguity (Eisenberg 1984) when *formulating* their visions and mission statements, their willingness to let employees interpret the corporate symbols freely is the exception more often than the rule (Fairhurst, forthcoming). Instead, we see corporate managers and consultants of corporate identity eager to expound the *exact* meaning of corporate symbols to the world around them. Bang & Olufsen is now trying to convince its employees that its organization and its products can be properly described with the values of 'excellence, synthesis, and poetry'. While these values *may* be compelling, consider how the identity of the organization in this and similar cases is articulated by a relatively small group of members. It is ironic that so many organizations still issue in a controlled and top-down manner messages that are expected to be 'owned' by all segments of the organization's membership.

Even corporate buildings are, as Berg and Kreiner (1990: 62) point out, 'seldom left to speak for themselves' by top management. Rather, their description and interpretation are a privilege assumed by CEOs, communication managers, and other architects of organizational identity. Explaining the significance of Volvo's pentagon-shaped Kalmar plant, the vice president of corporate planning suggested that 'it was a signal to the whole company that we were fully backing up what we were saying about work democracy, technological innovations, etc.' (cited in Berg and Kreiner 1990: 57). Such accounts not only work as retrospective rationalizations within the group of responsible identity managers but can also be seen as purposeful *over*determinations through which organizations make sure that their symbols are always interpreted 'correctly'. This point is clearly illustrated in another interesting example from Berg and Kreiner in which a marketing manager of a leading Swedish office furniture manufacturer explains the round shapes used in the organization's headquarters (cited in Berg and Kreiner 1990: 49):

The domed roof, in its form and design, consequently symbolizes the rounded details in our assortment. In the interior we have rounded doors and some corners are similarly rounded instead of being right-angled in order to accentuate the identity of the product . . . In the exterior, logo, architecture, and product program we are everywhere confronted with the same round basic form. From the moment we enter the reception we are also confronted with the positive sense of well-being associated with success. No communication problems here.

Many identity-handlers believe their outward symbols to have a direct relationship to 'what's inside' the organization. And often they speak unreflectively about capturing the organization's 'essence' (Christensen and Askegaard, forthcoming). When architects of corporate identity are insistent in articulating what the organization's identity *is*, they presume to allow for the identity to rise up out of the work relations and culture of the organization. Attempts to create, control, and project corporate identities are thus taken very seriously, with the expectation that a variety of stakeholders will join in the worship of the organization.

Interpretive Flexibility

The absorption of contemporary organizations into their own symbolic constructions is thus narrowed down to a relatively small clique of decision-makers speaking on behalf of the rest of the organization. Within this clique and in stark contrast to the passive role left for other organizational members, a great deal of creativity with respect to the expression of corporate identity is unfolded. Again, the Bang & Olufsen example mentioned above is an interesting case in point. Using philosophers and artists to articulate and present the company's new values of excellence, synthesis, and poetry to staff members, Bang & Olufsen emphasizes that, whereas other organizations simply *invent* values, Bang & Olufsen has *found* these values in the organization's own culture. Excellence, synthesis, and poetry are, in other words, described as being 'naturally' and almost inevitably linked to the corporate 'soul'.

Considering that corporate symbols of identity are seen as being integral to the organization, the interpretive flexibility for decision-makers and consultants in periods of organizational change is striking. What used to be held as natural and inevitable will suddenly be dissonant and out of place. The adeptness of managers to reinterpret the history or the logo of their organization is all the more remarkable when seen in the light of the basic assumptions of much identity management that *continuity* is important and that organizations need to be true to their history (e.g. Olins 1989). Large department stores—like, for example, Sears and Penney's in the USA—are careful to craft their new lines of clothing and their products in ways that situate them within the store's traditions. What is continuity, however, in this context? And what does it mean to be 'true' to the history of the company? Although it is widely accepted that continuity is an important dimension of *individual* identity (e.g. Mead 1934; Erikson 1968), it is not clear in exactly what respects this observation applies to organizational identity.

Most organizations want their audiences to see them as stable yet responsive entities, with an inspiring history and a reliable presence. This, however, is not easy to accomplish in a world that seems to be demanding radical changes and almost unlimited flexibility. Organizations today confront a rhetorical situation that simultaneously demands consistency and celebrates change as an unmitigated and unquestioned good. To manage organizational identity under such constraints requires a creative ability to reinterpret the mission of the organization and to link rhetorically the changes of the organization with central symbols of its past. As the changes become more fundamental, the ability to redefine continuity becomes all the more pressing. As Ashforth and Mael (1996: 27) put it: 'Indeed, managers of organizations undergoing a radical transformation often attempt to foster the perception of continuity by simply couching the OI [organizational identity] at a higher level of abstraction (e.g. a stable and mechanistic retailer in the process of becoming a dynamic and organic one may be said to be reaffirming its dedication to service excellence).' Such attempts to recast the past are not always successful in the eyes of employees and other audiences. Still, their significance should not be underestimated. To management, they represent a sense of control, a sense of ability to master and orchestrate the symbolic significance of the organization *vis-à-vis* its various publics or stakeholders. In fact, value-based abstract terms, such as those used in many corporate identity campaigns, are interesting for their abilities to command emotional allegiance yet conceal differences or even deny specificity (Cheney 1999; see also Eisenberg 1984).

CORPORATE SELF-SEDUCTION

Leadership is sometimes described as the ability to manage and reorganize symbols on behalf of others (Smircich and Stubbart 1985; Berg 1986). And, indeed, managers often believe that their role is to 'foster and maintain a system of more or less shared meanings so that coordinated behavior can occur' (Ashforth and Mael 1996: 35). However, coordinated behavior is not necessarily an indication of *shared* meanings. Although the linkage may sometimes be there, we find that, within the realm of identity management, there is great potential for self-delusion and self-seduction on the part of the sender. This is true when we look both at the behavior of organizational members and at the behavior of various external audiences.

The Illusion of Shared Meanings

As Donnellon *et al.* (1986) have illustrated, individuals in organizations account for common experiences in many different ways. People participating in, for example, a demonstration or a strike typically explain their behavior so differently that the notion of shared meaning becomes problematic to uphold. Schwartzman's (1989) research demonstrates this clearly with something as seemingly straightforward as a meeting: the gathering signifies a variety of things for various participants, on both content and relational levels. Thus, what appears to the observer as coordinated behavior rooted in shared understandings and interpretations of a situation is often an illusion.

People enter organizations with different capabilities, preferences, and interests and often want to accomplish different things. Such differences typically persist within the shared structure provided by the organization. As Weick (1979: 91) illustrates so well, 'it is not essential to agree on ends in order to implement interdependence'. Rather, the community assumed to exist behind this interdependence is easier to maintain if its exact meaning is not expounded too explicitly (Weick 1995). While the development of common ends and shared goals is a product of interdependence, *not* its starting point, the 'sharedness' observed by managers is typically an explanation constructed *retrospectively*—that is, after the fact. These processes are rarely visible or clear to organizational members. Most organizing takes place under the *assumption* of sharedness and commonality. And recent efforts to identify and express *core* organizational values are good examples (see also Dahler-Larsen 1997*b*; 1998).

Occasionally, however, the assumption of unity of meaning is challenged. Most employees of organizations are not dupes. And, just as cynicism about programs such as 'empowerment' is on the rise (Argyris 1998), so we find attempts to manipulate corporate symbols such as mission statements to labor's advantage. Fairhurst, Jordan, and Neuwirth (1997) have found in both private- and public-sector organizations counter-efforts by employees at lower levels to 'manage the meaning of the mission', largely in response to the masking of authoritarian management practices by an avowed interest in 'participative decision-making'.

A major reason to question the assumption of shared meaning is related to the fact that lay members of an organization are rarely *as* involved in corporate symbols as policy-makers and top managers tend to believe. Obviously, because organizations have become an important source of identification for many people in the industrialized world (Cheney 1983; Cheney and Tompkins 1987; Christensen 1997; see also Burke 1950), it would be a mistake to assume that employees are not interested in the identity of their workplace. Even in an age with changing employment patterns, a decline in job loyalty, and the blurring of organizational boundaries, evidence shows a widespread desire to link individual selves to organizations of all sorts (Scott *et al.* 1998). This interest, however, should not be mistaken with the *deep* involvement or profound concern for formal identity campaigns that we find among managers or other architects of corporate identity. In general, employees like to know that their organization is doing well in the marketplace, that its activities are accepted in the wider community, and that it is able to communicate professionally in its surroundings. Sometimes employees even demand more and better market communication from their organizations (Christensen 1994). Recent research shows that many employees prefer organizational change programs that are generally consistent with how they see the organization's image: for example, in retaining old wooden floorboards in a newly remodeled grocery store (Rousseau 1998). In this respect, the organization can be seen as an integral part of the employee's 'extended self' (cf. Belk 1988). However, to assume that most members of an organization are deeply involved in the complex and elaborate narratives that their leaders construct on their behalf is to miss the point that most audiences, including employees, are often indifferent to what organizations have to say. Active involvement requires participation and voice; paradoxically, management typically sees the issue of identity as *too* important to allow for that.

Being fascinated with their own ideas and their own communication and eager to share this fascination with their surroundings, managers often forget that their framework of relevance is different both from that of other members of the organization and from that of external audiences.

Reversed Seduction

To support the assumption that the world is genuinely involved in what organizations have to say—an assumption often reproduced in the scholarly literature—we are told about critical and inquisitive stakeholders, unpredictable, demanding, and political consumers, news-hungry media, and opportune politicians willing to follow any whim on the popular agenda. Indeed, many organizations have come to realize that they can no longer hide behind fancy images or well-polished façades and that their activities have become 'transparent' to the critical gaze of their constituencies (e.g. Bernstein 1992). This critical gaze, however, is often mistaken for a general *interest* or even *involvement* in the organization and its communication.

Obviously, few organizations pretend to speak to *everyone*. Rather, they segment the world into different audiences and stakeholder groups, under the assumption that each will respond differently to the organization's messages. Hence, Coca-Cola uses polar bears to reach its youngest audiences, while fast-moving and more fragmented images are employed to address teenagers. Likewise, advertising messages for Silk Cut cigarettes do not address all cigarette-smokers but are designed to reach a specific audience with an interest in aesthetic and sophisticated symbols. And clearly, when it comes to the art of creating attention through fancy and precisely targeted images, many organizations have a very realistic understanding of their various audiences. However, attention does not necessarily entail interest, let alone involvement, on the organization's *own* terms. As Buhl (1991) has demonstrated, consumers are involved in advertising messages to the extent that these messages allow them to confirm or augment their own self-projects. The reception of advertising messages, in other words, is self-referential in the sense that the receiver reads meaning into the message by importing relevant information from his or her own world (see also Iser 1974; Eco 1979). Still, many organizations tend to believe that high attention scores and interest in their products translate into a general involvement in the specifics of their identities. Extending an example introduced earlier, marketing managers at Bang & Olufsen thus imagine that the values of excellence, synthesis, and poetry introduced to reorient the organization internally are important also to consumers when choosing between different hi-fi brands. Besides the obvious problems of linking internal symbols with external concerns, we see here a tendency for an organization to become seduced by its own symbolic constructions. This tendency is often augmented when organizations set out to analyze the reception of their communication.

Believing that their target audiences genuinely care about what they have to say, organizations find themselves deeply involved in surveys and research designed to test the salience of their identities in their surroundings. In such surveys, target consumers and other constituencies are asked detailed questions about their *attitudes* toward a number of social issues, about their *knowledge* of various advertisements and logos, about their *preferences* among different brands, and about their *intentions* to buy specific products. Consumers often participate willingly in such interrogations, either because of curiosity or because they feel that participation is an *obligation*—not only in the democratic, political system but also in the sphere of consumption (cf. Laufer and Paradeise 1990). But what does this process tell organizations about their own identities?

As social psychology has taught us, people often change their behavior when surveyed or otherwise engaged by social scientists. And, the 'Hawthorne Effect' even extends to active playfulness toward the observer by the observed (Gillespie 1991; see also Baudrillard 1990). While some people feel honored by the attention they receive by the researcher and perhaps even experience a sense of guilt when they are less than fully knowledgeable about the topics of the interview, others develop a certain cynicism or blasé attitude towards the whole poling institution.

As we have noticed observing surveys about brands and corporate identities, uncertainty is produced when consumers seek to conceal their lack of knowledge or when their ignorance is translated into prespecified types of answers that do not take the lack of knowledge into proper consideration. In such cases, lack of knowledge is sometimes hidden under preset response categories, such as, for example, 'perhaps' or 'to some degree'. Obviously, when such responses are added up, the total picture will reflect only little of the ignorance behind the answers. In other cases, the limited validity of the data obtained is due to indifference, and sometimes even outright cynicism, on the part of the interviewee. Here participation does not reflect interest, let alone involvement, but may simply represent what Baudrillard (1990; see also Baudrillard 1983) refers to as the ironic strategy of the object—that is, its seductive willingness to 'play the game'. Everyone is expected to readily participate in this game; to be able to produce *some* kind of message that suggests awareness, involvement, or concern. 'Sure, I'll tell you what I think of that ad.' (see Fig. 15.2). What we experience here is a case of *reversed* seduction. Whereas marketing and other kinds of persuasive communication are often seen as systems of one-way seduction, the actual behavior of consumers, or electorates, may well reverse the process and seduce corporate communicators to believe that the world actually cares about what their corporations are saying (cf. Laufer and Paradeise 1990).

As a consequence, the idea, suggested by Ashforth and Mael (1996: 35), that 'the major task of top management is to foster and maintain a system of more or less shared meanings so that coordinated behavior can occur' takes on strikingly new meanings. Coordinated behavior involving consumers and

'Oh, just give me a pack of whatever the guys in the marketing are targeting for jerks like me.'

Fig. 15.2. 'Jerks like me'

other constituencies may well occur in the sense that these groups respond to surveys and other analyses in ways that lend support to corporate ideas, plans, and self-images. However, since such responses may be a product of indifference or irony in a blasé and 'over-communicated' world, the coordinated behavior may reflect nothing more than a passing convergence in the research situation. In this way, organizations often operate in a polling universe of maximum uncertainty. Still, they assign equal importance to and perceive equal salience for all survey findings and so-called expressions of public opinion.

The Simulated Situation

Even when participation and the answers given reflect a genuine interest on the part of the external audience in providing information, the testing of the salience of corporate identities and their reception in public does not necessarily reflect the life of corporate signifiers in the public sphere. As Fornell (1976: 162) carefully puts it:

By and large . . . marketing research is a company-initiated communication, and as such it tends to perform the function of a feedback that represents consumer reaction to stimuli determined by the firm. This type of marketing research runs the risk of providing information that is heavily biased by the company's perception of what the relevant consumer and marketing problems actually are.

According to Fornell, marketing often determines in advance what information is needed and thus puts research on a certain track. The problem of measuring external perceptions, however, goes deeper than Fornell's comment indicates. As Baudrillard (1983) argues, much testing of opinions can be seen as *simulation* that enact the opinions it sets out to uncover (see also Weick 1979; Laufer and Paradeise 1990). For example, interviewees in such tests are rarely asked to talk in general terms about their perception of various corporate identities, but are guided through a delimited world of carefully chosen corporate signifiers, organized in order to elicit answers of specific relevance to the organization itself. When the LEGO corporation, for example, performs its elaborate image analyses, it distinguishes clearly between 'nice-to-know' and 'need-to-know' information, where the latter refers to consumer answers to questions directly related to LEGO's own marketing model. This approach makes sense in a world crowded with information, but it tends to become self-seductive by providing only the kind of information that organizations are asking for. A similar thing is going on when organizations focus too much attention on the ideal—but *a*typical—heavy user of their product. In their constant search for new ideas, advertising agencies often fall prey to this approach, because heavy users of a product are typically able to provide thicker and more interesting descriptions of their consumption than the average consumer (Schudson 1993). This practice, which is not confined to the advertising industry, is clearly self-seductive.

The social situation enacted by external analyses thus has little in common with real-life encounters between corporate symbols and their average external audience (cf. Alvesson 1996). As Holbrook (1980: 36) points out, most consumers 'don't give a damn' about the details that organizations associate with their products and their brands:

Yes, we can build multiattribute models that predict preference toward toothpaste; we can generate complex multidimensional spaces that represent perceptions of cigarettes; we can construct devilishly clever procedures that trace the acquisition of information on cereal brands; we can—with our bare hands—construct mighty regression analyses that relate detergent usage to 300 separate life-style variables. In short—when it comes to factors of least importance to the consumer's emotional, cultural, and spiritual existence—we excel.

Most market research has, as Schudson (1993: 65) puts it, 'very limited goals and a very narrow focus and it often concentrates on product categories where the stakes for business are high but the interest of consumers low'. As a consequence, the answers provided by the interviewees may well be simulated too. Consider, again, the notion of a corporate image analysis. The assumption behind such analyses is the idea that the organization has one or several images 'out there'—images that can, or should, be captured by an analysis, almost like butterflies can be caught by a net. Assuming that its target audience is involved in its communication, the organization asks select members of this audience to respond to its symbols and perhaps even to rank them in relation to the symbols of its competitors. As it appears, the final product of such exercises—the 'corporate image'—is not something that pre-exists the analysis but is a methodological artifact—that is, a notion constructed in the process (Christensen and Askegaard, forthcoming). Thus, we see how ritualistic surveys can yield methodological constructs with the polling organization and its sponsor seeing largely what they want to see.

Under the circumstances outlined above, it makes little sense to suggest that 'images that prevail internally for the organization are those that survive a "reality test" against external points of reference' (Ashforth and Mael 1996: 40). In fact, there may be little connection between the two sets of images and identities for an organization: those held by employees and those projected in organizational communication campaigns (Treadwell and Harrison 1994). While some images may fail because they are explicitly rejected by external stakeholders—the attempts by Royal Dutch Shell to promote itself as environmentally responsible may well be rejected—most corporate images exist in a simulated universe, relatively independent of the concerns and interests of people in their day-to-day lives. Thus, reality tests, in the sense suggested by Ashforth and Mael, may rarely take place. To the extent that the world is willing to 'play the game' and perhaps even appropriate the identity language of contemporary organizations, their indifference or ignorance may never dawn on those organizations (see Fig. 15.3).

CONCLUSION

Although some of the claims and illustrations in this chapter are expressed quite strongly, we do so in order to make an important point about taken-for-granted assumptions in the management of corporate identity. Large corporations and other organizations have become so preoccupied with carefully crafted, elaborate, and univocal expressions of their mission and 'essence' that they often overlook penetrating questions about stakeholder involvement. Also, many organizations fail to establish sensible priorities for the variety of messages they produce. Further, with a few exceptions (e.g. Hatch and Schultz 1997) we see the same blind spots in recent academic writings on corporate identity management. This unfortunately narrow viewpoint pushes out considerations of how employees may consider the identity of 'their' organization. Even when demographic information from and surveys of employees are used to 'construct' a unified corporate identity, the multiplicity of meanings is obscured and the issue of *degree* of attachment or concern is downplayed.

With reference to 'outside' stakeholders or audiences, such as consumers, the process of corporate identity management inside the organization is often

'I can't decide. I'm having a brand identity crisis.'

Fig. 15.3. 'I can't decide'

overwhelmed by a strong presumption of interest and 'ownership'. More specifically, we find patterns of both self-absorption and self-seduction in identity management, and these tendencies are often beyond the full awareness of executives and technical experts working in the arena of corporate identity. At the most concrete level, we have suggested that the very ways in which data are gathered and interpreted in the process of creating an organizational identity can serve as much to self-confirm organizational communications campaigns as they do to 'reach out' beyond the perceptual world of the organization.

We believe that most large organizations do not fully appreciate the extent to which the problem of identity is 'recursive', in that an organization's very assertions of it become part of its own self-narrative and the construction of the future identities it chooses to project. With a century of study of identity behind us, we can say that identity should be understood much more as a process than as a thing that can easily be apprehended or held constant. This aspect of identity development makes it especially easy for organizations that invest a lot in telling their story or in saying who they are to be completely wrapped up in their own message making. The new organizational self-reflexivity envisioned by the editors of this volume should, therefore include a strong self-critical dimension able to capture the tendencies of self-absorption and self-seduction described in this chapter.

In a world saturated with symbols, where there is a great demand for every organization to keep communicating, it is easy to think that each message and every campaign are taken seriously and received in the ways designed. But such meanings are often malleable, unstable, and of only ephemeral interest. In fact, in many cases, cynicism may be the most prominent outcome.

Our closing message is simply that organizations should not *assume* either that their identities 'are' what they tell them to be or that people *necessarily care*. At the very least, such basic assumptions need to be examined. While we cannot easily disprove them, neither can they remain established today with the kind of certainty that seems to prevail.

NOTE

1 In this chapter, we focus on expressions of identity. Thus, we do not distinguish sharply between the notions of corporate identity and organizational identity. Although we acknowledge an emergent tradition to reserve the former to symbols, designs, names, logos, and other malleable signifiers of the organization and the latter to 'deeper' layers of organizational life, like, for example, tacit meanings, values, and processes of identification (see e.g. the special issue on identity in the *European Journal of Marketing* [1997], 31: 5–6), we find that such a distinction reifies the organization 'behind' its symbols and ignores the fact that the organization and its symbols are coexisting dimensions of the same process of signification. From a semiotic perspective, Christensen and Askegaard (forthcoming) are arguing that our access to organizations are always mediated by representations, these being not only carefully designed—and sometimes superficial—symbols, but also values, narratives, and corporate behaviors. As a consequence, whatever we refer to as 'organizational' is no less semiotic (in the sense of being a sign that refers to something else) than the 'corporate'.

REFERENCES

Alvesson, M. (1996), 'Leadership Studies: From Procedure and Abstraction to Reflexivity and Situation', *Leadership Quarterly*, 7/4: 455–85.

Argyris, C. (1998), 'Empowerment: The Emperor's New Clothes', *Harvard Business Review*, May–June: 98–107.

Ashforth, B. E., and Mael, F. A. (1996), 'Organizational Identity and Strategy as a Context for the Individual', *Advances in Strategic Management*, 13: 19–64.

Baudrillard, J. (1983), *In the Shadow of the Silent Majorities* (New York: Semiotext(e)).

—— (1988), *The Ecstasy of Communication* (New York: Semiotext(e)).

—— (1990), *Fatal Strategies* (New York: Semiotext(e)).

Belch, G. E., Belch, M. A., and Villarreal, A. (1987), 'Effects of Advertising Communications: Review of Research', *Research in Marketing*, 9: 59–117.

Belk, R. (1988), 'Possessions and the Extended Self', *Journal of Consumer Research*, 15: 139–68.

Berg, P. O. (1986), 'The Symbolic Management of Human Resources', *Human Resource Management*, 25/4: 557–79.

—— and Gagliardi, P. (1985), 'Corporate Images: A Symbolic Perspective of the Organization–Environment Interface', paper presented at the SCOS conference on Corporate Images, Antibes, France.

—— and Kreiner, K. (1990), 'Corporate Architecture: Turning Physical Settings into Symbolic Resources', in P. Gagliardi (ed.), *Symbols and Artifacts: Views of the Corporate Landscape* (Berlin: Walter de Gruyter), 41–67.

Bergquist, W. (1993), *The Postmodern Organization: Mastering the Art of Irreversible Change* (San Francisco: Jossey-Bass Publishers).

Bernstein, D. (1992), *In the Company of Green: Corporate Communications for the New Environment* (London: ISBA Publications).

Broms, H., and Gahmberg, H. (1983), 'Communication to Self in Organizations and Cultures', *Administrative Science Quarterly*, 28: 482–95.

Buhl, C. (1991), 'The Consumer's Ad: The Art of Making Sense of Advertising', in H. H. Larsen, D. G. Mick, and C. Alsted (eds.), *Marketing and Semiotics* (Copenhagen: Handelshøjskolens Forlag), 104–27.

Burke, K. (1950), *A Rhetoric of Motives* (Berkeley and Los Angeles: University of California Press).

Cheney, G. (1983), 'The Rhetoric of Identification and the Study of Organizational Communication', *Quarterly Journal of Speech*, 69: 143–58.

—— (1991), *Rhetoric in an Organizational Society: Managing Multiple Identities* (Colombia, SC: University of South Carolina Press).

—— (1999), *Values at Work: Employee Participation Meets Market Pressure at Mondragón* (Ithaca, NY: Cornell University Press).

—— and Christensen, L. T. (forthcoming), 'Identity at Issue: Linkages between "Internal" and "External" Organizational Communication', in F. M. Jablin and L. L. Putnam (eds.), *New Handbook of Organizational Communication* (Thousand Oaks, Calif.: Sage).

—— and Tompkins, P. K. (1987), 'Coming to Terms with Organizational Identification and Commitment', *Central States Speech Journal*, 38: 1–15.

Christensen, L. T. (1994), *Markedskommunikation som organiseringsmåde: En kulturteoretisk analyse* (Copenhagen: Akademisk Forlag).

—— (1995), 'Buffering Organizational Identity in the Marketing Culture', *Organization Studies*, 16/4: 651–72.

—— (1997), 'Marketing as Auto-Communication', *Consumption, Markets and Culture*, 1/3: 197–227.

—— (1999), 'Reklame i selvsving: Selvreference og auto-kommunikation i reklamens univers', unpublished manuscript.

—— and Askegaard, S. (forthcoming), 'Corporate Identity and Corporate Image Revisited: A Semiotic Perspective', *European Journal of Marketing*.

—— and Cheney, G. (1994), 'Articulating Identity in an Organizational Age', in S. A. Deetz (ed.), *Communication Yearbook 17* (Thousand Oaks, Calif.: Sage), 222–35.

Crable, R. E., and Vibbert, S. L. (1983), 'Mobil's Epideictic Advocacy: Observations of Prometheus-Bound', *Communication Monographs*, 50: 380–94.

Czarniawska, B. (1997), *Narrating the Organization: Dramas of Institutional Identity* (Chicago: University of Chicago Press).

Dahler-Larsen, P. (1997*a*), 'Moral Functionality and Organizational Identity: A Perspective on the New "Moralized Discourses" in Organizations', in M. A. Rahim and R. T. Golembiewsky (eds.), *Current Topics in Management* (Greenwich, Conn.: JAI Press), 2: 305–26.

—— (1997*b*), 'Organizational Identity as a "Crowded Category": A Case of Multiple and Quickly-Shifting We-Typifications', in S. Sackman (ed.), *Cultural Complexity in Organizations: Inherent Contrasts and Contradictions* (Thousand Oaks, Calif.: Sage), 367–90.

—— (1998), 'What 18 Case Studies of Organizational Culture Tell Us about Counter-Intentional Effects of Attempts to Establish Shared Values in Organizations', in M. A. Rahim, R. T. Golembiewsky, and C. C. Lundberg (eds.), *Current Topics in Management* (Stanford, Conn.: JAI Press), 3: 151–73.

Donnellon, A., Gray, B., and Bougon, M. G. (1986), 'Communication, Meaning and Organized Action', *Administrative Science Quarterly*, 31: 43–55.

Eco, U. (1979), *The Role of the Reader* (Bloomington, Ind.: Indiana University Press).

Eisenberg, E. (1984), 'Ambiguity as Strategy in Organizational Communication', *Communication Monographs*, 51: 227–42.

Erikson, E. H. (1968), *Identity—Youth and Crises* (New York: Norton).

Fairhurst, G. T. (forthcoming), 'Dualisms in Leadership', in F. M. Jablin and L. L. Putnam (eds.), *New Handbook of Organizational Communication* (Thousand Oaks, Calif.: Sage).

—— Jordan, J. M., and Neuwirth, K. (1997), 'Why are We Here? Managing the Meaning of the Organizational Mission', *Journal of Applied Communication Research*, 25: 243–63.

Fombrun, C. J., and van Riel, C. (1997), 'The Reputational Landscape', *Corporate Reputation Review*, 1/1: 5–13.

Fornell, C. (1976), *Consumer Input for Marketing Decisions: A Study of Corporate Departments for Consumer Affairs* (New York: Praeger).

Gillespie, R. (1991), *Manufacturing Knowledge: A History of the Hawthorne Experiment* (Cambridge: Cambridge University Press).

Hatch, M. J., and Schultz, M. (1997), 'Relations between Organizational Culture, Identity and Image', *European Journal of Marketing*, 31/5–6: 356–65.

Hirschhorn, L., and Gilmore, T. (1992), 'The New Boundaries of the "Boundaryless Company"', *Harvard Business Review*, May–June: 104–15.

Holbrook, M. B. (1980), 'Introduction: The Esthetic Imperative in Consumer Research', in E. C. Hirschman and M. B. Holbrook (eds.), *Symbolic Consumer Behavior* (Ann Arbor: Association of Consumer Research), 36.

Iser, W. (1974), *The Implied Reader* (Baltimore: Johns Hopkins University Press).

Kaufman, H. (1960), *The Forest Ranger: A Study in Administrative Behavior* (Baltimore: Johns Hopkins University Press).

Kotler, P. (1987), 'Semiotics of Person and Nation Marketing', in J. Umiker-Sebeok (ed.), *Marketing and Semiotics: New Directions in the Study of Signs for Sale* (Berlin: Mouton de Gruyter), 3–12.

Kunda, G. (1992), *Engineering Culture: Control and Commitment in a High-Tech Corporation* (Philadelphia: Temple University Press).

Laufer, R., and Paradeise, C. (1990), *Marketing Democracy: Public Opinion and Media Formation in Democratic Societies* (New Brunswick, NJ: Transaction).

Leitch, S., and Motion, J. (1999), 'The Truth Games of Corporate Identity', paper presented at the ICCIS conference on Corporate Identity, University of Strathclyde, Scotland.

Lotman, Y. M. (1990), *Universe of the Mind: A Semiotic Theory of Culture* (London: I. B. Tauris).

Luhmann, N. (1990), *Essays of Self-Reference* (New York: Columbia University Press).

Marchand, R. (1998), *Creating the Corporate Soul: The Rise of Public Relations and Corporate Imagery in American Big Business* (Berkeley and California: University of California Press).

Mead, G. H. (1934), *Mind, Self and Society* (Chicago: University of Chicago Press).

Olins, W. (1989), *Corporate Identity: Making Business Strategy Visible through Design* (London: Thames and Hudson).

Onkvisit, S., and Shaw, J. J. (1987), 'Standardized International Advertising', *Colombia Journal of World Business*, Fall: 43–55.

Phelps, J., Plumley, J., and Johnson, E. (1994), 'Integrated Marketing Communications: Who's Doing What?', *Proceedings of the American Academy of Advertising Conference*, 143–5.

Rousseau, D. (1998), 'Why Workers Still Identify With Organizations', *Journal of Organizational Behavior*, 19: 217–34.

Schmitt, B., and Simonson, A. (1997), *Marketing Aesthetics: The Strategic Management of Brands, Identity, and Image* (New York: Free Press).

Schudson, M. (1993), *Advertising, the Uneasy Persuasion: Its Dubious Impact on American Society* (New York: Basic Books).

Schultz, D. E., Tannenbaum, S. I., and Lauterborn, R. F. (1994), *The New Marketing Paradigm: Integrated Marketing Communications* (Chicago: NTC Business Books).

Schwartzman, H. (1989), *The Meeting: Gatherings in Organizations and Communities* (New York: Plenum Press).

Scott, C. R., Corman, S. R., and Cheney, G. (1998), 'Development of a Structurational Model of Identification in the Organization', *Communication Theory*, 8: 298–336.

Sherry, J. F. (1987), 'Advertising as a Cultural System', in J. Umiker-Sebeok (ed.), *Marketing and Semiotics: New Directions in the Study of Signs for Sale* (Berlin: Mouton de Gruyter), 441–61.

Smircich, L., and Stubbart, C. (1985), 'Strategic Management in an Enacted World', *Academy of Management Review*, 10: 724–36.

Treadwell, D. F., and Harrison, T. M. (1994), 'Conceptualizing and Assessing Organizational Image: Model Images, Commitment, and Communication', *Communication Monographs*, 61: 63–85.

Weick, K. E. (1979), *The Social Psychology of Organizing* (Reading, Mass.: Addison-Wesley).

—— (1995), *Sensemaking in Organizations* (London: Sage).

16

Identity Lost or Identity Found? Celebration and Lamentation over the Postmodern View of Identity in Social Science and Fiction

Barbara Czarniawska

One persistent topic in the recent wave of so-called postmodernist thinking is that of individual identity. The insertion of the problematizing adjective 'so-called' suggests at the outset that there is some doubt as to the kind of thinking that may be called 'postmodern'.

Indeed, the adjectives 'postmodern' and 'postmodernist' are frequently used in social science and humanities writing nowadays. Sometimes they stand contrasted to 'modern' and 'modernist', sometimes not; sometimes they are used synonymously, sometimes not. I have no ambition to sort out various semantic confusions once and for all, but I wish to propose a temporary order for the purposes of this chapter. I shall use the word 'postmodern' to denote a special kind of attitude, a sensibility that has its roots in one or another kind of disenchantment with what Lyotard (1979/1987) calls 'The Modern Project'. It often comes in one of two versions: despairing or celebratory. The former concentrates on a feeling of disorientation, meaninglessness, and fragmentation (Wilson 1991). The latter is a feeling that now, at last, an era of true freedom has come, of endless experimentation with no rules and no limitations. Rosenau (1995) calls it an 'upbeat postmodernism' and locates it in North America.

I would claim that it is also possible to distinguish a third attitude, that of skepticism towards the solutions of modernism ('more control, better control') combined with the realization that actions aimed at wringing order out of disorder seem to be necessary, albeit they are at best only temporarily successful. In other words, it is the attitude of an ironic observer who sees the paradoxicality of life and yet, as an actor, bravely engages in daily efforts to deparadoxify (Luhmann 1991) with few expectations of predictable results or lasting effects, and the acceptance of the inevitability of unexpected consequences. This is an attitude that permeates the present chapter.

The despairing and celebratory attitudes can easily be located in the writings on identity in social science in general and in organization studies in particular. Before I embark on illustrating and interpreting this trend, however, let me restate what previous authors in this volume have already taken up—that is, the connection between individual and organizational identities.

It is likely that the analogy between the formal organization and a person has its roots in the concept of *legal persona*, an invention demanded by and justified by its central place in the core set of institutions in the present Western institutional order: the market, the state, and the individual (Meyer 1986). In spite of many populist interpretations that contrast the individual with the other two, Meyer claims that the notion and the institution of the individual are necessary for the existence of both markets and states. His claim finds support in a thesis concerning the importance of *systemic* accountability in the modern order (Douglas 1986; Giddens 1991). Accordingly, the state assumes its citizens are accountable and the market requires accountable producers and consumers. The invention of the legal persona simply apportions accountability to a collective on the same principle as it would to an individual.

This social institution, or, as Karin Knorr-Cetina (1994) would have called it, societal fiction, has left many metaphorical traces in organization theory. As I have pointed out before (Czarniawska-Joerges 1994; Czarniawska 1997), organization theory, more often than not, treats organizations as super-persons, and therefore ascribes to them many anthropomorphic properties. Organizations make decisions, behave, learn, fail, and, of course, 'have' and 'exhibit' identities. The recent increase of interest in the concept of individual identity in the social sciences (see e.g. Gergen and Davis 1985; Gergen 1991, 1994; Giddens 1991; Kellner 1992) was joined by a similar increase of the interest in the concept of organizational identity. A recent example is the anthology edited by Whetten and Godfrey (1998).

In what follows, I will first look for a difference between what can be called an inherited view and an emerging view on individual identity. I will then examine the reasons for celebration and lamentation provoked by this emerging view.[1] I will end with a suggestion that both celebration and lamentation are still grounded in the inherited view of identity, and that one way to consider the possible consequences of the emerging view on identity is to look to science-fiction writings, which are less constricted in their ways of interpreting the world than is organization theory. By doing so, I will try to conscript science fiction (or some of it) into the ironic attitude.

IDENTITY: AN INHERITED AND AN EMERGING VIEW

The inherited view on identity can be briefly and with considerable simplification summarized as conceptualizing the individual identity as an expression of a 'true' Self—that is, a Self that is authentic,[2] coherent, and deep (a 'core' of one's personality). The diacritical view on language explains that these concepts are understood by virtue of not denoting what is seen as the opposite, referring to an expression of the Self that is faked, fragmented, and superficial. Thus the organizational literature postulated that an organization's identity should be equated with what the organization's members believe to be its distinctive, central, and enduring characteristics (see e.g. Albert and Whetten 1985; Dutton and Dukerich 1991; Alvesson and Björkman 1992; but observe that these authors will develop and complexify their views in time: see e.g. Dukerich *et al.* 1998).

The emerging view can be equally characterized in brief as conceptualizing identity as a social institution (Meyer 1986), historically and geographically contingent (MacIntyre 1981/1990; Rorty 1991), where *institution* is understood as a repetitive pattern of collective practices legitimated by a normative justification (Czarniawska 1997). An identity can thus be usefully conceptualized as a legitimate prescription (or prescriptions) for identity construction typical for a given time and place. Such a conceptualization necessitates historical and geographical comparisons and, indeed, there could be no better argument for the institutional and constructed view of identity than a comparison between a prescription for modern identity and that for a premodern one—for example, the ancient Roman (MacIntyre 1981/1990; Pitkin 1984). The latter, claims MacIntyre, was a combination of *particularity*, or the taking of a particular stance in a given community, and *accountability* towards that community, not towards the abstract system, as Giddens (1991) shows in his discussion of modern identity. Particularity and accountability formed the frame of an identity, which was to be filled with varying degrees of achievement of traditional Roman virtues, such as *pietas* (reverence for the past), *gravitas* (bearing the sacred weight of the past), *dignitas* (a manner worthy of one's task and station), and *constantia* (faithfulness to tradition) (Pitkin 1984). In other words, the identity of a person did not lie in his or her individuality, but in his or her relationship to the community in which he or she lived.

A prescription for a modern identity is based in the notion of individuation (Berger *et al.* 1974)—that is, of distancing and distinguishing the Self from any given community. One part of it concerns the way of composing the Self into a whole. This is to be achieved, claims Kavolis (Brown 1989: 195), by striving to achieve a *coherence* between the individual's experience and the way this experience is expressed, to produce a lasting memory (in the individual and other people) of a *continuity* in the course of the individual's life, and a conscious but not excessive *commitment* to the manner in which the individual expresses his or her Self. The entity thus composed differentiates him- or herself from others by demonstrating *self-respect* (independent of others' opinion), *efficiency* (capacity to accomplish one's own projects), *autonomy* (no need to rely on others), and *flexibility* (varying commitment to issues and projects) (Meyer 1986).

In other words, an ancient Roman would be a non-identity thrown outside his or her community (until he or she acquired a new stance in the new community), whereas a modern person would be expected to be 'himself' or 'herself' no matter what community or circumstances prevailed. Or, as MacIntyre puts it, the modern identity is plotted against a person's life history, whereas the Roman one was plotted against that of the community.

Life experience tells us that, according to the title of the book by Latour (1993), 'we have never been modern', not completely at any rate. While the prescription for modern identity is never successfully fulfilled, there are many elements of the premodern identity to be found in actions and self-presentations of both people and organizations. Particularity might be defined by a profession or a place in the production system, while dignity is still a virtue.[3] One's identity within an organization may be plotted against the history of the organization ('it was not until the merger occurred that Smith's special talents were revealed'). By reverse analogy, it is possible that the ancient Romans built their new identities in Britain around the abstract image of the Empire, because the barbarians would understand nothing about the soldiers' actual positions within their community. To continue, contemporary organization members are as accountable to the organization as the Romans were, but to an organization as a system, not as a community. And again, the creation of a family-like image of organization is but a way of evoking accountability towards an actual community, and not an abstract system. The Romans were much more modern than we assume,[4] whereas we are much more premodern that we sometimes wish to admit.

A systematic reflection thus reveals, in tune with ironist postmodernist thinking, that the breach between the premodern and the modern has been never successfully completed. Accordingly, a more complex picture of identity, though still grounded in individuation, may give a more accurate description—but not a prescription—of contemporary identity. Whether it is identity itself that is changing or simply how it is viewed is impossible and perhaps unnecessary to judge. After all, identity is an abstract concept that has to be filled with concrete contents with its every use.

Such a view on identity would see it not as found or exhibited, but as produced and reproduced in interactions, and thus Davies and Harré (1991) speak of *positioning* and Gergen (1994) of a *net of relationships*. Such an identity would be stable, assuming the persistence of a *memory of past interactions* (thus the 'cultural shock' of a person whose direct environment does not share her memory with her). As contemporary people move around and constantly remake their nets of relationships, identity becomes de-centered and multiple, which is counteracted by an effort of *self-narration* ('what I just did may seem strange to you, but you see, in my culture . . .'). The act of self-narration is present in premodern and modern identity prescriptions, but a different function is ascribed to it. Self-narration was seen as a simple report of life's events in the pre-modern era, as an account of these events against a life project in a modern era, and as a collage-like composition of these events aimed at producing coherence in our own times.

Such a collaged identity is *susceptible to fashion*—that is, it re-forms itself according to various identity prescriptions that dominate at certain times and places ('a green company', 'an innovative company', 'a company devoted to its tradition', etc.). Various events become composed differently depending on the prescription chosen ('We have always been attentive to the natural environment', or 'By introducing the environmental program, we were the first to break with a tradition that . . .').

While such a way of understanding identity may not be especially problematic in its metaphorical uses—that is, when applied to companies—it baffles those analysts of individual identity who formerly grounded their definition of identity in the notion of 'the true Self'. This notion cannot be preserved in the new context. 'Self . . . must be treated as a construction that, so to speak, proceeds from the outside in as well as from the inside out, from culture to mind as well as from mind to culture' (Bruner 1990: 108).

After all, says Rorty (1991: 192), the human self is just a self-reweaving web of beliefs that are revealed as habits of action. This web is centerless and contingent, connecting the self 'to those with similar tastes and similar identities'. The Self is historical, and is both constituted by and constitutive of a community. If the community conceives itself to be an abstract system, as is the case with formal organizations, the resulting selves will also be conceived of in abstract terms—a feature that often baffles an outsider witnessing organizational presentations. '"I hold a Chair in Management." "Then you must be the head of the department." "Oh, no, gods forbid!"' Thus proceeds a constructivist spiral, where I present myself in abstract, systemic terms, as the convention requires, but, in order to make them understandable, I have to resort to the history of a particular community: 'You see, in Sweden professors are not the heads of departments anymore.'

What becomes clear is that identities are performed in conversation, that what we achieve in conversation is positioning *vis-à-vis* other people, and against the background of a plot that is negotiated by those taking part in the conversation (Davies and Harré 1991). Whether this background is the history of the community or one's life project may vary from one conversation to another. Thus, the Self is produced, reproduced, and maintained in conversations, past and present. It is community constituted, as Rorty says, in the sense of being created by those who take part in a conversation; it is historical because past conversations are evoked in the course of present ones.

Such a view evokes different reactions. If there is no 'true Self', the question of authenticity is no longer pertinent. To those who lament, this means a moral downfall: in society where identity is 'just' narrated, fakes and masks will prevail, and nobody will be what they claim to be. The same assumption causes delight to those who celebrate: freed from the tyranny of authenticity, everybody will be who they want to be. Both these reactions return in fact to the inherited view of identity: the true Self is still there, but covered up or hidden. Both reactions ignore the *social* character of identity construction and do not understand the importance of positioning. Narrating an identity does not mean that the audience will accept it as such; positioning assumes an interaction. For example, throughout the 1980s Swedish public administrations made every effort to present themselves as a 'new' type of organization: efficient and cost-effective, with a glossy image. The reaction of the audience was to see them as effectively destroying their traditional identity, rooted deeply in the history of the particular community, and dedicating the 1990s to a desperate search for some kind of identity, imitating other countries and other models, and failing to find a coherent self-narrative (Czarniawska 1997). Authenticity does not seem to be in great demand anymore; one could say that it went out of fashion after having been deconstructed. The modern procedures for proving authenticity and for falsifying identifications are themselves in doubt, as Eco (1990: 200) convincingly shows: 'As a matter of fact, there is no ontological guarantee that the John I meet today is the same as the John I met yesterday. John undergoes physical (biological) changes much more so than a painting or a statue. Moreover, John can intentionally disguise himself in order to look like Tom.'

This brings us to the issue of the multiple and de-centered identities, which seem to be but a stronger expression of what was already seen as a defect of the modern identity: fragmentation (Berger *et al.* 1974). Again, those who despair predict that people deprived of a center will develop the symptoms of multiphrenia, or multiple personality disorder, and indeed quote many occurrences of this psychiatric disorder. Those who celebrate are enchanted with a vision of human kaleidoscopes or chameleons, armies of Zeligs (the infinitely adaptive hero of a Woody Allen movie by the same title). Both neglect the narrative rule of coherence, which differs from coherence demanded by a modern identity prescription and the *constantia* of the Romans. A successful identity presentation does not require that today's action conforms to yesterday's, but demands a convincing explanation ('my whole life changed after I went into therapy' and 'the new management team reworked all the principles upon which the company previously operated').

But the biggest worry for those who lament—and the biggest hope for those who celebrate—is yet another consequence that might be drawn from the emerging description of a contemporary identity. If identity is produced, reproduced, and maintained, machines can be used to produce it for people ('avatars') and produce it for themselves. What happens then? Will it be the end of the world, or the beginning of a Brave New one? Organization theorists do not engage in this discussion, although they should, as I shall argue at the end. Few social scientists do either (e.g. Latour 1996). The bulk of the discussion and speculation on this issue takes place in science fiction, a source that I shall use in the next section.

SOME NEW QUESTIONS CONCERNING PEOPLE AND MACHINES

'Modernist' science fiction used to consider the issue of machine and human identity as being an issue of control. Asimov's *I, Robot* (1950/1996), with the three famous 'laws of robotics', is an excellent example. He addressed such questions as how to prevent robots from hurting people, and whether a human being can love a robot, and, if so, whether it would gain control over humans. Asimov's collection of stories ends up with a provocative suggestion that Marvin Minsky must have loved: robots are more responsible than people, therefore human beings should relinquish their control to machines. Robots obedient to the three laws of robotics (specifying and proscribing situations threatening to human beings) will know better how to save the human race than the humans themselves.

The science-fiction novels back then always offered a useful insight for the students of identity: creating machines, people project into them the knowledge they possess about themselves. They hope that machines will lack certain defects humans have, or that they will acquire skills humans do not have. Machines, or at least cyborgs, are the sum of the self-knowledge that humans possess at any given time.

What is directly relevant to organizational life, however, is the new type of questions addressed by science-fiction writers today. For example, all kinds of interactive devices are being developed, although at the turn of the twenty-first century they are but crude imitations of the actual interactions between humans, and the positioning that takes place in such interactions is only rudimentary. But what if, asks Neal Stephenson in *The Diamond Age, or A Young Lady's Illustrated Primer* (1995), a truly interactive educative device can be designed? There is no doubt that companies would be extremely interested in a primer that socializes new members into the doings of their workplace. Such a primer needs to be only somewhat more advanced than the Macintosh interactive introduction to an Apple computer.

Stephenson boldly takes up the issue of multiple identities and their narrative glue: in his land of the future, identity prescriptions from different epochs will be mixed and exchanged. Money and power permitting, a disenchanted New York Jew can become a Neovictorian or a Confucian Chinese. In *The Diamond Age*, Judge Fang of the Coastal Republic, where 'he had rebuilt his own life after his career as a hoodlum in Lower Manhattan had brought him to a dead end' (Stephenson 1995: 133), contemplates a new turn:

'Actually, I am satisfied with my career, but dissatisfied with my tribal affiliation. I have grown disgusted with the Coastal Republic and have concluded that my true home lies in the Celestial Kingdom. I have often wondered whether the Celestial Kingdom is in need of magistrates, even those as poorly qualified as I.'

'This is a question I will have to take up with my superiors,' Dr. X said. 'However, given that the Celestial Kingdom currently has no magistrates whatsoever and therefore no judicial system, I deem it likely that some role can be found for one with your superb qualifications.' (Stephenson 1995: 153)

Judge's reasoning sounds like a satirical rendition of biographical narratives from Finnish engineers who became expatriates, as reported by Peltonen (1999). Far-fetched as it may seem, frequent changes of employment by many young computer specialists may be interpreted, in traditional terms, as a search for an environment that offers them a chance to express their true Self, or, in the terms of this text, as a search for environments that offer new, more exciting identities.

It should be added that Judge Fang's decision to change his tribal affiliation is not quite voluntary, but has to do with certain conditions stated by Dr X. Take a step further, and you will enter Margaret Atwood's dystopia *The Handmaid's Tale* (1985), where a totalitarian regime enforces invented identities on its citizens, so that all became Neopuritans in the America of the future. Although there have been no other totalitarian stories written after 1989 (a naïve optimism or an acute diagnosis of the *zeitgeist*?), it is not impossible to realize that changes of identity—tribal/organizational affiliation, place of residence—are often more or less forced on the employees of contemporary organizations.

Memory of interactions past, that cornerstone in identity construction, can also prove movable. *Fools* (Cadigan 1992) presents a vision of a world where the memory of interaction can be registered, and therefore sold, bought, and produced. As the back-cover text succinctly informs the reader, 'In a world of brainsuckers and bodysnatchers, you can't take anything for granted. Not even your own identity.' Since the work of producing narrative coherence in such a world would be even more frantic than in the one in which we live at present, new questions arise: What kind of an identity can a memory-junkie have—or afford? And yet the leading AI-researchers of our time, Hans Moravec and Marvin Minsky, work on exactly this kind of project—of recording memory and experience. *The Experience Economy: Work is Theater & Every Business a Stage*, says the title of the newest book by Harvard Business School's authors B. Joseph Pine II and James Gilmore (1999). Goods and services are not what the contemporary economy is about, say the authors: experience is what sells, so you had better learn how to produce it. And, on a more metaphorical level, what kind of organizational identity do mergers and acquisitions produce? Indeed—what kind of experience is produced thereby?

One interesting aspect of the novels I mentioned is that they take place in a world saturated with organizations. All identity construction is embedded in an organizational context—one might conclude that this is the plot against which the contemporary identities are narrated—no longer the history of community (which community?) nor the life project (which one?). Even William Gibson's (1996) cyberpunks are entrepreneurs who make a living on the margins of, or at the expense of, big corporations. Gibson's message, at least, is very clear if paradoxical: the more organizations there are, the more chaotic the world becomes (chaos, in most science fiction, is seen as a post-modern and positive alternative to totalitarianism).

This short chapter does not allow for a systematic registration and interpretation of all the portents of the changes that the emerging view on individual and organizational identities might bring. My intention is to suggest that, instead of restating the old dilemmas of authenticity or fragmentation, we should look for inspiration in texts and other creations that are not bound by conventional science requirements in their ways of interpreting the world. After all, as Kundera (1988: 32) says, 'The novel dealt with the unconscious before Freud, the class struggle before Marx, it practiced phenomenology . . . before the phenomenologists'. But before you reach for the science-fiction shelf, let us remain with scientific endeavors for awhile: let me introduce Olga, a machine-produced identity authored by several organizations.

WHO/WHAT IS OLGA?

Olga (Box 16.1) is not an organizational identity, but an identity created by five cooperating organizations: two departments at Stockholm Royal Polytechnic, one department at Stockholm University, and one public and one private company, and produced by (several) computers and a considerable amount of software. I saw Olga for the first time at a Winter School organized by the Art and Communication Center at Malmö University from 24 to 26 November 1998. My presence there was legitimated by a talk on the same topic that I am developing in this chapter. Olga, introduced to us after my talk, revealed to me the problems we now face with current non-fictional identity construction.

Olga is a personal assistant with whom you can interact, and we shall see many more of these helping us to sail through the abysses of information. They will search the web for us and help us decide, as Olga did, which microwave oven to choose. In the meantime, the creators of Olga shared with the conference participants the problems they encountered in creating the artificial identity. There was an interesting conflict between the linguists and the designers. The linguists insisted that, in order for Olga's speech to be understood, she must be made as humanoid as possible. The designers (and the conference audience) were of an opinion that the animated Olga (as seen in all the figures but the last) was much more 'humanoid' and attractive. The audience reported feeling that the humanoid Olga (Box 16.1) looked like Frankenstein's monster. This opinion was not only an idiosyncratic judgment, but was also corroborated by the long and extremely successful experience of animated films. The linguists remained unruffled in their belief in realist representation. This conflict between 'authenticity' and 'successful positioning' has been replayed on yet another stage.

Regardless of how the battle over Olga is resolved, I believe that future organizations will be busier fabricating these kinds of fictitious identities than

Box 16.1. Olga

'Olga is a 3-dimensional animated figure that the user can speak to. She helps the documentation user find and sort information from databases.'

'Olga may also on own initiative, for example, give advice and tips.'

'The goal with the Olga-project was to test multimodal user interfaces, combining technical system speech with direct-manipulation.'

'This is how Olga actually looks. The model was made with Alias/Wavefront and the Olga-figure contains 4356 polygons.'

Source: CID NADA KTH, THM KTH, Lingvistik SU, SICS, & Nordvis AB. Created 970701 (htttp://www.nada.kth.se/~osu/olga/).

dealing with their own. In fact, I expect that various Olgas will represent their owners, much as Benneton's advertising stands for Benneton without ever mentioning its products or the company structure. The production of Olga-like identities is where organization theorists interested in identity issues ought to direct their attention next, not the least because, in constructing Olga, her designers project onto her their own ideas as to how identities are produced and maintained.

Thus Olgas will represent companies, but they will also reflect what software people believe is an attractive identity to position oneself against. Are Olgas going to be all-knowing experts or cute little women a client can patronize? As this text is being sent to print, the newspapers show pictures of 'Ananova', a virtual financial news presenter created by New Media, a daughter company of the British Press Association. Judging from the pictures, she is both.

The process of creating Olga is a good illustration of research problems that emerge. There is a conventional issue of cooperation between different organizations that is, however, more actual nowadays than ever before, as organizations act within networks of organizations and frequently dissolve and re-establish their boundaries. There is a less conventional issue of differing perceptions of what a 'human' identity is. There is also an unconventional issue regarding what it is machines permit their creators to do: what kind of technology is needed to achieve the effect of 'humanity'? We used to believe that a heap of clay was enough.

Of course, Olga-phenomenon can be easily turned into a reason for celebration or lamentation. We can either say that Olgas will replace human salespeople and contribute to growing unemployment, or that Olgas will forge the way to developing a variety of avatars that people can use for their private purposes. Imagine one company's Olga talking to another company's Olga.

Predictably, I stand by the ironists, and shall draw support for this stance from Anthony Giddens (1991: 7), who says: 'In general, whether in personal life or in broader social milieu, processes of reappropriation and empowerment intertwine with expropriation and loss.' It is not up to us to make the final count, but to depict and interpret the phenomena of the postmodern era. In order to be able to do that, we have to abandon time-honored frames of reference and look for new ones, not out of disrespect, but out of curiosity, to better catch up with the times.

NOTES

1 An interesting collection containing both is Lash and Friedman (1992).
2 Not in the sense Heidegger uses the term.
3 Although *dignitas* should more properly be translated as 'honor' and contrasted with 'dignity'. Honor is a premodern virtue (Berger *et al.* 1974) but, at least according to d'Iribarne (1989), lies at the core of French management. On conflicts between the American code of dignity and other cultures' codes of honor, see Carbaugh (1993).
4 A recent exhibition of the Pompei findings at the Archeological National Museum at Naples, called 'Homo Faber' (closed April 1999), revealed work organization and technology that, without the proper background, could easily be mistaken for that which originated in the 1700s.

REFERENCES

Albert, S., and Whetten, D. A. (1985), 'Organizational Identity', in L. L. Cummings, and B. M. Staw (eds.), *Research in Organizational Behavior, Volume 7* (Greenwich, Conn.: JAI Press), 263–95.

Alvesson, M., and Björkman, I. (1992), *Organisatorisk identitet* (Lund: Studentlitteratur).

Asimov, I. (1950/1996), *I, Robot* (London: HarperCollins).

Atwood, M. (1985), *The Handmaid's Tale* (Toronto: McClelland & Stewart).

Berger, P. L., Berger, B., and Kellner, H. (1974), *The Homeless Mind* (London: Penguin).

Brown, R. H. (1989), *Social Science as Civic Discourse* (Chicago, Ill.: University of Chicago Press).

Bruner, J. (1990), *Acts of Meaning* (Cambridge, Mass.: Harvard University Press).

Cadigan, P. (1992), *Fools* (London: HarperCollins).

Carbaugh, D. (1993), 'Personhood, Positioning and Cultural Pragmatics: American Dignity in Cross-Cultural Perspective', in S. A. Deetz (ed.), *Communication Yearbook 17* (Thousand Oaks, Calif.: Sage), 159–86.

Czarniawska, B. (1997), *Narrating the Organization: Dramas of Institutional Identity* (Chicago: University of Chicago Press).

Czarniawska-Joerges, B. (1994), 'Narratives of Individual and Organizational Identities', in S. A. Deetz (ed.), *Communication Yearbook 17* (Thousand Oaks, Calif.: Sage), 193–221.

Davies, B., and Harré, R. (1991), 'Positioning: The Discursive Production of Selves'. *Journal for the Theory of Social Behavior*, 20/1: 43–63.

d'Iribarne, P. (1989), *La Logique de l'honneur: Gestion des enterprises et traditions nationales* (Paris: Seuil).

Douglas, M. (1986), *How Institutions Think* (London: Routledge & Kegan Paul).

Dukerich, J. M., Kramer, R., and McLean-Parks, J. (1998), 'The Dark Side of Organizational Identification', in D. A. Whetten, and P. C. Godfrey (eds.), *Identity in Organizations: Building Theory through Conversations* (Thousand Oaks, Calif.: Sage), 245–56.

Dutton, J. E., and Dukerich, J. M. (1991), 'Keeping an Eye on the Mirror: Image and Identity in Organizational Adaptation', *Academy of Management Journal*, 34/3: 517–54.

Eco, U. (1990), *The Limits of Interpretation* (Bloomington, Ind.: Indiana University Press).

Gergen, K. J. (1991), *The Saturated Self: Dilemmas of Identity in Contemporary Life* (New York: Basic Books).

—— (1994), *Realities and Relationships: Soundings in Social Construction* (Cambridge, Mass.: Harvard University Press).

—— and Davis, K. E. (1985) (eds.), *The Social Construction of a Person* (Berlin: Springer-Verlag).

Gibson, W. (1996), *Idoru* (London: Penguin).

Giddens, A. G. (1991), *Modernity and Self-Identity: Self and Society in the Late Modern Age* (Cambridge: Polity Press).

http://www.nada. kth.se/~osu/olga/.

Kellner, D. (1992), 'Popular Culture and the Construction of Postmodern Identities', in S. Lash and J. Friedman (eds.), *Modernity and Identity* (Oxford: Blackwell), 141–77.

Knorr-Cetina, K. (1994), 'Primitive Classification and Postmodernity: Towards a Sociological Notion of Fiction', *Theory, Culture & Society*, 11: 1–22.

Kundera, M. (1988), *The Art of the Novel* (London: Faber & Faber).

Lash, S., and Friedman, J. (1992) (eds.), *Modernity and Identity* (Oxford: Blackwell).

Latour, B. (1993), *We Have Never Been Modern* (Cambridge, Mass.: Harvard University Press).

—— (1996), *Aramis or the Love of Technology* (Cambridge, Mass.: Harvard University Press).

Luhmann, N. (1991), 'Stenographie und Euryalistik', in H.-U. Gumbrecht and K.-L. Pfeiffer (eds.), *Paradoxien, Dissonanzen, Zusammenbrüche: Situationen offener Epistemologie* (Frankfurt: Suhrkamp), 58–82.

Lyotard, J.-F. (1979/1987), *The Postmodern Condition: A Report on Knowledge* (Manchester: Manchester University Press).

MacIntyre, A. (1981/1990), *After Virtue* (London: Duckworth Press).

Meyer, J. (1986), 'Myths of Socialization and of Personality', in T. C. Heller, M. Sosna, and D. E. Wellbery (eds.), *Reconstructing Individualism: Autonomy, Individuality and the Self in Western Thought* (Stanford, Calif.: Stanford University Press), 208–21.

Peltonen, T. (1999), 'Finnish Engineers Becoming Expatriates: Biographical Narratives and Subjectivity', *Studies in Cultures, Organizations and Societies*, 5/2: 1–31.

Pine, B. J., II, and Gilmore, J. (1999), *The Experience Economy: Work is Theater and Every Business a Stage* (Boston: Harvard Business School Press).

Pitkin, H. F. (1984), *Fortune is a Woman: Gender and Politics in the Thought of Niccoló Macchiavelli* (Berkeley and Los Angeles: University of California Press).

Rorty, R. (1991), 'Inquiry as Recontextualization: An Anti-Dualist Account of Interpretation', *Objectivity, Relativism and Truth* (New York: Cambridge University Press), 93–110.

Rosenau, P. M. (1995), 'Affirmatives and Skeptics', in W. T. Anderson (ed.), *The Truth about Truth: De-Confusing and Re-Constructing the Postmodern World* (New York: Tarcher/Putnam), 107–9.

Stephenson, N. (1995), *The Diamond Age, or A Young Lady's Illustrated Primer* (New York: Bantam Books).

Whetten, D. A., and Godfrey, P. C. (1998) (eds.), *Identity in Organizations: Building Theory through Conversations* (Thousand Oaks, Calif.: Sage).

Wilson, E. (1991), *The Sphinx in the City* (London: Virago Press).

INDEX

McDonald's 63, 123, 129, 249
MacIntyre, A. 273, 274
Mackie, D. 36
Macrae, C. 162
Mael, F. 15, 28, 37, 38, 41, 256, 258, 259, 262, 265
Maklan, S. 6, 138–52
Malone, M. S. 209, 213, 215, 216
Marchand, R. 249
Margulies, W. 13
market-based management (MBM) 43–5
market research 262–5
marketing 66, 70, 140
    cause 122–3
    green 122, 123
    to support brand strategy 130–3, 134
marketing planning 145–7
marketing studies 22, 23
Markus, H. 24
Martin, J. 25, 159
Martinez, A. 235
Martinko, M. 100
Mead, G. H. 258
meanings, shared 259–61
media:
    and corporate disclosure 159
    and dissemination of reputations 99, 248
Medin, D. L. 37
Meindl, J. 80
Menon, A. 122
Menon, A. and Menon, A. 121
Mercedes Benz 57–8, 62, 139
mergers, and corporate identity 14
Messick, D. 36
metaphor, use of 29
Meyer, J. 272, 273, 274
Miles, M. 81
Milgrom, P. 98
Miller, P. 66
mission statements 248
Mitchell, A. 151
Mitchell, H. G. 142
Mitchell, R. K. 102, 107–8, 160, 161, 162, 167
Mobil Corporation 250
Mollerup, P. 13, 14
moral philosophy, organizational identity as 36, 43–6
Motion, J. 256
Motorola 117
Mouritsen, J. 6, 208–28
Munter, M. 237
Murray, J. A. 140

narratives, *see* stories, corporate
NASA 101
Navistar 240–3, 244
Nestlé 14, 65
networks 143
Neuwirth, K. 260

Nike 63, 127, 130
Nixon, S. 66
Nohria, N. 233
Nordstrom 121
Nowak, G. J. 163
Nucor Steel 41

O'Driscoll, A. 140
O'Leary, T. 66
Olga 279–81
Olins, W. 5, 13, 14, 51–65, 163, 202, 249, 254, 258
Onkvisit, S. 255
opportunity costs, and organizational identity 39
organizational identity 4–5, 11, 12, 15–16, 19–31, 272, 273
    central character of 36
    communication of 18–19
    continuity of 258–9
    and core competence 37–8, 41
    and corporate identity contrasted 17–20
    as decision frame 36–7
    distinctiveness of 36–7, 39–40
    in diversified organizations 41–3
    economic value of 38–9
    imitation of 40–1
    internal/external perspectives on 21–2, 28–9
    as moral philosophy 36, 43–6
    narrative view of 16, 25
    and organizational culture 24–6
    and organizational image 21–4
    perspectival issues 17–18
    and recipients of identity messages 18
    and reputation 95, 103–4, 108, 109
    self/other perspective on 23, 29
    singularity of 24
    social complexity of 41
    and sustained competitive advantage 39–41
    temporal continuity of 36, 37
    values-based foundation of 43–6
organizational schema 37, 38
organizational structure, and corporate storytelling 190–1
Osborne, D. 67
outsourcing 58

Paradeise, C. 262, 264
parent visibility 167–8
particularity 273, 274
Pavlik, E. L. 209
Peck, H. 142
Peltonen, T. 278
Peppers, D. 150
Percy, L. 172
performance, product/service 142
Perrow, C. 98

Lightning Source UK Ltd.
Milton Keynes UK
178279UK00001B/10/P